Genre.   • Think about How presented
              on Stage - directions.
            Not just what is written.
            • Identify the conflict.   11/98

to say

/
Nothing
Repetitio
Values

Birmingham Metrop

139490   D0231266

21/6/99.
15/6/00

Edgar -

H E I N E M A N N

S H A K E S P E A R E

King Lear

edited by Frank Green

with additional notes and activities by
Rick Lee, Steven Croft and Helen Cross

Series Editor: John Seely

Heinemann Educational Publishers
Halley Court, Jordan Hill, Oxford OX2 8EJ
a division of Reed Educational & Professional Publishing Ltd
MELBOURNE   AUCKLAND
FLORENCE   PRAGUE   MADRID   ATHENS
SINGAPORE   TOKYO   SAO PAULO
CHICAGO   PORTSMOUTH (NH)   MEXICO
IBADAN   GABORONE   JOHANNESBURG
KAMPALA   NAIROBI

Introduction, notes and activities © Frank Green, John Seely,
Rick Lee, Steven Croft, Helen Cross, Ken Elliott 1995

Published in the *Heinemann Advanced Shakespeare* series 1995

99 98 97
10 9 8 7 6 5 4 3 2

A catalogue record for this book is available from the British Library on
request.
ISBN 0 435 19301 5

Cover design Miller Craig and Cocking
Cover photograph from Donald Cooper

Page make-up by Sharon Rudd

Produced by Celia Floyd, Basingstoke

Printed by Clays Ltd, St Ives plc

CONTENTS

How to use this book

This edition of *King Lear* has been prepared to provide students with several different kinds of information and guidance.

The introduction

Before the text of the play there is:
- a summary of the plot
- a brief analysis of how the plot works
- background information about where Shakespeare got the story from and how he adapted it for his purposes
- a brief explanation of Shakespeare's texts.

The text and commentary

On each right-hand page you will find the text of the play. On the facing left-hand pages there are three types of support material:
- a summary of the action
- detailed explanations of difficult words, phrases and longer sections of text
- suggestions of points you might find it useful to think about as you read the play.

End-of-act activities

After each act there is a set of activities. These can be tackled as you read the play. Many students, however, may want to leave these until they undertake a second reading. They consist of the following.

Keeping track: straightforward questions directing your attention to the action of the act.

Drama: practical drama activities to help you focus on key characters, relationships and situations.

Close study: work on the text of selected extracts from the play, designed to help you tackle Shakespeare's language in detail.

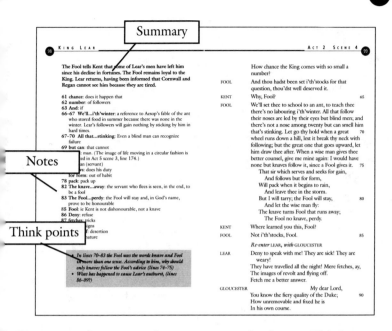

Key scene: a focus on an important scene in the act. This is intended to help you combine an understanding of the characters and broader themes of the play with the ability to comment on the text in detail.

Writing: progressive activities throughout the book help you to develop essay writing skills.

Explorations

At the end of the book there are a variety of items to draw together your thoughts and insights on the play as a whole:
- how to approach thinking about the whole play
- work on character
- work on the themes and issues
- guidance on how to tackle practical drama activities
- advice on preparing for an examination
- advice on essay writing, together with a sample essay written by an A level student, with comments
- practice essay questions
- glossary of technical terms

The plot

Lear, King of ancient Britain, decides in his old age that he wishes to retain the status of king without having any of the responsibilities.

He intends to divide the kingdom between his three daughters. He asks the daughters to declare the extent of their love for him before he announces what their share will be. When his youngest and favourite daughter, **Cordelia**, refuses to say what he wants to hear, Lear is angry and disinherits her. Her proposed share of the kingdom is divided between her sisters.

The older sisters, **Goneril** and **Regan**, turn against Lear and he is driven mad. Cordelia, now married to the **King of France**, returns with an army to help her father. Lear and Cordelia are reunited but lose the battle. They are taken prisoner. Goneril and Regan die as a result of jealousy of each other; Cordelia is killed in prison; and Lear dies of a broken heart.

At the same time a second plot runs through the play. It is more than a sub-plot: indeed, it might be considered parallel to the Lear plot although it is essentially convergent. The differences in the two plots ensure that we do not think of repetition, but the similarities reinforce the themes, and we appreciate that Lear's suffering is not an isolated circumstance.

The **Earl of Gloucester** has two sons, the legitimate **Edgar** and the bastard **Edmund**. As a result of Edmund's machinations Edgar is banished and Gloucester is cruelly blinded; and it is Edmund who is, directly or indirectly, responsible for the deaths of all of Lear's daughters.

Predominant plots, scene by scene

Act 1

Scene 1	LEAR
Scene 2	GLOUCESTER
Scene 3	LEAR
Scene 4	LEAR
Scene 5	LEAR

Act 2

Scene 1	GLOUCESTER
Scene 2	LEAR
Scene 3	GLOUCESTER
Scene 4	LEAR

Act 3

Scene 1	LEAR
Scene 2	LEAR
Scene 3	GLOUCESTER
Scene 4	LEAR/GLOUCESTER
Scene 5	GLOUCESTER
Scene 6	LEAR
Scene 7	GLOUCESTER

Act 4

Scene 1	GLOUCESTER
Scene 2	LEAR
Scene 3	LEAR
Scene 4	LEAR
Scene 5	LEAR
Scene 6	LEAR/GLOUCESTER
Scene 7	LEAR

Act 5

Scene 1	LEAR
Scene 2	GLOUCESTER
Scene 3	LEAR/GLOUCESTER

Background

The story

In English folk-tale there was a story of a king and his three daughters. It was a story that was often re-worked: Holinshed's *Chronicles* contains one version, and Spenser's *The Faerie Queene* another. A play, *The True Chronicle History of King Leir and His Three Daughters*, was performed towards the end of the sixteenth century, and it was this version of the story to which Shakespeare referred most closely.

It is interesting to note that Shakespeare's version of the story was the first in which Lear and Cordelia did not enjoy a happy ending.

Some considered that the tragic ending was too much for an audience to endure, and Nahum Tate rewrote the play to give it a happy ending. It was generally performed in this form from 1681 until Edmund Kean restored Shakespeare's ending in 1823. To the original story Shakespeare also added:

- Lear's madness
- the storm
- the Fool
- the 'Gloucester plot' and Poor Tom.

(It is worth noting that Nahum Tate cut the Fool from his version of the play, but the character was restored by Macready in 1838. The idea for the introduction of the plot involving Gloucester and his sons was taken from Sir Philip Sidney's *Arcadia*.)

The text of Shakespeare's plays

Shakespeare's work is generally treated with such immense respect that it may seem strange to admit that we cannot be certain exactly what he wrote. The reasons for this mystery lie in the circumstances of the theatre and publishing in the sixteenth and seventeenth centuries.

Shakespeare was a professional actor and shareholder in a company of actors, the Lord Chamberlain's Men, for whom he wrote his plays. Since copyright and performing rights did not exist before the eighteenth century, there was always the risk that if a play was successful other companies would perform it and reap the financial rewards. To avoid this problem, acting companies guarded the handwritten copy of a completed work. It was the company's most valuable resource and kept by the prompter: each actor was given only his own lines and his cues. None of these manuscripts survives to the present day.

This lack of printed texts seems strange to modern readers but, like the work of other playwrights of his time, Shakespeare's plays existed essentially as oral, not written, texts. His concern was with what they looked and sounded like on the stage, not what they looked like on the page.

However, there was money to be made from printed plays and, during his lifetime, nearly half of Shakespeare's plays were printed in what are known as quartos: paperback editions of single plays. Some of these, called 'bad' quartos, are pirated editions based on the memories of actors and audience. Others are much more accurate and may have been authorized by Shakespeare or the sharers in his company, perhaps to capitalize on a popular success which was about to go out on repertory, or to forestall a pirate edition. None, however, seems to have been supervised by the playwright and all differ, often considerably, from the key text of Shakespeare's plays, the *First Folio*.

The *First Folio*, published in 1623, is a collected edition of all Shakespeare's plays (with the exception of *Pericles*). It was edited by John Hemming and Henry Condell, two sharers in the Lord Chamberlain's Men, using 'good' quartos, prompt copies and other company papers to provide an accurate text as a fitting memorial to their partner. They did not start the editing process until after Shakespeare had died and apparently based their editorial decisions on what had happened in the theatre. We cannot be certain how far they represent what Shakespeare's ultimate intentions might have been. Even if Shakespeare had approved the text that went to the printer, it was the custom for writers to leave much of the detail of spelling and punctuation to the printer or to a scribe who made a fair copy from the playwright's rough drafts. The scribe and printer thus introduced their own interpretation and inaccuracies into the text. The *First Folio* was reprinted three times in the seventeenth century and each edition corrected some inaccuracies and introduced new errors.

A modern editor tries to provide a text which is easy to read and close to Shakespeare's presumed intentions. To do this, the editor may modernize spelling and change punctuation, add stage directions and scene divisions and make important decisions about which of several readings in quarto and folio editions is most acceptable.

If you are able to compare this edition of the play with other editions, you are likely to find many minor variations between them, as well as occasional major differences which could change your view of a character or situation.

King Lear

Evidence suggests that *King Lear* was written in the winter of 1604–1605. It was printed in 1608 as the first quarto, of which twelve copies still exist. However, there are ten different versions of the first quarto because proofreading was carried out as the printing progressed; this meant that alterations were made to some pages after uncorrected versions of those pages had already been produced. It has been calculated that there are one hundred and sixty-seven differences in the twelve copies – and to complicate matters further, some of the corrections are wrong! A second quarto was printed in 1619 (although it was dated 1608, presumably for commercial purposes).

The first folio appeared in 1623, and it is this version on which most editors base contemporary editions. It was produced, possibly, from a first quarto copy and a manuscript (possibly a prompt book). The folio version contains the addition of about 100 lines to the quarto text, and the omission of about 300 lines from it (including the 'mock trial' in Act 3 scene 6, the confrontation between Goneril and Albany in Act 4 scene 2 and the whole of Act 4 scene 3).

Some editors think that Shakespeare revised the play after it had been produced, and that the folio is the result. But most theatre directors believe that at least some of what it omits is essential to the play.

What this all means is that there is no definitive version of the play: no original manuscript has survived.

KING LEAR

CHARACTERS

LEAR, King of Britain
KING OF FRANCE
DUKE OF BURGUNDY
DUKE OF CORNWALL, husband to Regan
DUKE OF ALBANY, husband to Goneril
EARL OF KENT
EARL OF GLOUCESTER
EDGAR, son to Gloucester
EDMUND, bastard son to Gloucester
CURAN, a courtier
OSWALD, steward to Goneril
Old man, tenant to Gloucester
Doctor
Fool
An officer, employed by Edmund
Gentleman, attendant on Cordelia
A herald
Servants to Cornwall
GONERIL
REGAN   } daughters to Lear
CORDELIA

Knights of Lear's train, Officers, Messengers, Soldiers, and
Attendants

SCENE *Britain*

Plot
Character
Setting
Language
tone.

Simile
as

Metaphore
likeness to.

FRANCE = CORDELIA.
EDMUND = BASTARD

Symbolism. Irony-verbal.
theme. Situationa Irony-mismate
style. dramatic Irony.
tone = metaphors
simily-hidden.

**The Earl of Kent and the Earl of Gloucester await Lear's
announcement about the division of his kingdom. Gloucester
is accompanied by his illegitimate son, Edmund.**

 1 **had more affected**: preferred
 2 **Albany**: Albany was a region north from the Humber into
   what is now Scotland
 5 **values**: regards
 5–6 **equalities...moiety**: the division is so equal that neither of
   them, however fussy, can prefer the other's share
 8 **His breeding...charge**: I have paid for his upbringing or I am
   responsible for his conception
10 **brazed**: hardened (from, coated with brass)
11 **conceive**: understand (but Gloucester picks up on its other
   meaning – become pregnant)
15 **fault**: sin or loss of the scent by hounds. (Sin was often linked
   with a bad smell; hence the connection.)
16 **issue**: outcome/child
17 **proper**: handsome (but also the ironic meaning of
   'appropriate', being the result of sin)
18 **by order of law**: legitimate
19 **account**: estimation
20 **knave**: boy. (Again there may be irony because it also has the
   meaning 'villain'.)
   saucily: presumptuously, insolently
23 **whoreson**: fellow (only becomes an insult with the
   appropriate tone and language)

> - *Note that Lear has already decided on the division of
>   the kingdom because Kent and Gloucester know at
>   least some of the details.*
> - *Edmund hears his mother, and his own conception,
>   referred to in a most off-hand way (lines 12–14,
>   20–22).*

Act one

Scene 1

A state room in KING LEAR'S *palace*

Enter KENT, GLOUCESTER, *and* EDMUND

KENT   I thought the King had more affected the Duke of
            Albany than Cornwall.

GLOUCESTER It did always seem so to us; but now, in the division
            of the kingdom, it appears not which of the Dukes
            he values most; for equalities are so weighed that   5
            curiosity in neither can make choice of either's moiety.

KENT   Is not this your son, my Lord?

GLOUCESTER His breeding, Sir, hath been at my charge: I have
            so often blushed to acknowledge him, that now I
            am brazed to't.   10

KENT   I cannot conceive you.

GLOUCESTER Sir, this young fellow's mother could; whereupon
            she grew round-wombed, and had, indeed, Sir, a son
            for her cradle ere she had a husband for her bed. Do
            you smell a fault?   15

KENT   I cannot wish the fault undone, the issue of it being
            so proper.

GLOUCESTER But I have a son, Sir, by order of law, some year
            elder than this, who yet is no dearer in my account:
            though this knave came something saucily to the   20
            world before he was sent for, yet was his mother
            fair; there was good sport at his making, and the
            whoreson must be acknowledged. Do you know this
            noble gentleman, Edmund?

EDMUND   No, my Lord.   25

Lear announces that he intends to hand over his kingdom to his daughters so that he can live the remaining years of his life as king, but without the cares of state. He has divided the realm into three, and the daughter professing the greatest love for him will get the largest part.

28 services: duty

29 sue: beg

30 study deserving: work at deserving your respect

31 out: abroad

31–32 away...again: does Gloucester find Edmund a source of embarrassment, despite his claim in lines 9–10?

Stage directions *Sennet*: fanfare announcing a procession
coronet: small crown (symbol of Lear's power)

33 Attend: escort

34 liege: lord

35 we: royal plural
darker purpose: more secret intention. (Those who knew of Lear's plans to divide the kingdom were not aware of this part of the plan.)

37 fast: firm (a contrast with shake in the next line)
intent: intention

40 Unburthened: unburdened. (Crawl seems a strange word to link with a loss of worry and responsibility – unless he intends living to be extremely old!)

40 and 41: son: son-in-law

42 We have...publish: now I am determined to make known

43 several dowers: separate marriage portions

45 Great: noble

46 sojourn: stay
made...sojourn: visited for purposes of love

48 both: this precedes a list of three items, not two

49 Interest of territory: right to the land

51 largest bounty: most generous share

- *But the division for Goneril and Regan has already been decided (lines 3–7)!*
- *What can Lear's purpose be? Do we take Lear at face value (lines 43–44), or does he have another motive?*

GLOUCESTER My Lord of Kent: remember him hereafter as my
honourable friend.

EDMUND My services to your Lordship.

KENT I must love you, and sue to know you better.

EDMUND Sir, I shall study deserving. 30

GLOUCESTER He hath been out nine years, and away he shall
again. The King is coming.

Sennet. Enter one bearing a coronet, KING LEAR,
CORNWALL, ALBANY, GONERIL, REGAN, CORDELIA,
and Attendants

LEAR Attend the Lords of France and Burgundy,
Gloucester.

GLOUCESTER I shall, my Liege.

[*Exeunt* GLOUCESTER *and* EDMUND

LEAR Meantime, we shall express our darker purpose. 35
Give me the map there. Know that we have divided
In three our kingdom; and 'tis our fast intent
To shake all cares and business from our age,
Conferring them on younger strengths, while we
Unburthened crawl toward death. Our son of
Cornwall, 40
And you, our no less loving son of Albany,
We have this hour a constant will to publish
Our daughters' several dowers, that future strife
May be prevented now. The Princes, France and
Burgundy,
Great rivals in our youngest daughter's love, 45
Long in our court have made their amorous
sojourn,
And here are to be answered. Tell me, my
daughters,
(Since now we will divest us both of rule,
Interest of territory, cares of state)
Which of you shall we say doth love us most? 50
That we our largest bounty may extend

Goneril and Regan speak flatteringly to their father, and he tells them which parts of the kingdom will be theirs. His youngest daughter, Cordelia, has listened to her sisters with growing apprehension.

52 Where...challenge: to the one who is most deserving by her natural expression of love for me
54 wield the matter: express
55 space and liberty: room to move about and freedom to do so
58 As much...found: as much as any father found himself to be loved
59 breath: words
   unable: inadequate
60 all...much: all comparison
62 bounds: boundaries
63 champains: open country
   riched: enriched
64 wide-skirted meads: extensive meadows
65 issues: children
66 perpetual: for all time
68 self metal: same stuff, material (play on words – mettle means 'spirit')
69 prize me...worth: assess myself at her value. (This carries on the imagery of metal, to be continued with precious, line 73.)
70 deed: play on words – action/duty/legal document proving ownership
71 that: in that
73 the most...sense: which are found in well-balanced feelings. (Shakespeare probably had in mind the work of Pythagoras, the Greek thinker, who believed that the square symbolized the world of the senses.)
74 alone: only
   felicitate: made happy
75 poor: pitied/not rich
77 more ponderous: of more weight
78 hereditary ever: as perpetual, line 66
80 validity: value
82 last and least: youngest and smallest

- *What is the dramatic effect of Cordelia's 'asides'?*
- *What might be the reason for Lear's plan to give Cordelia the land which separates that of Goneril and Regan?*

Where <u>nature doth</u> with merit challenge. Goneril,
Our eldest-born, speak first.

GONERIL Sir, I love you more than word can wield the
matter;
Dearer than eye-sight, space and liberty;   55
Beyond what can be valued rich or rare;
No less than life, with grace, health, beauty,
honour;
As much as child e'er loved, or father found;
A love that makes breath poor and speech unable;
Beyond all manner of so much I love you.   60

CORDELIA [*Aside*] What shall Cordelia speak? Love, and be
silent.

LEAR Of all these bounds, even from this line to this,
With shadowy forests and with champains riched,
With plenteous rivers and wide-skirted meads,
We make thee lady: to thine and Albany's issues 65
Be this perpetual. What says our second daughter
Our dearest Regan, wife of Cornwall?

REGAN I am made of that self metal as my sister,
And prize me at her worth. In my true heart
I find she names my very deed of love;   70
Only she comes too short: that I profess
Myself an enemy to all other joys
Which the most precious square of sense possesses,
And find I am alone felicitate
In your dear highness' love.

CORDELIA [*Aside*]   Then poor
Cordelia!   75
And yet not so; since I am sure my love's
More ponderous than my tongue.

LEAR To thee and thine, hereditary ever,
Remain this ample third of our fair kingdom,
No less in space, validity, and pleasure,   80
Than that conferred on Goneril. Now, our joy,
Although our last, and least; to whose young love

Cordelia determinedly refuses to exaggerate her feelings.
She will only say that she loves Lear as a daughter should
love a father; and she is disowned by him.

83 **The vines...Burgundy**: the King of France (noted for its
   vineyards) and the Duke of Burgundy (a rich agricultural
   region)
84 **interested**: related
   draw: attract
85 **more opulent**: richer
92 **my bond**: my bounden duty
94 **mar**: spoil
   fortunes: play on words – chances/wealth
96 **are right fit**: is fitting
97 **Obey...honour you**: reminiscent of marriage vows
99 **all**:completely
   happily: haply, perhaps
100 **take my plight**: accept my marriage vow
103 **To love my father all**: to give all my love to my father
105 **untender**: unbending
106 **true**: straight
108 **sacred radiance of the sun**: Christianity was not the
    beginning of man's belief in a greater power; in pre-Christian
    times pagan beliefs encompassed various forms of
    diety/dieties
109 **Hecate**: (pronounced Hecket) goddess of the underworld
110 **operation of the orbs**: influence of the planets.
    (Compare the belief in astrology today.)
111 **From whom...to be**: controlling life and death
113 **Propinquity...blood**: nearness of relationship and blood-ties
114–115 **And as...for ever**: I do not recognize you from this
    time forth

> • *'A third more opulent...' What is Lear's purpose in*
>   *asking his daughters to proclaim their love for him*
>   *when he has already decided on the division of the*
>   *land? Is it his pride that causes him to do this? Does he*
>   *want to see his daughters subservient? Or is it that a*
>   *public acknowledgement of his wishes will be binding*
>   *on them after his death?*

The vines of France and milk of Burgundy
Strive to be interessed; what can you say to draw
A third more opulent than your sisters? Speak.   85

CORDELIA   Nothing, my lord.

LEAR   Nothing?

CORDELIA   Nothing.

LEAR   Nothing will come of nothing: speak again.

CORDELIA   Unhappy that I am, I cannot heave   90
My heart into my mouth: I love your Majesty
According to my bond; no more nor less.

LEAR   How, how, Cordelia! Mend your speech a little,
Lest you may mar your fortunes.

CORDELIA   Good my Lord,
You have begot me, bred me, loved me: I   95
Return those duties back as are right fit,
Obey you, love you, and most honour you.
Why have my sisters husbands, if they say
They love you all? Happily, when I shall wed,
That lord whose hand must take my plight shall
    carry   100
Half my love with him, half my care and duty:
Sure I shall never marry like my sisters,
To love my father all.

LEAR   But goes thy heart with this?

CORDELIA   Ay, my good Lord.

LEAR   So young, and so untender?   105

CORDELIA   So young, my Lord, and true.

LEAR   Let it be so; thy truth then be thy dower:
For, by the sacred radiance of the sun,
The mysteries of Hecate and the night,
By all the operation of the orbs   110
From whom we do exist and cease to be,
Here I disclaim all my paternal care,
Propinquity and property of blood,
And as a stranger to my heart and me

Cordelia's part of the kingdom is to be shared by the other daughters and their husbands. Lear intends to divide his time between Goneril and Regan in turn, on a monthly basis. To Lear's further displeasure, Kent speaks up for Cordelia.

115 **Scythian**: an inhabitant of what is now Russia; said to be savage and cruel
116 **makes his generation messes**: eats his offspring or parents
  messes: dishes, food
118 **neighboured**: closely regarded, treated as a neighbour
119 **sometime**: former
121 **Dragon**: emblem of the ancient British monarchy, symbolizing ruthless power
122 **set my rest**: repose in retirement/stake my all
123 **nursery**: nursing, care
124–125 **So be...from her**: so let me find peace in my grave, as now I remove my father's love from her
125 **Who stirs?**: come on, jump to it!
127 **digest**: incorporate
128 **plainness**: bluntness, plain-speaking
  marry her: be her dowry
129 **invest**: hand over to
130 **Pre-eminence**: superiority
130–131 **large...majesty**: great trappings of kingship
132 **With reservation**: keeping the right or privilege
133–134 **shall our abode Make**: shall live with
135 **th'addition**: titles and honours
  sway: rule
136 **Revenue**: income
  execution of the rest: carrying out all other authority
138 **part**: share
141 **patron**: benefactor
142 **The bow...shaft**: imagery of archery – the bow is pulled right back, do not stand in the path of the arrow. I have made up my mind: do not get in my way.
143–144 **Let it...heart**: let the arrow drop, even if it kills me
144 **be Kent unmannerly**: I would only be ill-mannered...

- *Is it unfair to suggest that Lear seems obsessed with pride, property, possessions, and power at this stage?*
- *How much more straightforward would it have been for Lear if he had had a son?*

Hold thee from this for ever. The barbarous
　　Scythian,　　　　　　　　　　　　　　115
Or he that makes his generation messes
To gorge his appetite, shall to my bosom
Be as well neighboured, pitied, and relieved,
As thou my sometime daughter.

KENT　　　　　　　　　　　　　　Good my Liege, –

LEAR　　Peace, Kent!　　　　　　　　　　120
Come not between the Dragon and his wrath.
I loved her most, and thought to set my rest
On her kind nursery. Hence, and avoid my sight!
So be my grave my peace, as here I give
Her father's heart from her! Call France. Who
　　stirs?　　　　　　　　　　　　　　125
Call Burgundy. Cornwall and Albany,
With my two daughters' dowers digest the third;
Let pride, which she calls plainness, marry her.
I do invest you jointly with my power,
Pre-eminence, and all the large effects　　　130
That troop with majesty. Ourself, by monthly
　　course,
With reservation of an hundred knights
By you to be sustained, shall our abode
Make with you by due turn. Only we shall retain
The name and all th'addition to a king; the
　　sway,　　　　　　　　　　　　　　135
Revenue, execution of the rest,
Beloved sons, be yours: which to confirm,
This coronet part between you.

KENT　　　　　　　　　　　　　　Royal Lear,
Whom I have ever honoured as my King,
Loved as my father, as my master followed,　　140
As my great patron thought on in my prayers, –

LEAR　　The bow is bent and drawn; make from the shaft.

KENT　　Let it fall rather, though the fork invade
The region of my heart: be Kent unmannerly,

Despite Lear's warnings, Kent continues to plead for
Cordelia. Lear's patience is exhausted as Kent persists.

145 When Lear is mad: ...if I thought you were mad
   thou: a form of address suggestive of intimacy, or used for
   equals or inferiors but never, in normal circumstances, by a
   subject to his king
   old man: see note, foot of page 38
146–148 Think'st...folly: do you think that the personification
   of duty (myself, Kent) is afraid to speak out when the
   personification of power (Lear) submits to the personification
   of flattery (Regan and Goneril)? Honour (Kent) must be
   blunt when majesty (Lear) is foolish.
148 Reserve thy state: keep your king-like qualities
149 in...consideration: after deepest reflection
150 answer...judgment: I will stake my life on my opinion
152–153 whose low...hollowness: whose quiet words do not
   ring with insincerity (ie who speak sincerely)
154–155 a pawn...To wage: a chess-piece of limited value to
   use in war, contest/a stake in a wager
156 motive: the reason for my action
157 still: always
158 blank: white. (This refers to the white centre of a target seen
   by Lear, rather than the white of his eye.)
157–158 let me...eye: through me you will see things clearly
159 Apollo: sun god (therefore connected with clear sight) – and
   god of archery (straight aiming, perhaps?)
160 vassal: inferior person; a subject, b base wretch
   miscreant: a unbeliever, b villain
161 forbear: don't go on (spoken to Kent)
162–163 Kill...disease: you want to kill the one who cares for
   you and bless those who cause your death
163 revoke: take back
164 vent clamour: utter a sound
165 recreant: traitor, deserter, villain
166 allegiance: loyalty
167 That: seeing that, because

> • *Kent is direct in his approach to Lear; some would
> accuse him of rudeness. What do you think about
> Kent's attitude to Lear?*

When Lear is mad. What would'st thou do, old
   man?   145
Think'st thou that duty shall have dread to speak
When power to flattery bows? To plainness
   honour's bound
When majesty falls to folly. Reserve thy state;
And, in thy best consideration, check
This hideous rashness: answer my life my
   judgment,   150
Thy youngest daughter does not love thee least;
Nor are those empty-hearted whose low sounds
Reverb no hollowness.

LEAR   Kent, on thy life, no more.

KENT   My life I never held but as a pawn
To wage against thine enemies; nor fear to lose
   it,   155
Thy safety being motive.

LEAR   Out of my sight!

KENT   See better, Lear; and let me still remain
The true blank of thine eye.

LEAR   Now, by Apollo, –

KENT   Now, by Apollo, King,
Thou swear'st thy Gods in vain.

LEAR   O, vassal!
   miscreant!   160
        [*Laying his hand upon his sword*

ALBANY,
CORNWALL   Dear Sir, forbear.

KENT   Kill thy physician, and the fee bestow
Upon the foul disease. Revoke thy gift;
Or, whilst I can vent clamour from my throat,
I'll tell thee thou dost evil.

LEAR   Hear me, recreant! 165
On thine allegiance, hear me!
That thou hast sought to make us break our vow,

Lear banishes Kent from the kingdom. The King of France
and the Duke of Burgundy are brought before Lear.
Burgundy is asked what he requires as a dowry if he marries
Cordelia. Burgundy says he will take what has already been
offered.

168 **durst never yet**: have never dared to do/have never
considered doing
strained: excessive
169 **betwixt...power**: between giving judgement and carrying it
out
170 **nor, nor**: neither, nor
place: position
171 **Our potency...reward**: I'll show you how I can use my
power – this is what you get! (Potency refers back to power,
line 169.)
172 **allot**: allow
172–173 **for provision...disasters**: to make sure you are
equipped to face misfortunes
176 **trunk**: body
177 **Jupiter**: the supreme god
179–180 **sith...is here**: since you insist on behaving like a
tyrant, you will be sending me away to freedom
181 **The Gods...take thee**: may the gods themselves protect you
183 **And your...approve**: I hope your actions back up your
grand words
186 **shape...course**: behave as before
Stage direction *Flourish*: a fanfare announcing important people
190 **rivalled**: competed
in the least: at the lowest
191 **present**: immediate
193 **crave**: ask for, desire
194 **tender**: offer

> • *Kent's farewell speech, lines 179–186, is in rhyming
>   couplets. Can you suggest why this might be?*
> • *Lear's proposed division of his kingdom into three has
>   not been the best kept of secrets, it would seem. Why do
>   you think so many people have known about it?*

Which we durst never yet, and with strained pride
To come betwixt our sentence and our power,
Which nor our nature nor our place can bear,   170
Our potency made good, take thy reward.
Five days we do allot thee for provision
To shield thee from disasters of the world;
And on the sixth to turn thy hated back
Upon our kingdom: if on the tenth day
   following   175
Thy banished trunk be found in our dominions,
The moment is thy death. Away! By Jupiter,
This shall not be revoked.

KENT   Fare thee well, King; sith thus thou wilt appear,
Freedom lives hence, and banishment is here.   180
[*To* CORDELIA] The Gods to their dear shelter take
   thee, maid,
That justly think'st and hast most rightly said!
[*To* GONERIL *and* REGAN] And your large speeches
   may your deeds approve,
That good effects may spring from words of love.
Thus Kent, O Princes! bids you all adieu;   185
He'll shape his old course in a country new.   [*Exit*

Flourish. Re-enter GLOUCESTER, *with* FRANCE,
BURGUNDY, *and Attendants*

GLOUCESTER   Here's France and Burgundy, my noble Lord.

LEAR   My Lord of Burgundy,
We first address toward you, who with this king
Hath rivalled for our daughter. What, in the
   least,   190
Will you require in present dower with her,
Or cease your quest of love?

BURGUNDY   Most royal Majesty,
I crave no more than hath your Highness offered,
Nor will you tender less.

LEAR   Right noble Burgundy,

Burgundy is stunned when he is told that Cordelia now has
no dowry at all. Lear advises the King of France to look
elsewhere for a bride, but France refuses to believe that
Cordelia has done something so outrageous that her father
has completely changed his opinion of her.

195 **dear**: a play on words (linked with price, line 196) –
beloved/greatly valued
197 **aught**: anything
little-seeming substance: there are two possible meanings,
depending on whether seeming refers to little or substance –
if we read that Cordelia seems to have little substance then
the meaning is 'person of no importance'; on the other hand,
if she is seen as a thing (or substance) who has little time for
seeming (pretence) then the meaning is 'one who values
reality and has no time for hypocrisy'
198 **with...pieced**: together with my displeasure
199 **fitly like**: please by its fitness
201 **infirmities**: disadvantages, drawbacks
owes: owns
with our oath: by my promise
205 **Election...up**: it is impossible to choose her
207 **tell**: enumerate, count out
For: as for
208 **make such a stray**: stray so far
211–212 **Nature...t'acknowledge hers**: (Lear is suggesting that
Cordelia is not only a stranger to him now, but also barely
recognized as being human)
213 **best object**: object of greatest love
214 **argument**: theme
balm: comfort
216 **dismantle**: strip away
217 **folds**: (the reference to clothing continues)
218 **unnatural**: again the 'natural'/'unnatural' theme
219 **That monsters it**: as to be monstrous
219–220 **fore-vouched...taint**: previously proclaimed love is suspect
220–222 **which to believe...in me**: without a miracle to
convince me I cannot believe that

- *Can you anticipate Lear's reaction to the comments of
the King of France?*
- *How do France's remarks compare with those of Kent?*
- *What did Kent actually say to offend Lear?*

When she was dear to us we did hold her so,   195
But now her price is fallen. Sir, there she stands:
If aught within that little-seeming substance,
Or all of it, with our displeasure pieced,
And nothing more, may fitly like your Grace,
She's there, and she is yours.

BURGUNDY   I know no answer. 200

LEAR   Will you, with those infirmities she owes,
Unfriended, new adopted to our hate,
Dowered with our curse and strangered with our
        oath,
Take her, or leave her?

BURGUNDY   Pardon me, royal Sir;
Election makes not up in such conditions.   205

LEAR   Then leave her, sir; for, by the power that made me,
I tell you all her wealth. [*To* FRANCE] For you,
        great King,
I would not from your love make such a stray
To match you where I hate; therefore beseech you
T'avert your liking a more worthier way   210
Than on a wretch whom Nature is ashamed
Almost t'acknowledge hers.

FRANCE   This is most strange,
That she, whom even but now was your best
        object,
The argument of your praise, balm of your age,
The best, the dearest, should in this trice of
        time   215
Commit a thing so monstrous, to dismantle
So many folds of favour. Sure, her offence
Must be of such unnatural degree
That monsters it, or your fore-vouched affection
Fall into taint; which to believe of her,   220
Must be a faith that reason without miracle
Should never plant in me.

Cordelia asks her father to make it clear that her 'crime' is that she has offended him: that she has not committed an outrage against society. Burgundy is no longer interested in marriage to Cordelia.

223 **If for I want**: if the trouble is that I lack
224 **purpose not**: not intend to put it into practice
224–225 **since what...before I speak**: it is because what I genuinely feel I shall have made clear by my actions rather than by talking about it
226 **blot**: stain on my character
murther: murder
227 **dishonoured**: dishonourable
229 **But even...richer**: but I am in your bad books because I do not have certain qualities, the lack of which makes me a better person
230 **still-soliciting**: always looking for the main chance
232 **lost**: ruined
234 **tardiness in nature**: natural reticence, holding back
235 **leaves...unspoke**: gives no spoken account
238 **regards**: considerations
239 **Aloof from...point**: remote from the essential issue (love)
241 **portion**: dowry
247 **respect and fortunes**: status and wealth
are his love: are what he thinks of as love
249–250 **that art...despised!**: (oxymoron – see GLOSSARY)

> '*Better thou*
> *Hadst not been born than not t'have pleased me better.*'
> • *There is another implied reference here to nature and 'natural' behaviour. In this case is Lear being unnatural, or not?*

CORDELIA   I yet beseech your
                         Majesty,
                         (If for I want that glib and oily art
                         To speak and purpose not, since what I well intend,
                         I'll do't before I speak), that you make known   225
                         It is no vicious blot, murther or foulness,
                         No unchaste action, or dishonoured step,
                         That hath deprived me of your grace and favour,
                         But even for want of that for which I am richer,
                         A still-soliciting eye, and such a tongue   230
                         That I am glad I have not, though not to have it
                         Hath lost me in your liking.

LEAR   Better thou
                         Hadst not been born than not t'have pleased me
                             better.

FRANCE   Is it but this? a tardiness in nature
                         Which often leaves the history unspoke   235
                         That it intends to do? My Lord of Burgundy,
                         What say you to the lady? Love's not love
                         When it is mingled with regards that stand
                         Aloof from th'entire point. Will you have her?
                         She is herself a dowry.

BURGUNDY   Royal King,   240
                         Give but that portion which yourself proposed,
                         And here I take Cordelia by the hand,
                         Duchess of Burgundy.

LEAR   Nothing: I have sworn; I am firm.

BURGUNDY   I am sorry, then, you have so lost a father   245
                         That you must lose a husband.

CORDELIA   Peace be with
                         Burgundy!
                         Since that respect and fortunes are his love,
                         I shall not be his wife.

FRANCE   Fairest Cordelia, that art most rich, being poor;
                         Most choice, forsaken; and most loved,
                             despised!   250

France is pleased to marry Cordelia, and the surprised Lear is dismissive of them both. Cordelia takes her leave of her sisters, reminding them that she knows them well.

253–264 Gods...benison: couplets summarize the attitudes which have been established

253 their: the gods'

254 thrown to my chance: it is my good fortune that she has come my way

257 wat'rish: implying weakness; **a** watering down the wine **b** prone to flooding

258 unprized precious: unappreciated but precious to me

259 unkind: unnatural

260 where: place elsewhere

264 benison: blessing

267 jewels: irony – see GLOSSARY
    washed: washed with tears/clear-sighted. (I know you for what you are!)

269 loth: reluctant

270 as they are named: by their proper name

271 professed bosoms: your alleged love

273 prefer: recommend

275 Prescribe not us: don't tell us
    study: effort

277 At Fortune's alms: as a charity gift from fortune
    scanted: skimped, lacked

278 well...wanted: deserve to lack affection as you showed lack of affection (to our father)

279 plighted: folded, concealed (pleated)/swearing as truth (as in the wedding ceremony, to plight one's troth)

> • *Do we learn more about Lear's character from his attitude towards Burgundy and the King of France?*

Thee and thy virtues here I seize upon:
Be it lawful I take up what's cast away.
Gods, gods! 'tis strange that from their cold'st
  neglect
My love should kindle to inflamed respect.
Thy dowerless daughter, King, thrown to my
  chance,   255
Is Queen of us, of ours, and our fair France:
Not all the dukes of wat'rish Burgundy
Can buy this unprized precious maid of me.
Bid them farewell, Cordelia, though unkind:
Thou losest here, a better where to find.   260

LEAR   Thou hast her, France; let her be thine, for we
            Have no such daughter, nor shall ever see
            That face of hers again; therefore be gone
            Without our grace, our love, our benison.
            Come, noble Burgundy.   265

            [*Flourish. Exeunt* LEAR, BURGUNDY, CORNWALL,
                    ALBANY, GLOUCESTER, *and Attendants*

FRANCE   Bid farewell to your sisters.

CORDELIA   The jewels of our father, with washed eyes
            Cordelia leaves you: I know you what you are;
            And like a sister am most loth to call
            Your faults as they are named. Love well our
              father: 270
            To your professed bosoms I commit him:
            But yet, alas! stood I within his grace,
            I would prefer him to a better place.
            So farewell to you both.

REGAN   Prescribe not us our duty.

GONERIL   Let your
              study   275
            Be to content your lord, who hath received you
            At Fortune's alms; you have obedience scanted,
            And well are worth the want that you have wanted.

CORDELIA   Time shall unfold what plighted cunning hides;

Goneril and Regan agree that they must discuss how to
ensure that Lear will not have control over their lives in the
future.

280 **Who covers...derides**: those who hide sins are revealed
   eventually, to their shame
283 **nearly appertains**: closely concerns
284 **hence**: go from here
291 **grossly**: obviously
292–293 **yet he hath...himself**: but he has never really known
   what he has been doing
294–298 **The best and...with them**: at his best he was hot
   headed, so at his time of life we must expect not only
   ingrained faults of character, but also the erratic moodiness
   of old age
299 **unconstant starts**: sudden fancies, changes of mind
301 **compliment**: ceremony
302 **hit**: act
303 **carry**: continues to use
304 **disposition**: temperament
   as he bears: that he has
304–305 **this last...offend us**: giving the kingdom to us will
   only bring us trouble
307 **i'th'heat**: strike while the iron is hot

> • *Can you suggest why Shakespeare has changed from
>   verse to prose at this point in the play?*

| | Who covers faults, at last with shame derides. 280 |
| | Well may you prosper! |

FRANCE   Come, my fair Cordelia.
                  [*Exeunt* FRANCE *and* CORDELIA

GONERIL   Sister, it is not little I have to say of what most
nearly appertains to us both. I think our father will
hence to-night.

REGAN   That's most certain, and with you; next month   285
with us.

GONERIL   You see how full of changes his age is; the
observation we have made of it hath not been little:
he always loved our sister most; and with what poor
judgment he hath now cast her off appears too   290
grossly.

REGAN   'Tis the infirmity of his age; yet he hath ever but
slenderly known himself.

GONERIL   The best and soundest of his time hath been but
rash; then must we look from his age, to receive 295
not alone the imperfections of long-engraffed
condition, but therewithal the unruly waywardness
that infirm and choleric years bring with them.

REGAN   Such unconstant starts are we like to have from him
as this of Kent's banishment.   300

GONERIL   There is further compliment of leave-taking
between France and him. Pray you, let us hit
together: if our father carry authority with such
disposition as he bears, this last surrender of his will
but offend us.   305

REGAN   We shall further think of it.

GONERIL   We must do something, and i'th'heat.   [*Exeunt*

Edmund is obsessed with his illegitimacy, and by means of a letter which he is carrying, he intends to denigrate his legitimate half-brother, Edgar. Gloucester enters, disturbed by Lear's recent behaviour.

1 **Nature**: fertility goddess/Mother Nature (a further reference to nature as a major theme)
  thy law: law of nature, the survival of the fittest

3 **Stand...custom**: be subject to the restrictions imposed on a bastard by customary law

4 **curiosity of nations**: the over-particular nature of national laws

5 **moonshines**: months

6 **Lag**: lagging behind
  bastard: base-born, illegitimate
  base: low, vile. (Note Edmund's obsession with the word base over the next few lines; despite having an aristocratic father Edmund is of common birth and he has no claim to any title or possessions – his illegitimacy makes him base, the bottom of the social pile –)

7 **my dimensions...compact**: I am as well-formed

8 **generous**: like a gentleman
  true: true to father's likeness

9 **honest madam's issue**: married woman's child

11–12 **in the lusty...quality**: being conceived in lust, secrecy and vigour have a fuller mixture of energetic qualities

13 **dull...bed**: (this shows a pessimistic view of marriage, and especially marriages of social convenience)

14 **fops**: fools

17 **is to**: is due as much to

19 **speed**: is successful

20 **invention**: plan (power of invention)

21 **top**: overcome

23 **in choler parted**: left in anger

24 **prescribed**: limited

25 **Confined to exhibition**: restricted to a small allowance

26 **Upon the gad**: impulsively (pricked by a goad, possibly), on the spur of the moment

> • *How does Shakespeare force his audience to think about the relationships in two different families?*
> • *How similar are the problems of the two families?*
> • *What are the differences?*

Scene

The Earl of Gloucester's castle

Enter EDMUND, *with a letter*

EDMUND   Thou, Nature, art my goddess; to thy law
                My services are bound. Wherefore should I
                Stand in the plague of custom, and permit
                The curiosity of nations to deprive me,
                For that I am some twelve or fourteen
                      moonshines   5
                Lag of a brother? Why bastard? Wherefore base?
                When my dimensions are as well compact,
                My mind as generous, and my shape as true,
                As honest madam's issue? Why brand they us
                With base? with baseness? bastardy? base, base?   10
                Who in the lusty stealth of nature take
                More composition and fierce quality
                Than doth, within a dull, stale, tired bed,
                Go to th'creating a whole tribe of fops,
                Got 'tween asleep and wake? Well then,   15
                Legitimate Edgar, I must have your land:
                Our father's love is to the bastard Edmund
                As to th'legitimate. Fine word, 'legitimate'!
                Well, my legitimate, if this letter speed,
                And my invention thrive, Edmund the base   20
                Shall top th'legitimate – : I grow, I prosper;
                Now, gods, stand up for bastards!

                Enter GLOUCESTER

GLOUCESTER Kent banished thus! And France in choler parted!
                And the King gone to-night! prescribed his power!
                Confined to exhibition! All this done   25
                Upon the gad! – Edmund, how now! What news?

EDMUND   So please your Lordship, none.

Edmund draws attention to the letter by seeming to want to hide it. Gloucester takes it from him and discovers what appears to be a plan by Edgar to kill Gloucester.

28 earnestly: eagerly
   put up: put away, hide
32 dispatch: haste/removal
34–35 Let's see...spectacles: dreadful irony (see GLOSSARY), considering later events, about 'seeing' and not needing spectacles
37 o'erread: read through
39 o'erlooking: inspection
41 detain: retain
46 essay or taste: trial or test
47 policy and reverence of age: policy of respecting old age
48 to the best of our times: in our prime
49 relish: enjoy
50 fond bondage: foolish slavery
51–52 sways...suffered: tells us what to do, not because he has authority but because we do not object
53–54 If our...waked him: if I had the power to decide whether our father should sleep or wake (ie he would sleep for ever because I should not wake him)

> • *Do you see any parallel between Gloucester's behaviour here and Lear's attitude to his children in Scene 1?*

[*Putting up the letter*

GLOUCESTER   Why so earnestly seek you to put up that letter?

EDMUND   I know no news, my Lord.

GLOUCESTER   What paper were you reading?   30

EDMUND   Nothing, my Lord.

GLOUCESTER   No? What needed then that terrible dispatch of it
into your pocket? The quality of nothing hath not
such need to hide itself. Let's see: come; if it be
nothing, I shall not need spectacles.   35

EDMUND   I beseech you, Sir, pardon me; it is a letter from my
brother that I have not all o'erread, and for so
much as I have perused, I find it not fit for your
o'erlooking.

GLOUCESTER   Give me the letter, sir.   40

EDMUND   I shall offend, either to detain or give it. The
contents, as in part I understand them, are to
blame.

GLOUCESTER   Let's see, let's see.

EDMUND   I hope, for my brother's justification, he wrote   45
this but as an essay or taste of my virtue.

GLOUCESTER   [*Reads*] *This policy and reverence of age makes
the world bitter to the best of our times; keeps our
fortunes from us till our oldness cannot relish them. I
begin to find an idle and fond bondage in the*   50
*oppression of aged tyranny, who sways, not as it
hath power, but as it is suffered. Come to me, that of
this I may speak more. If our father would sleep till I
waked him, you should enjoy half his revenue for ever,
and live the beloved of your brother,* EDGAR –   55
Hum! Conspiracy! 'Sleep till I waked him, – you
should enjoy half his revenue.' My son Edgar! Had
he a hand to write this? a heart and brain to breed it
in? When came you to this? Who brought it?

EDMUND   It was not brought me, my Lord; there's the   60
cunning of it; I found it thrown in at the

Gloucester is convinced that Edgar is plotting against him. Edmund seems to be pleading for Gloucester not to act with undue haste, but to give Edgar a chance to explain himself. Edmund suggests that Gloucester should overhear the next conversation between the brothers.

62 **casement**: window
closet: room
63 **character**: handwriting
64 **matter**: subject of the letter
65 **in respect of that**: considering the contents
fain: rather
70 **sounded you**: tried you out
73 **fit**: appropriate
at perfect age: mature
74 **declined**: past their prime
as ward to: under the protection of. (Usually a minor would be a 'ward' of a guardian who was legally responsible for the ward's affairs until s/he reached majority.)
77 **Abhorred**: hated
detested: detestable
78 **sirrah**: sir (used when addressing inferiors)
79 **apprehend**: seize
83 **testimony...intent**: evidence of what he means to do
83–84 **should run...course**: you would be adopting a safe plan
84 **where**: whereas
86 **shake in pieces...obedience**: destroy his faith in you
87 **pawn down**: stake
88 **feel**: test
89 **pretence of danger**: dangerous intention
91 **meet**: proper
92–93 **an auricular assurance**: hearing the proof for yourself

> • *Edmund has been abroad until recently. On such a short acquaintance, why is Gloucester prepared to believe him, to Edgar's discredit?*

casement of my closet.

GLOUCESTER You know the character to be your brother's?

EDMUND   If the matter were good, my Lord, I durst swear it
           were his; but, in respect of that, I would fain   65
           think it were not.

GLOUCESTER It is his.

EDMUND   It is his hand, my Lord; but I hope his heart is
           not in the contents.

GLOUCESTER Has he never before sounded you in this   70
           business?

EDMUND   Never, my Lord. But I have heard him oft
           maintain it to be fit that, sons at perfect age, and
           fathers declined, the father should be as ward to the
           son, and the son manage his revenue.   75

GLOUCESTER O villain, villain! His very opinion in the letter!
           Abhorred villain! Unnatural, detested, brutish
           villain! worse than brutish! Go, sirrah, seek him; I'll
           apprehend him. Abominable villain! Where is he?

EDMUND   I do not well know, my Lord. If it shall please   80
           you to suspend your indignation against my
           brother till you can derive from him better
           testimony of his intent, you should run a certain
           course; where, if you violently proceed against him,
           mistaking his purpose, it would make a great gap 85
           in your own honour, and shake in pieces the heart
           of his obedience. I dare pawn down my life for him,
           that he hath writ this to feel my affection to your
           honour, and to no other pretence of danger.

GLOUCESTER Think you so?   90

EDMUND   If your honour judge it meet, I will place you
           where you shall hear us confer of this, and by an
           auricular assurance have your satisfaction; and that
           without any further delay than this very evening.

GLOUCESTER He cannot be such a monster –   95

EDMUND   Nor is not, sure.

Gloucester asks Edmund to discover Edgar's true intent. He blames the recent breakdown in parent/child relationships (for himself and the king) on planetary influence. When Gloucester leaves, Edmund comments that man is too eager to blame his own faults and weaknesses on the stars.

99 **wind...him**: worm your way into his thoughts for me
99–100 **frame...wisdom**: organize it as you think best
100–101 **I would...resolution**: I would give up my status to be free from doubt
102 **presently**: at once
   convey: carry out
103 **find means**: see fit
105 **late**: recent
105–106 **These late...to us**: (it is not difficult to imagine that a superstitious people would interpret an eclipse as a sign of ill omen)
l06–108 **though...effects**: though science explains eclipses, man has to endure the disasters that follow
112 **villain**: Edgar
   comes...prediction: is such as was forecast
113–114 **falls...nature**: no longer shows natural affection
114–115 **We have...time**: things are not what they were
115 **machinations**: plotting
   hollowness: insincerity
117 **disquietly**: disturbingly
118 **it shall...nothing**: you will gain by it
121 **excellent foppery**: extreme stupidity
122 **we are...fortune**: things go against us
122–123 **often...behaviour**: often through our own excessive behaviour
125 **on**: by
126 **treachers**: traitors
127 **spherical predominance**: a planet being in the ascendant when we were born
129–130 **divine thrusting on**: supernatural compulsion
130 **admirable**: awesome, to be wondered at
131 **whoremaster**: lusting
   goatish: lecherous
132 **compounded**: came together

- *Point out the dramatic irony (see GLOSSARY) in lines 119–120.*

GLOUCESTER – to his father, that so tenderly and entirely loves
him. Heaven and earth! Edmund, seek him out;
wind me into him, I pray you: frame the business
after your own wisdom. I would unstate myself 100
to be in a due resolution.

EDMUND I will seek him, Sir, presently; convey the
business as I shall find means, and acquaint you
withal.

GLOUCESTER These late eclipses in the sun and moon 105
portend no good to us: though the wisdom of
Nature can reason it thus and thus, yet Nature finds
itself scourged by the sequent effects. Love cools,
friendship falls off, brothers divide: in cities,
mutinies; in countries, discord; in palaces, 110
treason; and the bond cracked 'twixt son and father.
This villain of mine comes under the prediction;
there's son against father: the King falls from bias of
nature; there's father against child. We have seen
the best of our time: machinations, hollowness, 115
treachery, and all ruinous disorders follow us
disquietly to our graves. Find out this villain,
Edmund; it shall lose thee nothing: do it carefully.
And the noble and true-hearted Kent banished! his
offence, honesty! 'Tis strange. [*Exit* 120

EDMUND This is the excellent foppery of the world, that,
when we are sick in fortune, often the surfeits
of our own behaviour, we make guilty of our
disasters the sun, the moon, and stars; as if we were
villains on necessity, fools by heavenly 125
compulsion, knaves, thieves, and treachers by
spherical predominance, drunkards, liars, and
adulterers by an enforced obedience of planetary
influence; and all that we are evil in, by a divine
thrusting on. An admirable evasion of 130
whoremaster man, to lay his goatish disposition to
the charge of a star! My father compounded with

Edgar appears. Although he has mocked Gloucester's
references to eclipses, Edmund tells his brother of the
influences which the planets are thought to have. He advises
Edgar to think seriously of how he might have offended
their father.

133 **dragon's tail**: a particular positioning of the sun and moon
    nativity: birth
134 **Ursa major**: the Great Bear, a constellation of stars
135 **Fut**: an exclamation, from 'sfoot or by Christ's foot
136 **that I am**: what I am
137 **bastardizing**: being conceived as a bastard
138 **pat**: at the right time
138–139 **like...comedy**: as predictably as the ending of an old
    comedy
139 **is**: for
140 **Tom o'Bedlam**: generic name for any mad beggar; taken
    from Bethlehem, or the Hospital of St Mary of Bethlehem,
    used as an asylum from the early fifteenth century. It is ironic
    that Edmund should refer to Tom o'Bedlam on Edgar's
    arrival, since this is the role to be adopted by Edgar later.
141 **divisions**: family conflicts/musical 'divisions' Fa, sol, la, mi:
    it has been suggested that these notes are discordant to
    reflect Edmund's character
144–145 **this other**: the other
147 **effects**: results
    succeed: turn out
149 **dearth**: famine
150–151 **menaces and maledictions**: threats and curses
152 **diffidences**: cases of lack of trust
152–153 **dissipation of cohorts**: breaking up of armies
153 **nuptial breaches**: failure of marriages
154 **sectary astronomical**: believer in astrology
160 **countenance**: look
163 **forbear his presence**: avoid meeting him
164 **qualified**: reduced

- *Why might it be said that lines 138–141 and 147–153
  indicate that Edmund is self-confident: quite sure of
  himself and the position which he has engineered with
  his father?*

my mother under the dragon's tail, and my nativity
was under *Ursa major*, so that it follows I am
rough and lecherous. Fut! I should have been   135
that I am had the maidenliest star in the firmament
twinkled on my bastardizing. Edgar –

Enter EDGAR

and pat he comes, like the catastrophe of the old
comedy: my cue is villanous melancholy, with a sigh
like Tom o' Bedlam. O! these eclipses do   140
portend these divisions. *Fa, sol, la, mi.*

EDGAR   How now, brother Edmund! What serious
contemplation are you in?

EDMUND   I am thinking, brother, of a prediction I read this
other day, what should follow these eclipses.   145

EDGAR   Do you busy yourself with that?

EDMUND   I promise you the effects he writes of succeed
unhappily; as of unnaturalness between the child
and the parent; death, dearth, dissolutions of
ancient amities; divisions in state; menaces and   150
maledictions against King and nobles; needless
diffidences, banishment of friends, dissipation of
cohorts, nuptial breaches, and I know not what.

EDGAR   How long have you been a sectary astronomical?

EDMUND   When saw you my father last?   155

EDGAR   The night gone by.

EDMUND   Spake you with him?

EDGAR   Ay, two hours together.

EDMUND   Parted you in good terms? Found you no
displeasure in him by word nor countenance?   160

EDGAR   None at all.

EDMUND   Bethink yourself wherein you may have offended
him; and at my entreaty forbear his presence until
some little time hath qualified the heat of his

Edgar protests that someone has blackened his character, but
Edmund tells him to keep out of Gloucester's way until such
time as their father cools down. Edmund gloats that it is too
easy to fool his father and brother.

166–167 with the...allay: even if he injured you it would
scarcely diminish
169–170 have...forbearance: restrain your feelings
172 fitly: at the right time
176–177 I am no...toward you: it would not be honest to
suggest that there is any good feeling towards you
179 faintly: only an impression
image and horror: horrible reality
181 anon: soon
183 credulous: gullible
186 practices: plots
I see the business: I know what I have to do
188 All...fit: everything will be right for me that I can influence
(ie if I have anything to do with it). He sees himself in
control of his own fate.

> • *Is there any reason why Gloucester and Edgar
> should be so gullible?*

Lear is spending his first month with Goneril. Goneril tells
her steward, Oswald, about her dissatisfaction with her
father's attitude.

4 By day and night: all the time (or simply a curse)

	displeasure, which at this instant so rageth in 165
	him that with the mischief of your person it would
	scarcely allay.
EDGAR	Some villain hath done me wrong.
EDMUND	That's my fear. I pray you have a continent
	forbearance till the speed of his rage goes 170
	slower, and as I say, retire with me to my lodging,
	from whence I will fitly bring you to hear my Lord
	speak. Pray ye, go; there's my key. If you do stir
	abroad, go armed.
EDGAR	Armed, brother! 175
EDMUND	Brother, I advise you to the best. I am no honest
	man if there be any good meaning toward you;
	I have told you what I have seen and heard; but
	faintly, nothing like the image and horror of it;
	pray you, away. 180
EDGAR	Shall I hear from you anon?
EDMUND	I do serve you in this business. [*Exit* EDGAR

    A credulous father, and a brother noble,
    Whose nature is so far from doing harms
    That he suspects none; on whose foolish honesty 185
    My practices ride easy! I see the business.
    Let me, if not by birth, have lands by wit:
    All with me's meet that I can fashion fit.   [*Exit*

Scene 3

A room in the Duke of Albany's palace

Enter GONERIL, *and* OSWALD, *her steward*

GONERIL	Did my father strike my gentleman for chiding of
	his Fool?
OSWALD	Ay, Madam.
GONERIL	By day and night, he wrongs me; every hour

Goneril orders Oswald to ensure that he and their staff
neglect Lear and his followers. She will use the complaints
that her father will make to her advantage. She intends to
write to Regan to enlist her co-operation in dealing
with Lear.

  5 **flashes**: suddenly breaks out
    crime: offence
  7 **upbraids us**: tells me off (note the royal plural)
 10 **come...services**: reduce the level of service
 11 **the fault...answer**: I'll be reponsible if there are complaints
 14 **I'd have...question**: I want him to make an issue of it
 15 **distaste**: dislike
 17 **Idle**: foolish
 21 **With checks...abused**: with punishment instead of flattery
    when flattery does not work
 25 **breed...occasions**: bring about opportunities
 26 **speak**: rebuke him
    straight: at once
 27 **To hold...course**: to take the same attitude as I do

> • *The information in this scene could have been conveyed
>   if Goneril had been speaking to her husband. But she
>   confides in Oswald. What does this suggest to us about
>   Goneril's relationship with Albany?*

Kent appears in disguise at the Duke of Albany's palace.

  1 **as well**: as successfully (as his disguise)
  2 **defuse**: disguise
  3 **carry...issue**: achieve my aim completely (the reconciliation of
    Lear and Cordelia)
  4 **razed my likeness**: obliterated, completely changed my
    appearance (shaved?)

He flashes into one gross crime or other,   5
That sets us all at odds: I'll not endure it:
His knights grow riotous, and himself upbraids us
On every trifle. When he returns from hunting
I will not speak with him; say I am sick:
If you come slack of former services,   10
You shall do well; the fault of it I'll answer.

OSWALD   He's coming, Madam; I hear him.   [*Horns within*

GONERIL   Put on what weary negligence you please,
You and your fellows; I'd have it come to question:
If he distaste it, let him to my sister,   15
Whose mind and mine, I know, in that are one,
Not to be over-ruled. Idle old man,
That still would manage those authorities
That he hath given away! Now, by my life,
Old fools are babes again, and must be used   20
With checks as flatteries, when they are seen
    abused.
Remember what I have said.

OSWALD   Well, Madam.

GONERIL   And let his knights have colder looks among you;
What grows of it, no matter; advise your fellows so:
I would breed from hence occasions, and I shall, 25
That I may speak: I'll write straight to my sister
To hold my very course. Prepare for dinner.

                                              [*Exeunt*

Scene 4

A hall in the same

Enter KENT, *disguised*

KENT   If but as well I other accents borrow,
That can my speech defuse, my good intent
May carry through itself to that full issue
For which I razed my likeness. Now, banished Kent,

The disguised Kent offers to serve Lear.

4–7 If thou...labours: if Lear will take you into his service then your beloved King will find you hard-working

Stage direction *Horns*: hunting horns

8 stay a jot: wait a moment

11 What...profess?: what is your profession?

13 profess: (play on words) claim

no less...seem: the suggestion is that he is much more than he seems

14 put me in trust: give me a position of trust

16 judgment: Judgement Day

16–17 when...choose: when I have to

17 to eat no fish: possibly eating fish was associated with weakness, and/or womanizing; it seems to be an example of the rough humour in which Kent, as Caius, indulges

19–20 as poor...King: who has given away everything!

27 countenance: appearance (not just 'face')

32 honest counsel: honourable secrets

curious: elaborate

> • *Look again at the note on line 145, page 12. What can you say about the use of 'thou' and 'you' here?*

If thou canst serve where thou dost stand
    condemned,   5
So may it come, thy master, whom thou lov'st,
Shall find thee full of labours.

Horns within. Enter LEAR, KNIGHTS, *and*
ATTENDANTS

LEAR	Let me not stay a jot for dinner: go, get it ready.
	[*Exit an* ATTENDANT
	How now! what art thou?
KENT	A man, Sir. 10
LEAR	What dost thou profess? What would'st thou with us?
KENT	I do profess to be no less than I seem; to serve him truly that will put me in trust; to love him that is honest; to converse with him that is wise, and 15 says little; to fear judgment; to fight when I cannot choose; and to eat no fish.
LEAR	What art thou?
KENT	A very honest-hearted fellow, and as poor as the King. 20
LEAR	If thou be'st as poor for a subject as he is for a King, thou art poor enough. What would'st thou?
KENT	Service.
LEAR	Who would'st thou serve?
KENT	You. 25
LEAR	Dost thou know me, fellow?
KENT	No, Sir; but you have that in your countenance which I would fain call master.
LEAR	What's that?
KENT	Authority. 30
LEAR	What services canst thou do?
KENT	I can keep honest counsel, ride, run, mar a curious

Lear takes Kent into his service on a trial basis. Oswald is off-hand to Lear, and one of Lear's knights has noticed that the King's party is being treated with much less respect than formerly.

35 **diligence**: taking pains, conscientiousness
42 **knave**: young servant, boy
   Fool: court jester. (A jester would often have a unique and particularly close relationship with his monarch; in this case he is very much like the son whom Lear never had.)
45 **So please you**: he is carrying out Goneril's orders
46 **clotpoll**: blockhead
48 **mongrel**: (addressing Oswald) term of abuse
52 **roundest**: rudest
56 **entertained**: treated
57 **ceremonious affection**: ceremonial (due to king) and affection (due to father)
   wont: used to
58 **abatement**: reduction
59 **dependants**: servants

	tale in telling it, and deliver a plain message bluntly; that which ordinary men are fit for, I am qualified in, and the best of me is diligence. 35

LEAR   How old art thou?

KENT   Not so young, Sir, to love a woman for singing, nor so old to dote on her for anything; I have years on my back forty-eight.

LEAR   Follow me; thou shalt serve me; if I like thee no 40 worse after dinner I will not part from thee yet. Dinner, ho! dinner! Where's my knave? my Fool? Go you and call my Fool hither.

                                             [*Exit an* ATTENDANT

Enter OSWALD

    You, you, sirrah, where's my daughter?

OSWALD   So please you –   [*Exit* 45

LEAR   What says the fellow there? Call the clotpoll back.

                                        [*Exit a* KNIGHT

    Where's my Fool, ho? I think the world's asleep.

Re-enter KNIGHT

    How now! Where's that mongrel?

KNIGHT   He says, my Lord, your daughter is not well.

LEAR   Why came not the slave back to me when I   50 called him?

KNIGHT   Sir, he answered me in the roundest manner, he would not.

LEAR   He would not!

KNIGHT   My Lord, I know not what the matter is; but, to 55 my judgment, your Highness is not entertained with that ceremonious affection as you were wont; there's a great abatement of kindness appears as well in the general dependants as in the Duke himself also and your daughter.   60

Lear has been aware of the change in the way he has been
treated, but he has wondered if he has been over-sensitive.
Oswald is insolent to Lear, and he is struck by the King and
tripped by Kent.

65 rememb'rest: remindest
66 conception: idea
   faint: off-hand
68 jealous curiosity: paranoia
   very pretence: actual intention
70 this: these (for)
72 pined away: languished, wasted away (from grief)
78 My Lady's father: by his own actions Lear has become
   dependent on his daughters; he has relinquished his authority
83 bandy: exchange (from exchanging shots in tennis)
85 base foot-ball player: game associated with the lower classes –
   as distinct from tennis
88 differences: ie differences in position, status

> • *In lines 71–73 the knight comments on the Fool and
>   Lear responds. What do these lines tell us about
>   Cordelia, the Fool and Lear?*

LEAR	Ha! say'st thou so?
KNIGHT	I beseech you, pardon me, my Lord, if I be mistaken; for my duty cannot be silent when I think your Highness wronged.
LEAR	Thou but rememb'rest me of mine own 65 conception: I have perceived a most faint neglect of late; which I have rather blamed as mine own jealous curiosity than as a very pretence and purpose of unkindness: I will look further into't. But where's my Fool? I have not seen him this two days. 70
KNIGHT	Since my young Lady's going into France, Sir, the Fool hath much pined away.
LEAR	No more of that; I have noted it well. Go you, and tell my daughter I would speak with her.

                              [Exit an ATTENDANT

	Go you, call hither my Fool. 75

                              [Exit an ATTENDANT

Re-enter OSWALD

	O! you sir, you, come you hither, sir. Who am I, sir?
OSWALD	My Lady's father.
LEAR	'My Lady's father!' my Lord's knave: you whore-son dog! you slave! you cur! 80
OSWALD	I am none of these, my Lord; I beseech your pardon.
LEAR	Do you bandy looks with me, you rascal? [*Striking him*
OSWALD	I'll not be strucken, my Lord.
KENT	Nor tripped neither, you base foot-ball player. 85 [*Tripping up his heels*
LEAR	I thank thee, fellow; thou serv'st me, and I'll love thee.
KENT	Come, sir, arise, away! I'll teach you differences:

Despite being warned by Lear that he is going too far, the
Fool rebukes his master for his foolish behaviour.

89 **lubber**: clumsy fellow
90–91 **have you wisdom?**: do you know what's good for you?
93 **earnest**: a down payment
94 **coxcomb**: fool's cap
95 **pretty knave**: fine fellow
96 **were best**: had better
98 **part**: side
99–100 **and thou...shortly**: if you do not back the stronger
side you will soon be in trouble
101 **banished**: Lear has handed over his kingdom to Goneril and
Regan, and they will turn their backs on him now; it seems
that he has banished them, and not Cordelia
102 **did...blessing**: Cordelia found genuine love
104 **Nuncle**: a corruption of 'mine uncle', and a common form of
address used by jesters
107 **living**: possessions (that enable me to live)
coxcombs: signs of foolishness
108 **beg...daughters**: try asking your daughters for something
and they will soon show you how foolish you have been
109 **the whip**: a punishment for Fools
110 **to kennel**: to be driven out of the house
111 **Brach**: hound bitch. (Dogs were associated with flattery.)
113 **A pestilent...me**: this is noxious and bitter to me
117–126 **Have more...score**: the gist of the rhyme is, be
prudent to accumulate wealth. Presumably the lesson which
is being pointed is that Lear has done the opposite: he has
been rash and thrown away his wealth.
119 **owest**: own

> • *In line 113, why might it be said that Lear could be
> referring to the Fool, to Oswald and the other servants,
> or even to Lear himself?*

	away, away! If you will measure your lubber's
	length again, tarry; but away! Go to; have you 90
	wisdom? [*Exit* OSWALD] So.
LEAR	Now, my friendly knave, I thank thee: there's
	earnest of thy service. [*Gives* KENT *money*

Enter FOOL

FOOL	Let me hire him too: here's my coxcomb.
	[*Offers* KENT *his cap*
LEAR	How now, my pretty knave! how dost thou? 95
FOOL	Sirrah, you were best take my coxcomb.
KENT	Why, Fool?
FOOL	Why? for taking one's part that's out of favour.
	Nay, and thou canst not smile as the wind sits,
	thou'lt catch cold shortly: there, take my 100
	coxcomb. Why, this fellow has banished two on's
	daughters, and did the third a blessing against his
	will: if thou follow him thou must needs wear my
	coxcomb. How now, Nuncle! Would I had two
	coxcombs and two daughters! 105
LEAR	Why, my boy?
FOOL	If I gave them all my living, I'd keep my coxcombs
	myself. There's mine; beg another of thy daughters.
LEAR	Take heed, sirrah; the whip.
FOOL	Truth's a dog must to kennel; he must be 110
	whipped out when the Lady's Brach may stand by
	th'fire and stink.
LEAR	A pestilent gall to me!
FOOL	Sirrah, I'll teach thee a speech.
LEAR	Do. 115
FOOL	Mark it, Nuncle:
	Have more than thou showest,
	Speak less than thou knowest,
	Lend less than thou owest,

Using rhyme and riddle, the Fool maintains his attack on the King.

120 **goest**: walk
121 **Learn...trowest**: listen to more than you believe
122 **Set...throwest**: gamble moderately
124 **in-a-door**: indoors
126 **Than two...score**: than you would expect
127 **nothing**: nonsense
128 **unfeed**: unpaid. (Lawyers were notorious for working not on the promise of payment, but only when cash was forthcoming – no fee, no plea!)
129–130 **Can you...Nuncle?**: surely something can be made of anything
131 **nothing...nothing**: see Act 1 scene 1 line 89
132–133 **so much...comes to**: how much his tenants paid (for which he did nothing!)
134 **bitter**: sarcastic
138 **lord**: Lear himself
141 **Do...stand**: impersonate him
143 **presently**: immediately
144 **motley**: Fool's multi-coloured clothing
145 **found out**: discovered
    there: he points to where Lear is standing
147–148 **that...born with**: you are a born fool/we are all as foolish as new-born babies
149 **This is...Fool**: this is not wholly foolish/this man is not a complete fool
151 **monopoly**: exclusive privilege (of selling some item or trading with a particular country); the privilege was 'conferred by the state', but in Elizabethan times, often at a price!
151–153 **if I had...snatching**: the Fool takes Kent's remark to mean this is not foolishness all together or you will not find every bit of foolishness in this one man. I do not have stupidity all to myself; lords and ladies have their share of it.

> • *Can you suggest why King Lear seems prepared to take this barrage of criticism from the Fool?*

	Ride more than thou goest,	120
	Learn more than thou trowest,	
	Set less than thou throwest;	
	Leave thy drink and thy whore,	
	And keep in-a-door,	
	And thou shalt have more	125
	Than two tens to a score.	

KENT   This is nothing, Fool.

FOOL   Then 'tis like the breath of an unfeed lawyer; you
gave me nothing for't. Can you make no use of
nothing, Nuncle?   130

LEAR   Why no, boy; nothing can be made out of nothing.

FOOL   [*To* KENT] Prithee, tell him, so much the rent of his
land comes to: he will not believe a Fool.

LEAR   A bitter Fool!

FOOL   Dost thou know the difference, my boy,   135
between a bitter Fool and a sweet one?

LEAR   No, lad; teach me.

FOOL
    That lord that counselled thee
      To give away thy land,
    Come place him here by me,   140
      Do thou for him stand:
    The sweet and bitter fool
      Will presently appear;
    The one in motley here,
      The other found out there.   145

LEAR   Dost thou call me fool, boy?

FOOL   All thy other titles thou hast given away; that thou
wast born with.

KENT   This is not altogether Fool, my Lord.

FOOL   No, faith, lords and great men will not   150
let me; if I had a monopoly out, they would have
part on't: and ladies too, they will not let me have
all the fool to myself; they'll be snatching. Nuncle,

The Fool continues to rebuke Lear.

157 crowns: pieces of shell
158 clovest: split
159–160 bor'st...dirt: referring to the fable of the old man who was worried about overloading his ass so he carried him
160 bald crown: bald head
162 myself: a fool
164–167 Fools had...apish: fools were never less popular because even wise men are behaving foolishly, but they do not know how to be truly witty since they only have imitative skills
168 When...wont: how long have you been accustomed
169–171 since thou...breeches: since you gave your daughters the power to keep you in line
172–173 Then they...sung: they weep for joy and I sing in sorrow (illustrating the topsy-turvy world which Lear's decision has created)
174–175 play...among: hide himself amongst fools
178 And: if
179 I marvel what kin: I wonder at the relationship
184–185 thou hast...sides: your sense has been whittled away on two sides
186 parings: shavings
187 what makes...on?: what are you doing wearing that headband (of a frown)?

> • *What seem to be the necessary qualities for a king's Fool?*

give me an egg, and I'll give thee two crowns.

LEAR   What two crowns shall they be?   155

FOOL   Why, after I have cut the egg i'th'middle and eat
up the meat, the two crowns of the egg. When
thou clovest thy crown i'th'middle, and gav'st away
both parts, thou bor'st thine ass on thy back o'er
the dirt: thou hadst little wit in thy bald crown   160
when thou gav'st thy golden one away. If I speak
like myself in this let him be whipped that first finds
it so.
    Fools had ne'er less grace in a year;
        For wise men are grown foppish,   165
    And know not how their wits to wear,
        Their manners are so apish.

LEAR   When were you wont to be so full of songs, sirrah?

FOOL   I have used it, Nuncle, e'er since thou mad'st thy
daughters thy mothers; for when thou gav'st   170
them the rod and putt'st down thine own breeches,
    Then they for sudden joy did weep,
        And I for sorrow sung,
    That such a king should play bo-peep,
        And go the fools among.   175
Prithee, Nuncle, keep a schoolmaster that can
teach thy Fool to lie: I would fain learn to lie.

LEAR   And you lie, sirrah, we'll have you whipped.

FOOL   I marvel what kin thou and thy daughters are:
they'll have me whipped for speaking true,   180
thou'lt have me whipped for lying; and sometimes I
am whipped for holding my peace. I had rather be
any kind o'thing than a fool; and yet I would not
be thee, Nuncle; thou hast pared thy wit o'both
sides, and left nothing i'th'middle: here comes   185
one o'the parings.

Enter GONERIL

LEAR   How now, daughter! what makes that frontlet on?

Goneril takes Lear to task about the behaviour of his
followers. The Fool is not impressed that the King is being
told what to do.

189 pretty: fine, manly
190–191 an 0...figure: a zero without a preceding figure to give
it value
196–197 He that...want some: he who gives everything away
because he is tired of it will one day want some of it back
198 shealed peascod: empty peapod
199 all-licensed: free to do as he pleases
201 carp: find fault, complain
202 rank: gross
204 safe redress: sure remedy
205 too late: only too recently
206 course: of action
206–212 put it on...discreet proceeding: encourage it by not
showing disapproval; if you do this I will rebuke you for it,
and the remedies will be swift. These remedies might offend
you and in other circumstances that would be a shame, but
they will be necessary in the interests of a healthy state, and
considered to be wise measures.
214–215 The hedge-sparrow...young: probably a proverb,
obviously an illustration of ingratitude
215 it: its
216 candle: light of the state (Lear)
darkling: in the dark
219 fraught: loaded
220 dispositions: states of mind
222 May not...horse?: even a Fool can see when things are the
wrong way round (Lear being told what to do)

You are too much of late i'th'frown.

FOOL   Thou wast a pretty fellow when thou hadst no need
to care for her frowning; now thou art an O   190
without a figure. I am better than thou art now; I
am a Fool, thou art nothing. [*To* GONERIL] Yes,
forsooth, I will hold my tongue; so your face bids
me, though you say nothing.
         Mum, Mum: 195
         He that keeps nor crust nor crumb,
         Weary of all, shall want some.
That's a shealed peascod.   [*Pointing to* LEAR

GONERIL Not only, Sir, this your all-licensed Fool,
But other of your insolent retinue   200
Do hourly carp and quarrel, breaking forth
In rank and not-to-be-endured riots. Sir,
I had thought, by making this well known unto
     you,
To have found a safe redress; but now grow fearful,
By what yourself too late have spoke and done,   205
That you protect this course, and put it on
By your allowance; which if you should, the fault
Would not 'scape censure, nor the redresses sleep,
Which, in the tender of a wholesome weal,
Might in their working do you that offence,   210
Which else were shame, that then necessity
Will call discreet proceeding.

FOOL   For you know, Nuncle,
         The hedge-sparrow fed the cuckoo so long,
         That it's had it head bit off by it young.   215
So out went the candle, and we were left darkling.

LEAR   Are you our daughter?

GONERIL I would you would make use of your good wisdom,
Whereof I know you are fraught; and put away
These dispositions which of late transport you   220
From what you rightly are.

FOOL   May not an ass know when a cart draws the horse?

Lear does not appear to take Goneril seriously until she demands that he reduce the number of his followers. He decides to go immediately to Regan.

223 Jug: familiar name for Joan/container for ale
   Whoop...thee: possibly from a popular song
226 notion: mental capacity
226–227 discernings Are lethargied: senses are drugged
   waking?: am I awake? (He assumes he is dreaming.)
230 that: who I am
230–231 for by...daughters: if I were to judge by my kingship, my knowledge and my reason (which lead me to think that I am Lear) I should wrongly assume that I had daughters
233 Which: whom
235 admiration: pretended astonishment
   o'th'savour: the same taste
236 pranks: childish games
240 disordered: disorderly
   deboshed: debauched, undisciplined
   bold: insolent
242 Shows: appears
   epicurism: gluttony. (Epicurus was a Greek philosopher who believed that intellectual pleasure was the goal of life; however, misinterpretation of his philosophy has led to his being linked exclusively with sensual pleasures.)
244 graced: by the King's presence
244–245 doth speak For: demands
247 disquantity your train: reduce the number of your followers
248 remainders...depend: those who stay with you
249 besort: be suitable for
250 Which know...you: who know their position – and you
252 Degenerate: treacherous
   bastard: he is suggesting that Goneril is not behaving like his daughter
253 daughter: Regan
254 You strike my people: see Act 1 scene 4 line 83

- *Lear's mocking questions and comments (lines 217, 224–228, 230–232, 234) might be influenced by the Fool's attitude in the scene so far. (Ironically he will need these questions answering later.)*
- *How does Goneril convince Lear that she means business?*

	Whoop, Jug! I love thee.	
LEAR	Does any here know me? This is not Lear:	
	Does Lear walk thus? speak thus? Where are his	
	eyes?	225
	Either his notion weakens, his discernings	
	Are lethargied – Ha! waking? 'tis not so.	
	Who is it that can tell me who I am?	
FOOL	Lear's shadow.	
LEAR	I would learn that; for by the marks of	230
	sovereignty, knowledge, and reason, I should be	
	false persuaded I had daughters.	
FOOL	Which they will make an obedient father.	
LEAR	Your name, fair gentlewoman?	
GONERIL	This admiration, Sir, is much o'th'savour	235
	Of other your new pranks. I do beseech you	
	To understand my purposes aright:	
	As you are old and reverend, should be wise.	
	Here do you keep a hundred knights and squires;	
	Men so disordered, so deboshed, and bold,	240
	That this our court, infected with their manners,	
	Shows like a riotous inn: epicurism and lust	
	Makes it more like a tavern or a brothel	
	Than a graced palace. The shame itself doth speak	
	For instant remedy; be then desired	245
	By her, that else will take the thing she begs,	
	A little to disquantity your train;	
	And the remainders, that shall still depend,	
	To be such men as may besort your age,	
	Which know themselves and you.	
LEAR	Darkness and	
	devils!	250
	Saddle my horses; call my train together.	
	Degenerate bastard! I'll not trouble thee:	
	Yet have I left a daughter.	
GONERIL	You strike my people, and your disordered rabble	

Lear is beginning to compare Goneril's ingratitude with Cordelia's previous 'offence'. He calls on the gods to make Goneril infertile, or to help her to produce a child to make her life a misery.

256 **Woe**: woe to the person
Woe...repents: speaking to Goneril, thinking about his treatment of Cordelia
257 **Is it your will?**: do you agree with this?
261 **kite**: scavenging bird, and hence a person who preys on others
263 **particulars**: finer points
264 **exact regard**: precise detail
264–265 **support...name**: live up to the honour of their reputation
265–266 **O most...show**: it was a minor indiscretion but how important it seemed at the time! (Cordelia's failure to declare her love openly is now insignificant.)
267 **engine**: machine/implement
frame of nature: natural disposition
269 **gall**: bitterness
270 **gate**: head
271 **dear**: precious to me
279 **derogate**: dishonoured, debased
280 **teem**: produce children
281 **spleen**: malice, evil
282 **thwart disnatured**: perverse and unnatural

- *What is the significance of lines 265–266?*
  In lines 274–288 we see an extremely bitter curse for a father to inflict on his daughter.
- *Does he have good reason for it?*
- *Is Lear's present bitterness in any way connected with his previous treatment of Cordelia?*

Make servants of their betters.   255

Enter ALBANY

LEAR   Woe, that too late repents; O! Sir, are you come?
            Is it your will? Speak, Sir. Prepare my horses.
            Ingratitude, thou marble-hearted fiend,
            More hideous, when thou show'st thee in a child,
            Than the sea-monster.

ALBANY   Pray, Sir, be patient.   260

LEAR   [*To* GONERIL] Detested kite! thou liest.
            My train are men of choice and rarest parts,
            That all particulars of duty know,
            And in the most exact regard support
            The worships of their name. O most small fault, 265
            How ugly didst thou in Cordelia show!
            Which, like an engine, wrenched my frame of
                nature
            From the fixed place, drew from my heart all love,
            And added to the gall. O Lear, Lear, Lear!
            Beat at this gate, that let thy folly in,   [*Striking his
                                                        head* 270
            And thy dear judgment out! Go, go my people.
                            [*Exeunt* KENT *and* KNIGHTS

ALBANY   My Lord, I am guiltless, as I am ignorant
            Of what hath moved you.

LEAR   It may be so, my Lord.
            Hear, Nature, hear! dear Goddess, hear!
            Suspend thy purpose, if thou didst intend   275
            To make this creature fruitful!
            Into her womb convey sterility!
            Dry up in her the organs of increase,
            And from her derogate body never spring
            A babe to honour her! If she must teem,   280
            Create her child of spleen, that it may live
            And be a thwart disnatured torment to her!
            Let it stamp wrinkles in her brow of youth,

Lear condemns Goneril, convinced that Regan will take his
side in the argument. Albany is puzzled by the events that
are going on around him: they seem beyond his
understanding, and are certainly beyond his control.

284 cadent: falling
   fret: cut, wear away
285–286 Turn all...contempt: laugh scornfully at her
   troubles, treat her joys with contempt
291–292 But let...gives it: let his ill-humour play itself out as it
   always does with old people
293 clap: stroke
294 Within a fortnight!: only two weeks previously 100 had
   been agreed on
297 perforce: unavoidably
298 Should...them: make it seem that you are worthy of a king's
   tears
299 Th'untented woundings: wounds too deep to be cleaned
   with lint
300 fond: foolish
301 Beweep this cause: if you shed tears about this matter
302 loose: emit
303 temper: soften
305 comfortable: comforting
307 flay: skin
   visage: face
308–309 I'll resume...for ever: (ie becoming king again)
308 shape: appearance
311–312 partial...To: biased because of

> • *Note Lear seems to believe that he can take off and put
>   on 'kingship' as he fancies (lines 308–309).*
> • *Is Goneril right to suspect Lear of treason (line 310)?*

	With cadent tears fret channels in her cheeks,	
	Turn all her mother's pains and benefits	285
	To laughter and contempt, that she may feel	
	How sharper than a serpent's tooth it is	
	To have a thankless child! Away, away! [*Exit*	
ALBANY	Now, Gods that we adore, whereof comes this?	
GONERIL	Never afflict yourself to know more of it:	290
	But let his disposition have that scope	
	As dotage gives it.	

Re-enter LEAR

LEAR	What! fifty of my followers at a clap;	
	Within a fortnight!	
ALBANY	What's the matter, Sir?	
LEAR	I'll tell thee. [*To* GONERIL] Life and death! I am ashamed	295
	That thou hast power to shake my manhood thus,	
	That these hot tears, which break from me perforce,	
	Should make thee worth them. Blasts and fogs upon thee!	
	Th'untented woundings of a father's curse	
	Pierce every sense about thee! Old fond eyes,	300
	Beweep this cause again, I'll pluck ye out,	
	And cast you, with the waters that you loose,	
	To temper clay. Yea, is't come to this?	
	Ha! Let it be so: I have another daughter,	
	Who, I am sure, is kind and comfortable:	305
	When she shall hear this of thee, with her nails	
	She'll flay thy wolvish visage. Thou shalt find	
	That I'll resume the shape which thou dost think	
	I have cast off for ever. [*Exit*	
GONERIL	Do you mark that?	310
ALBANY	I cannot be so partial, Goneril,	
	To the great love I bear you, –	

After her father's departure, Goneril says it is important to
reduce the number of Lear's knights so that he will not
present a threat. Albany suggests she might have gone too
far but she does not listen. She sends Oswald to Regan with
a letter asking for her sister's support.

315 **tarry**: wait
   take...with thee: take me with you/go with the description
   of fool (this was a common quip on parting)
316–321 **A fox...after**: these were all end-rhymes in Elizabethan
   English; the verse shows the Fool's contempt for Goneril
319 **sure**: certainly be sent
323 **politic**: shrewd, prudent
324 **At point**: armed
325 **buzz**: rumour
   fancy: fantasy, product of the imagination
326 **He may enguard...powers**: he may protect his old age with
   these forces
327 **in mercy**: at his mercy
328 **fear too far**: be over-cautious
329 **still**: always
330 **Not fear...taken**: rather than live in fear of being overtaken
   by harms
332 **sustain**: looks after
337 **particular**: personal
339 **compact**: strengthen, reinforce

> • *From what you have seen of Oswald so far would you*
> *judge him to be a typical servant?*

GONERIL	Pray you, content. What, Oswald, ho!
	[*To the* FOOL] You, sir, more knave than fool, after
	your master.
FOOL	Nuncle Lear, Nuncle Lear! tarry, take the Fool 315
	with thee.
	A fox, when one has caught her,
	And such a daughter,
	Should sure to the slaughter,
	If my cap would buy a halter; 320
	So the Fool follows after. [*Exit*
GONERIL	This man hath had good counsel. A hundred
	knights!
	'Tis politic and safe to let him keep
	At point a hundred knights; yes, that on every
	dream,
	Each buzz, each fancy, each complaint, dislike, 325
	He may enguard his dotage with their powers,
	And hold our lives in mercy. Oswald, I say!
ALBANY	Well, you may fear too far.
GONERIL	Safer than trust too far.
	Let me still take away the harms I fear,
	Not fear still to be taken: I know his heart. 330
	What he hath uttered I have writ my sister;
	If she sustain him and his hundred knights,
	When I have showed th'unfitness, –
	Re-enter OSWALD
	How now,
	Oswald!
	What, have you writ that letter to my sister?
OSWALD	Ay, madam. 335
GONERIL	Take you some company, and away to horse:
	Inform her full of my particular fear;
	And thereto add such reasons of your own
	As may compact it more. Get you gone,
	And hasten your return. [*Exit* OSWALD

Goneril accuses Albany of being naive in his attitude to Lear.

341 This milky...course: mild and gentle course of action
343 attaxed: complained of
344 harmful: ie dangerous to the state
346 Striving...well: compare the current American phrase, If it
ain't broke, don't fix it
348 th'event: let's see what happens

**Lear sends Kent to Regan with a letter, presumably
announcing Lear's arrival. The Fool tells the King that
Regan will be just like Goneril.**

1 before: ahead
Gloucester: the town
2–4 Acquaint...letter: only answer my daughter's questions
about the letter; do not volunteer information
4 diligence: dispatch, carrying this out
8 were't: it meaning brain
9 kibes: chilblains
11–12 thy wit...slipshod: you will not need slippers for
chilblains because you have no brains
14 kindly: like her kind (cruelly)
15 this: Goneril
crab: sour apple
18 She will...crab: your experience with one will be as sour as
with the other

	No, no, my Lord,	340
	This milky gentleness and course of yours	
	Though I condemn not, yet, under pardon,	
	You are much more attaxed for want of wisdom	
	Than praised for harmful mildness.	

| ALBANY | How far your eyes may pierce I cannot tell: 345 |
| | Striving to better, oft we mar what's well. |

| GONERIL | Nay, then – |

| ALBANY | Well, well; th'event.   [*Exeunt* |

Scene 5

Court before the same

Enter LEAR, KENT, *and* FOOL

| LEAR | Go you before to Gloucester with these letters. Acquaint my daughter no further with any thing you know than comes from her demand out of the letter. If your diligence be not speedy I shall be there afore you. 5 |

| KENT | I will not sleep, my Lord, till I have delivered your letter.   [*Exit* |

| FOOL | If a man's brains were in's heels, were't not in danger of kibes? |

| LEAR | Ay, boy. 10 |

| FOOL | Then, I prithee, be merry; thy wit shall not go slip-shod. |

| LEAR | Ha, ha, ha! |

| FOOL | Shalt see thy other daughter will use thee kindly; for though she's as like this as a crab's like an 15 apple, yet I can tell what I can tell. |

| LEAR | What canst tell, boy? |

| FOOL | She will taste as like this as a crab does to a crab. Thou canst tell why one's nose stands i'th'middle |

The Fool tries to keep up Lear's spirits by making light
hearted observations which have a serious intent. Lear is
experiencing difficulty in concentrating on what is said to
him.

20 on's: of one's
22–23 Why...spy into: man will not do anything silly if he uses
his senses properly
30 horns: sexual innuendo
31 forget my nature: cease to be a kind father/go mad
33 Thy asses...'em: your fools have gone to see to them
34 seven stars: the constellation Pleiades
mo: more
37 To take't...perforce: to regain the kingdom by force
Monster: monstrous
43–44 O! let...mad: is this a premonition? There is an irony that,
in his uncertain state of mind, this is the one thing that he is
definite about.
44 temper: normal state of mind
48–49 She that's...shorter: the virgin who does not understand
the seriousness of the situation will be too simple to preserve
her chastity
departure, ...shorter: a rhyme in Elizabethan English
49 unless...shorter: coarse reference to cutting short the penis, so
prolonging the girl's virginity
long, shorter: a play on words

- *Despite the Fool's jocular conversation and quips, Lear
  is distracted. What is he thinking about at lines 24, 31
  and 37?*
- *With Lear's mind in turmoil, how helpful is it that the
  Fool keeps up a constant babble of riddle and critical
  comment. Do you hold the Fool partly responsible for
  Lear's state of mind?*

	on's face?	20
LEAR	No.	
FOOL	Why, to keep one's eyes of either side's nose, that what a man cannot smell out, he may spy into.	
LEAR	I did her wrong, –	
FOOL	Canst tell how an oyster makes his shell?	25
LEAR	No.	
FOOL	Nor I neither; but I can tell why a snail has a house.	
LEAR	Why?	
FOOL	Why, to put's head in; not to give it away to his daughters, and leave his horns without a case.	30
LEAR	I will forget my nature. So kind a father! Be my horses ready?	
FOOL	Thy asses are gone about 'em. The reason why the seven stars are no mo than seven is a pretty reason.	
LEAR	Because they are not eight?	35
FOOL	Yes, indeed: thou would'st make a good Fool.	
LEAR	To take't again perforce! Monster Ingratitude!	
FOOL	If thou wert my Fool, Nuncle, I'd have thee beaten for being old before thy time.	
LEAR	How's that?	40
FOOL	Thou should'st not have been old till thou hadst been wise.	
LEAR	O! let me not be mad, not mad, sweet heaven; Keep me in temper; I would not be mad!	

Enter GENTLEMAN.

	How now! Are the horses ready?	45
GENTLEMAN	Ready, my Lord.	
LEAR	Come, boy.	
FOOL	She that's a maid now, and laughs at my departure, Shall not be a maid long, unless things be cut shorter.	

[*Exeunt*

ACTIVITIES

Keeping track

Scene 1

1 In the opening dialogue between Kent and Gloucester, what do we learn about:
   • the King and the current 'political' situation
   • Gloucester's relationships with his two sons?
2 What does Lear say he wants to achieve by dividing his kingdom between his daughters? Are there any signs that it will not be as straightforward as Lear anticipates?
3 How and why does Cordelia '*mar her fortunes*'?
4 What is the reason for Lear's banishment of Kent?
5 At the end of the scene Goneril and Regan discuss their father's behaviour. What does this dialogue add to our knowledge of the two sisters themselves, their father and their family relationships?

Scene 2

6 What are Edmund's views on legitimacy and illegitimacy?
7 What are the differences between what Edmund appears to believe in, and what his father believes in?
8 How does Edmund set his trap for Gloucester and Edgar?

Scene 3

9 Now that he has abdicated his power, how is Lear behaving, according to Goneril? What does she intend to do about it?

Scene 4

10 How does Kent manage to continue serving Lear despite his banishment?
11 There is growing tension between Lear and his knights, and Goneril's household. Which incidents bring it to a head? Are your sympathies entirely with Lear in this matter? Do the Fool's comments affect your attitude?

Scene 5

12 In this scene:
   • what is the Fool trying to do

- how does he go about it
- can you suggest why he takes this approach?

Drama

1 Use FORUM THEATRE (see page 273) to explore the moment (Act 1 scene 1 line 86) when Cordelia says, '*Nothing, my Lord.*'
2 Use the 'Mirror, Mirror' technique (see page 272) to explore Goneril or Regan's thoughts after they have returned home at the end of scene 1.
3 Edmund has no one in whom to confide. After re-reading his opening speech in scene 2 work in pairs, one as Edmund and one as a friend who tries to talk him out of his chosen path.
4 The appearance of the Fool is crucial to a successful production of the play. How would you portray him (see also 8, below)? Consider mannerisms, costume, way of speaking, and accent. Look at some of the first exchanges with Lear in Act 1 scene 4. Select one or two of these exchanges and in pairs try to find the timing required to make this particular type of 'black' wordplay comical.
5 If you were to present an up-dated or even modern version of this act, there are a number of decisions you would have to make
   – and justify – before beginning on production details:
   - the exact period in which the action takes place
   - the situation/status of the Lear and Gloucester families
   - the 'settings' of each scene
   - the role and costume of the Fool
   - the costumes of the different characters
   - Kent's disguise.
   Do you have any suggestions for solving these problems?

Close study

1 Make sure that you are absolutely clear in your mind about the central event/s of Act 1 scene 1 because this is crucial to subsequent actions and reactions in the play.
   Explain:
   - what Lear is planning to do as King of Britain
   - what effect he anticipates this will have on his children
   - what upsets Lear's plan
   - what he does as a result of this
   - what this tells us about Lear as a king, as a father and as a human being.
2 Look at the responses of the three sisters to Lear's request:
   Goneril, lines 54–60
   Regan, lines 68–74
   Cordelia, lines 90–92 and 94–103.

- The vocabulary used by Goneril and Regan includes words associated with personal possessions or profit: dearer (line 55) valued (line 56) poor (line 59) prize (line 69) deed (line 70) precious (line 73).

  Is this a coincidence or does it show what is uppermost in their minds?

- Cordelia says that she must remain true to herself. By the end of the act we have seen already some of the repercussions of her honesty. Her apprehension (lines 60, 75–77) shows us that she might suspect something of the sort.

  If she feels that way, is it self-indulgent of her to disregard the consequences and answer her father as she does?

  What harm would it have done to answer in the same vein as her sisters?

3 Explain any similarities in, or differences between, the way in which the following are feeling at the end of scene one about what Lear has done:
- Cordelia and Kent
- Goneril and Regan
- France and Burgundy.

What do such reactions tell us about these characters?

4 Part of Shakespeare's skill is his bringing together of different themes. Note how he deals with these different themes (see page 00) in the early lines of the play:

1 human relationships and conflicts
2 the influence on man of the natural universe
3 the influence of gods and the supernatural
4 the structure of society
5 the transfer of power.

In Act 1 scene 1 the following lines refer to these (numbered) themes.

Lines				
	12–14	1	94–103	1
	36–41	4 and 5	108–111	2 and 3
	48–51	1 and 5	112–115	1
	62–65	1 and 5	122–125	1
	82–84	1	134–135	4 and 5
	90–92	1	145–148	4

Complete the references for the rest of scene 1:

Lines		
	146–147	246–248
	151	253–254
	159–160	268–270
	171–178	287
	181–182	289–291
	188–205	292

211–212	295–298
217–220	303–305

5 Often a theme is dealt with most memorably by the use of imagery and/or metaphor. In *King Lear* recurrent images concern:
   • nature/the natural world
   • health/sickness/old age
   • family/fertility/sex
   • money/position/power.
   In Act 1 scene 1 the imagery of nature can be seen in lines 115–117 and 121; the imagery of health is evident in lines 162–163 and 214.
   Find similar references to family and money.
   (You are advised to keep note of the imagery as you read through the play, together with line references and/or quotations. It will prove useful for answering later questions.)

Key scene

Lear's clash with Goneril: Act 1 scene 4 lines 187–309

Keying it in

1 This encounter comes about because Lear challenged Goneril about her cold and unwelcoming attitude. Look at Act 1 scene 3.
   • Why is Goneril angry here?
   • What other cause of irritation does she claim?
   • What instruction does she give her servants? Why?
2 At the beginning of Act 1 scene 4 we see the disguised Kent determined to continue to serve Lear. Read again lines 1–93.
   • What is the effect of Kent's display of allegiance to Lear?
   • What is the significance of what the knight has to tell Lear? How would you describe the knight's manner and behaviour here?
   • How is Oswald involved in this scene and what is the significance of his reply to Lear's question, '*Who am I, sir?*' (line 77)?
3 In the section immediately prior to Lear's confrontation with Goneril we see the Fool commenting on Lear's actions.
   • What is the effect of his jokes and comments about Lear being a fool for having given away his kingdom?
   • What do you think about the way that Lear responds to the Fool's comments?
   • What is the significance of the Fool's comment:
   '*I had rather be
   any kind o'thing than a fool; and yet I would not
   be thee*' (lines 182–184)?

The scene itself

4 lines 187–212

Goneril enters and it is immediately clear from her frowns that she is displeased.

- How does the Fool's comment to Lear:
  '*I am better than thou art now; I
  am a Fool, thou art nothing*' (lines 191–192)
  sound the key note here?
- What does Goneril complain of (lines 199–212)?
- What do you make of her attitude to her father?

5 lines 213–223

- What is the significance of the Fool's comments:
  '*The hedge-sparrow fed the cuckoo so long
  That it's had it head bit off by it young*' (lines 214–215) and
  '*May not an ass know when a cart draws the horse?*' (line 222)?
- What is the significance of Lear's, '*Are you our daughter?*' (line 217)?

6 lines 224–233

The question of 'identity' already touched on in lines 77 and 217 is at the heart of Lear's speech here.

- Why do you think Lear questions his identity at this point?
- What state of mind do you think he is in?

7 lines 234–250

- What further complaints does Goneril put forward here?
- How does she view Lear?
- What offer does she make to her father?
- What do you think her motives are?

8 lines 250–271

- What do you think about the language in which Lear responds to his daughter?
- What kind of imagery predominates?
- What happens to the verse structure in this section?
- How has Lear's view of Cordelia's '*fault*' now changed, and why is this change significant?
- Why do you think Lear dismisses his knights at the end of this section?

9 lines 272–288

Lear now lays a terrible curse on Goneril.

- Make a list of all the images he uses in this verbal attack on his daughter.
- Which particular images do you find most powerful? Why?

10 lines 289–309

Albany looks on amazed at what is happening as he does not know
what is wrong with Lear.
- What is Goneril's attitude to her father's wild words?
- What do you think is significant about Lear threatening to pluck
  out his own eyes?
- What does Lear's conviction that he will find comfort and
  protection with Regan tell us about him?
- How would you sum up Lear's state of mind as he leaves?

Overview

This scene is important because it marks Lear's first step towards
self-knowledge and realizing the full extent of the foolishness of
his behaviour.
- In what ways does Lear begin to see the truth of things?
- How does the scene help to clarify our view of the characters?
- How far do you sympathize with Lear at the end of this scene?

Writing

1 Imagine that you are one of the characters referred to in CLOSE
   STUDY, question 2, page 65. At the end of Act 1 scene 1:
   - how do you feel about what has happened
   - how do you feel about the person/people responsible for what has
     happened
   - and, briefly, how do you think you might be affected in the future
     by what has happened?
   Your writing can be in the form of a diary entry or an interior
   monologue.
2 Briefly, in note form if you wish, what differences are you already
   aware of in the characters of Edgar and Edmund? Are there any
   similarities?
3 In scene 1 Regan says of her father, '*he hath ever but slenderly
   known himself*' (lines 292–293). In scene 5 Lear says he is afraid that
   he might be losing touch with reality:
       '*O! let me not be mad, not mad, sweet heaven*' (lines 43–44).
   In note form, and giving quotations and/or line references, what
   evidence have you seen so far to support Regan's view and Lear's
   apprehension? (These notes will be useful for work in Act 3 and Act 4.)

It is dark. Edmund, on his way to see Edgar, is told that the
Duke of Cornwall and Regan are to visit the Earl of
Gloucester. There are rumours of a conflict between Cornwall
and Albany. Edmund tells Edgar that he can use the darkness
to avoid their father.

 1 **Save**: God save (common greeting)
 8 **ear-bussing**: ear-kissing (ie whispered)
    arguments: topics of conversation
10 **toward**: imminent
14 **The better**: so much the better
15 **This weaves...business**: inevitably this news fits neatly into my
    plans
16 **take**: capture
17 **queasy question**: delicate matter (queasy, liable to vomit)
18 **Briefness...work**: prompt action and good luck help me
19 **descend**: come down. (Edgar is in Edmund's room/s – see Act
    1 scene 2 lines 171–173.)
21 **Intelligence**: information

> • *(Lines 10–11) There are other references in the play to*
>   *this conflict, but nothing materializes.*
>   *Elizabethans generally believed that a land could not*
>   *be ruled satisfactorily by more than one person. They*
>   *would expect civil war to result from the situation which*
>   *Lear has created.*

Act two

Scene **1**

A court within the castle of the Earl of Gloucester

Enter EDMUND *and* CURAN, *meeting*

EDMUND   Save thee, Curan.

CURAN   And you, sir. I have been with your father, and
given him notice that the Duke of Cornwall and
Regan his Duchess will be here with him this night.

EDMUND   How comes that?   5

CURAN   Nay, I know not. You have heard of the news
abroad? I mean the whispered ones, for they are yet
but ear-bussing arguments.

EDMUND   Not I: pray you, what are they?

CURAN   Have you heard of no likely wars toward, 'twixt   10
the Dukes of Cornwall and Albany?

EDMUND   Not a word.

CURAN   You may do then, in time. Fare you well, sir.   [*Exit*

EDMUND   The Duke be here to-night! The better! best!
This weaves itself perforce into my business.   15
My father hath set guard to take my brother;
And I have one thing, of a queasy question,
Which I must act. Briefness and Fortune, work!
Brother, a word; descend: brother, I say!

Enter EDGAR

My father watches: O Sir! fly this place;   20
Intelligence is given where you are hid;
You have now the good advantage of the night.
Have you not spoken 'gainst the Duke of

Edmund persuades Edgar to take part in a mock sword
fight, knowing that Gloucester is approaching. When Edgar
has fled, Edmund wounds himself and convinces his father
that he has been injured because he refused to co-operate
with Edgar's wishes to murder Gloucester.

24 i'th'haste: in great haste
26 Upon his party: on his side
27 Advise yourself: think about it
29 cunning: pretence
30 seem to defend: give the appearance of defending
  quit you well: give a good account of yourself
33–34 beget...endeavour: give the impression that I had really
  been in a fight
34–35 drunkards...sport: dashing young men in Elizabethan
  times would often mix their own blood with wine to drink a
  toast to loved ones
38 Mumbling...charms: he is playing on Gloucester's
  superstition
38–39 conjuring...mistress: calling upon the moon to watch
  over him
40 Look, Sir, I bleed: a delaying tactic – he must convince
  Gloucester of Edgar's guilt before allowing them to meet
41 Fled this way: he points in the wrong direction
43 murther: murder
45 parricides: murders of fathers
  bend: aim

- *Can you work out what is happening in lines 31–32?*
- *Edgar might seem naive to play into Edmund's hands
  with the sword fight, but look how Edmund has
  unsettled him in a very short time: in lines 20–26 how
  many enemies has he suggested that Edgar has?*

Cornwall?
He's coming hither, now, i'th'night, i'th'haste,
And Regan with him; have you nothing said   25
Upon his party 'gainst the Duke of Albany?
Advise yourself.

EDGAR   I am sure on't, not a word.

EDMUND   I hear my father coming; pardon me;
In cunning I must draw my sword upon you;
Draw; seem to defend yourself; now quit you
    well.   30
Yield; come before my father. Light, ho! here!
Fly, brother. Torches! torches! So, farewell.
                                        [*Exit* EDGAR
Some blood drawn on me would beget opinion
                                        [*Wounds his arm*
Of my more fierce endeavour: I have seen
    drunkards
Do more than this in sport. Father! father!   35
Stop, stop! No help?

Enter GLOUCESTER, *and* SERVANTS *with torches*

GLOUCESTER   Now, Edmund, where's the
             villain?

EDMUND   Here stood he in the dark, his sharp sword out,
Mumbling of wicked charms, conjuring the moon
To stand auspicious mistress.

GLOUCESTER   But where is he?

EDMUND   Look, Sir, I bleed.

GLOUCESTER   Where is the villain, Edmund? 40

EDMUND   Fled this way, Sir, when by no means he could –

GLOUCESTER Pursue him, ho! Go after.   [*Exeunt some* SERVANTS
                                        'By no means' what?

EDMUND   Persuade me to the murther of your lordship;
But that I told him, the revenging Gods
'Gainst parricides did all the thunder bend;   45

Edmund describes Edgar's 'attack' on him. Gloucester says that, with Cornwall's help, Edgar will be caught and put to death. Anticipating Edgar's capture, Edmund says that his brother has told him that he will deny all and blame Edmund; and, as the legitimate son, Edgar will expect to be believed.

46 **Spoke with...bond**: explained in how many ways and with how strong a bond
47 **in fine**: finally
48 **loathly opposite**: bitterly opposed
49 **fell motion**: fierce thrust
50 **prepared**: unsheathed
51 **unprovided**: unprotected
  lanched: pierced
52 **alarumed**: roused (as to the sound of battle)
53 **quarrel's right**: justice of the cause
54 **gasted**: terrified
57 **And found – dispatch**: once found – death!
  arch and patron: chief patron (hendiadys – see GLOSSARY)
61 **to the stake**: to get his desserts
62 **death**: will be put to death
64 **pight**: firmly fixed (from 'pitched')
  curst speech: angry words
65 **discover**: reveal
66 **unpossessing**: unable to inherit by right
67–69 **If I...faithed?**: if I deny what you say, do you have any qualities which would make people believe you?
69–72 **No: what I...practice**: no, I would deny everything, you can be sure, even if you produced my own handwriting as evidence; and I'd blame it all on you – the idea, the scheming and the wicked plan
73 **make a...world**: suppose everyone to be very stupid
75 **pregnant**: promising
  potential spirits: powerful driving forces
76 **strange**: unnatural
  fast'ned: hardened
77 **got**: begot
  I never got him: I am not his father
Stage direction *Tucket*: personal fanfare of Cornwall

• *'Thou unpossessing bastard!' is a particularly telling phrase. Why does Edmund use it, do you think?*

Spoke with how manifold and strong a bond
The child was bound to th'father; Sir, in fine,
Seeing how loathly opposite I stood
To his unnatural purpose, in fell motion,
With his prepared sword he charges home   50
My unprovided body, lanched mine arm:
And when he saw my best alarumed spirits
Bold in the quarrel's right, roused to th'encounter,
Or whether gasted by the noise I made,
Full suddenly he fled.

GLOUCESTER   Let him fly far: 55
Not in this land shall he remain uncaught;
And found – dispatch. The noble Duke my master,
My worthy arch and patron, comes to-night:
By his authority I will proclaim it,
That he which finds him shall deserve our
         thanks,   60
Bringing the murderous coward to the stake;
He that conceals him, death.

EDMUND   When I dissuaded him from his intent,
And found him pight to do it, with curst speech
I threatened to discover him: he replied,   65
'Thou unpossessing bastard! dost thou think,
If I would stand against thee, would the reposal
Of any trust, virtue, or worth in thee
Make thy words faithed? No: what I should deny, –
As this I would; ay, though thou didst produce   70
My very character – I'ld turn it all
To thy suggestion, plot, and damned practice:
And thou must make a dullard of the world,
If they not thought the profits of my death
Were very pregnant and potential spirits   75
To make thee seek it.'

GLOUCESTER   O strange and fast'ned
         villain!
Would he deny his letter, said he? I never got him.
                                        [*Tucket within*

Gloucester praises Edmund, and says he will make sure that he can inherit his land. Cornwall and Regan arrive because they have heard from Goneril and do not want to be at home when Lear turns up. They are surprised by Edgar's behaviour which Regan blames on her father's influence.

79 **ports**: seaports/gates (means of exit)
80 **The Duke...that**: he is seeking the support of the man who now rules this part of the country
83 **natural**: illegitimate/showing natural affection
83–84 **work the means...capable**: make legal an inheritance for you
86 **I can...now**: is only a short time ago
87 **comes too short**: is inadequate
88 **Which can...th'offender**: with which the offender can be punished
96 **consort**: company (the implication is gang, mob)
97 **affected**: disposed
98 **put him on**: incited him to
99 **expense**: spending
    waste: squandering
101 **cautions:** warnings
102 **sojourn**: stay
    my house: Regan sees herself in control.
104–105 **I hear...office**: dramatic irony – see GLOSSARY
105 **child-like office**: true son's affection

- *What does the repetition of lines 89, 92 and 95 show us about Gloucester's state of mind?*
- *How does Regan seek to associate all evil with Lear; and how does Edmund quickly establish a rapport with Regan?*

Hark! the Duke's trumpets. I know not why he
    comes.
All ports I'll bar; the villain shall not 'scape;
The Duke must grant me that: besides his
    picture   80
I will send far and near, that all the kingdom
May have due note of him; and of my land,
Loyal and natural boy, I'll work the means
To make thee capable.

Enter CORNWALL, REGAN, *and* ATTENDANTS

CORNWALL   How now, my noble friend! since I came hither 85
    Which I can call but now, I have heard strange news.

REGAN   If it be true, all vengeance comes too short
    Which can pursue th'offender. How dost, my Lord?

GLOUCESTER   O! Madam, my old heart is cracked, it's cracked.

REGAN   What! did my father's godson seek your life? 90
    He whom my father named, your Edgar?

GLOUCESTER   O! Lady, Lady, shame would have it hid.

REGAN   Was he not companion with the riotous knights
    That tended upon my father?

GLOUCESTER   I know not, Madam; 'tis too bad, too bad. 95

EDMUND   Yes, Madam, he was of that consort.

REGAN   No marvel then though he were ill affected;
    'Tis they have put him on the old man's death,
    To have th'expense and waste of his revenues.
    I have this present evening from my sister 100
    Been well informed of them, and with such
        cautions
    That if they come to sojourn at my house,
    I'll not be there.

CORNWALL   Nor I, assure thee, Regan.
    Edmund, I hear that you have shown your father
    A child-like office.

Edmund accepts Cornwall's invitation to enter his service.
Regan tells Gloucester that they have come to him for advice.

106 **bewray his practice**: expose his scheming
107 **apprehend**: arrest
110–111 **make your...please**: carry out your intention (to
capture Edgar) and use my influence as you see fit
113 **ours**: a follower of mine (and given protection). Note the
use of the royal plural.
115 **seize on**: claim
116 **Truly, however else**: loyally, even if I might be lacking in
other respects
118 **out of season**: at a time not of our choosing
threading...night: threading our way through the night.
(The implication of threading a needle in the dark
emphasizes the difficulty of their situation as Regan sees it:
on the other hand, acting in the dark suggests that there is
something to hide.)
119 **Occasions**: reasons
prize: importance
122 **differences**: disputes
123 **from**: away from
123–124 **the several...dispatch**: each messenger waits to be sent
back (with a reply)
125 **Lay...bosom**: find peace at heart
125–126 **bestow...businesses**: we need you to give us advice
about our affairs
127 **Which craves...use**: demand immediate attention

> • *What do Regan's 'my house' (line 102, previous page)
> and her interruption here (line 118) tell us about the
> relationship between Cornwall and Regan?*

EDMUND	It was my duty, Sir.	105

GLOUCESTER He did bewray his practice; and received
This hurt you see, striving to apprehend him.

CORNWALL Is he pursued?

GLOUCESTER   Ay, my good Lord.

CORNWALL If he be taken he shall never more
Be feared of doing harm; make your own
    purpose,   110
How in my strength you please. For you,
    Edmund,
Whose virtue and obedience doth this instant
So much commend itself, you shall be ours:
Natures of such deep trust we shall much need;
You we first seize on.

EDMUND   I shall serve you, Sir,   115
Truly, however else.

GLOUCESTER   For him I thank your Grace.

CORNWALL You know not why we came to visit you, –

REGAN Thus out of season, threading dark-eyed night:
Occasions, noble Gloucester, of some prize,
Wherein we must have use of your advice.   120
Our father he hath writ, so hath our sister,
Of differences, which I best thought it fit
To answer from our home; the several messengers
From hence attend dispatch. Our good old friend,
Lay comforts to your bosom, and bestow   125
Your needful counsel to our businesses,
Which craves the instant use.

GLOUCESTER   I serve you, Madam.
Your Graces are right welcome.
                                    [*Flourish. Exeunt*

Kent meets Oswald outside Gloucester's castle. Oswald does not recognise Kent, but he has to withstand a stream of abuse.

1 **dawning**: it is still dark
2 **Ay**: not true, but Kent plays along with Oswald
4 **mire**: mud
5 **if thou lov'st me**: please
7 **care not for**: don't like
8 **pinfold**: pen for stray animals
   Lipsbury pinfold: there is no trace of a place called Lipsbury, so it is usually taken to mean the space between the lips; the phrase is interpreted as teeth
9 **care**: worry (play on words from line 7)
13 **broken meats**: left-overs
14 **three-suited**: menial servants were given three suits a year
14–15 **hundred-pound**: James I sold knighthoods for £100; the implication is that Oswald is claiming to be better than he is
15 **worsted-stocking**: real gentlemen wore silk
15–16 **lily-livered**: cowardly (bloodless, white-livered)
16 **action-taking**: going to law
   glass-gazing: vain (looking in the mirror)
17 **super-serviceable**: over-anxious to serve
   finical: fussy
   one trunk-inheriting: owning only enough to fit into one trunk
18–19 **be a bawd...service**: be prepared to do any disgusting service if it was asked of you
19 **composition**: compound
20 **pandar**: procurer (for improper purposes, as bawd). In literature, Pandarus or Pandaro was the go-between who procured for Troilus the love of Cressida.
23 **thy addition**: these titles
24 **rail**: pour abuse
26 **varlet**: menial servant

- *How might lines 13–23 be seen as relief from the tension of the previous scene?*
- *How might the same lines be said to demonstrate in some way the themes with which the play is concerned?*

Scene 2

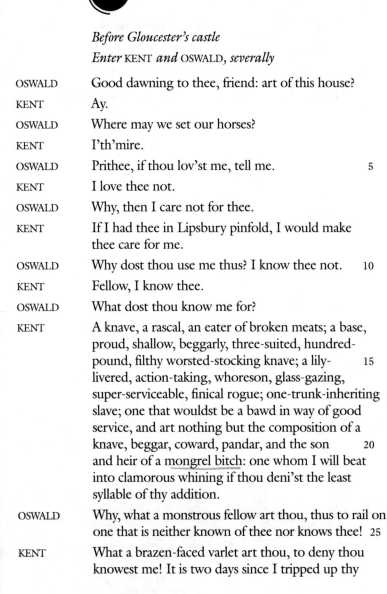

Before Gloucester's castle
Enter KENT *and* OSWALD, *severally*

OSWALD	Good dawning to thee, friend: art of this house?
KENT	Ay.
OSWALD	Where may we set our horses?
KENT	I'th'mire.
OSWALD	Prithee, if thou lov'st me, tell me. 5
KENT	I love thee not.
OSWALD	Why, then I care not for thee.
KENT	If I had thee in Lipsbury pinfold, I would make thee care for me.
OSWALD	Why dost thou use me thus? I know thee not. 10
KENT	Fellow, I know thee.
OSWALD	What dost thou know me for?
KENT	A knave, a rascal, an eater of broken meats; a base, proud, shallow, beggarly, three-suited, hundred-pound, filthy worsted-stocking knave; a lily- 15 livered, action-taking, whoreson, glass-gazing, super-serviceable, finical rogue; one-trunk-inheriting slave; one that wouldst be a bawd in way of good service, and art nothing but the composition of a knave, beggar, coward, pandar, and the son 20 and heir of a mongrel bitch: one whom I will beat into clamorous whining if thou deni'st the least syllable of thy addition.
OSWALD	Why, what a monstrous fellow art thou, thus to rail on one that is neither known of thee nor knows thee! 25
KENT	What a brazen-faced varlet art thou, to deny thou knowest me! It is two days since I tripped up thy

Kent challenges Oswald to fight. Oswald cries for help, and
Kent beats him until Edmund, Cornwall, Regan and
Gloucester intervene. Kent's anger cannot be contained.

30 sop: something which soaks up a liquid (usually bread soaking
up milk, milk-sop)

29–30 I'll make...of you: I'll see to it that you soak up the
moonlight (ie I'll knock you to the ground which the shining
moon is 'flooding')

31 cullionly: rascally (a word full of scorn – cullion means
testicle)

barber-monger: one who is always at the barber's

34 Vanity the puppet: Goneril (seen as a figure of self- interest as
portrayed in a puppet show)

36 carbonado your shanks: criss-cross your legs with sword-cuts

36–37 come your ways: come on

39–40 neat slave: elegant rascal

42 matter: subject of the quarrel

43 With...please: I'll fight with you, fine fellow, if you like

44 flesh: initiate

49 difference: quarrel

52 disclaims in thee: denies any part in making you

52–53 a tailor made thee: you are only what your clothes make
you

55 tailor: tailors were regarded with little respect

heels and beat thee before the King? Draw, you
rogue; for though it be night, yet the moon shines:
I'll make a sop o'th'moonshine of you.   30
                                      [*Drawing his sword*
You whoreson cullionly barber-monger, draw.

OSWALD   Away! I have nothing to do with thee.

KENT   Draw, you rascal; you come with letters against the
            King, and take Vanity the puppet's part against the
            royalty of her father. Draw, you rogue, or I'll so 35
            carbonado your shanks: draw, you rascal; come
            your ways.

OSWALD   Help, ho! murther! help!

KENT   Strike, you slave; stand, rogue, stand; you neat
            slave, strike.   [*Beats him* 40

OSWALD   Help, ho! murther! murther!

Enter EDMUND, *with his rapier drawn*

EDMUND   How now! What's the matter? Part!

KENT   With you, goodman boy, if you please: come, I'll
            flesh ye; come on, young master.

Enter CORNWALL, REGAN, GLOUCESTER, *and*
SERVANTS

GLOUCESTER Weapons! arms! What's the matter here?   45

CORNWALL   Keep peace, upon your lives:
            He dies that strikes again. What is the matter?

REGAN   The messengers from our sister and the King.

CORNWALL   What is your difference? speak.

OSWALD   I am scarce in breath, my Lord.   50

KENT   No marvel, you have so bestirred your valour.
            You cowardly rascal, nature disclaims in thee: a
            tailor made thee.

CORNWALL   Thou art a strange fellow; a tailor make a man?

KENT   A tailor, sir: a stone-cutter or a painter could not 55

Cornwall tries to find out the cause of the dispute. Oswald says he did not fight because of Kent's age, at which Kent resumes his abuse of Oswald.

59–60 at suit: in consideration

61 unnecessary letter: z is little used in English and not used at all in Latin

63 unbolted: unsifted

64 jakes: lavatory
wagtail: a term of abuse; specifically it could mean wanton (suggesting effeminacy)/not standing still

66 beastly: as an animal
reverence: respect

69–70 wear a sword...honesty: carry the symbol of manhood but have no honour

70 smiling rogues: those whose appearance is a deliberate cover for despicable acts

71 holy cords: natural bonds – husband/wife, father/son, King/subject

72 intrince: intricate, tangled
smooth: encourage by means of flattery

75 renege: deny
halcyon: kingfisher

75–76 turn their...gale: it was believed that if a kingfisher was hung up by its beak it would turn in the wind

78 epileptic: presumably Oswald is twitching with emotion at Kent's attack on him

79 Smoile: smile at (dialect)

80 Goose: fool
Sarum: Salisbury

80–81 if I had...Camelot: the connection between goose and cackling is obvious; the gist is 'if you were in my charge I would soon knock you into shape'

81 Camelot: thought to be Winchester

84 No contraries...antipathy: no two things could be more opposite

86 fault: offence

> • *Are you clear what it is about Oswald that Kent despises (lines 69–77); and how this is connected to one of the central issues of the play?*

have made him so ill, though they had been but
two years o'th'trade.

CORNWALL   Speak yet, how grew your quarrel?

OSWALD   This ancient ruffian, Sir, whose life I have spared at
suit of his grey beard, –   60

KENT   Thou whoreson zed! thou unnecessary letter! My
Lord, if you will give me leave, I will tread this
unbolted villain into mortar, and daub the wall of a
jakes with him. Spare my grey beard, you wagtail?

CORNWALL   Peace, sirrah!   65
You beastly knave, know you no reverence?

KENT   Yes, sir; but anger hath a privilege.

CORNWALL   Why art thou angry?

KENT   That such a slave as this should wear a sword,
Who wears no honesty. Such smiling rogues as
  these,   70
Like rats, oft bite the holy cords a-twain
Which are too intrince t'unloose; smooth every
  passion
That in the natures of their lords rebel;
Bring oil to fire, snow to their colder moods;
Renege, affirm, and turn their halcyon beaks   75
With every gale and vary of their masters,
Knowing nought, like dogs, but following.
A plague upon your epileptic visage!
Smoile you my speeches, as I were a Fool?
Goose, if I had you upon Sarum plain,   80
I'd drive ye cackling home to Camelot.

CORNWALL   What! art thou mad, old fellow?

GLOUCESTER   How fell you out? say that.

KENT   No contraries hold more antipathy
Than I and such a knave.   85

CORNWALL   Why dost thou call him knave? What is his fault?

Kent offends Cornwall, who accuses him of using plain-speaking as an artful technique. Kent mockingly uses the language of flattering courtiers. Oswald begins giving his side of the story to the increasingly-impatient Cornwall.

87 likes me not: does not please me

92–101 This is...duties nicely: (Cornwall comments on Kent's criticism of Oswald, lines 69–81)

93 affect: pretend

94–95 constrains...nature: putting on this roughness is not natural to him

97 And they...plain: if people accept his rudeness, then that is fine; if they object, he claims he is just speaking plainly

99 Harbour more craft: hides more craftiness (the marine metaphor is obvious)
more corrupter: double comparative for emphasis

100 silly-ducking observants: low-bowing attendants

101 stretch...nicely: strain to carry out their duties with refinement

102–105 Sir...Phoebus' front: (Kent picks up Cornwall's reference to 'observants', and he speaks satirically)

103 aspect: appearance/position of planets

104 influence: astrological power

104–105 radiant fire...front: fiery forehead of the sun. (Phoebus is another name for Apollo, the sun-god.)

106 dialect: manner of speaking
discommend: disapprove of

107 he: a man such as Cornwall has described

108 beguiled: charmed (irony – see GLOSSARY)

109–110 which for my part...me to't: I will not be a '*plain knave*' even though I know I should win you over from your present displeasure if I were to act towards you in that way. (Scholars disagree on the interpretation of these lines.)

113 very late: recently

114 his misconstruction: the King's misunderstanding

115 he...displeasure: Kent, in league with the King, and gratifying the King's anger

• *Kent is accused of being artificially blunt. What is the effect of his use of courtly parody?*

KENT   His countenance likes me not.

CORNWALL   No more, perchance, does mine, nor his, nor hers.

KENT   Sir, 'tis my occupation to be plain:
            I have seen better faces in my time   90
            Than stands on any shoulder that I see
            Before me at this instant.

CORNWALL   This is some fellow,
            Who, having been praised for bluntness, doth affect
            A saucy roughness, and constrains the garb
            Quite from his nature: he cannot flatter, he,   95
            An honest mind and plain, he must speak truth:
            And they will take it, so; if not, he's plain.
            These kind of knaves I know, which in this
                plainness
            Harbour more craft and more corrupter ends
            Than twenty silly-ducking observants,   100
            That stretch their duties nicely.

KENT   Sir, in good faith, in sincere verity,
            Under th'allowance of your great aspect,
            Whose influence, like the wreath of radiant fire
            On flick'ring Phœbus' front, –

CORNWALL   What mean'st by
                this?   105

KENT   To go out of my dialect, which you discommend
            so much. I know, sir, I am no flatterer: he that
            beguiled you in a plain accent was a plain knave;
            which for my part I will not be, though I should
            win your displeasure to entreat me to't.   110

CORNWALL   What was th'offence you gave him?

OSWALD   I never gave him any:
            It pleased the King his master very late
            To strike at me, upon his misconstruction;
            When he, compact, and flattering his
                displeasure,   115
            Tripped me behind; being down, insulted, railed,

Cornwall finally orders that Kent should be put in the stocks. Kent protests that he serves the King but he is ignored. Gloucester warns that Lear will be offended.

117–118 put upon...him: gave all the appearance of a hero so that he was thought worthy
119 attempting: attacking
self-subdued: did not retaliate
120 in the fleshment: encouraged by the first success
121 Drew: his sword
121–122 None...fool: Ajax (a Greek hero) is a fool alongside people like these
122 stocks: an instrument of punishment in which the victim was placed in a sitting position with the ankles locked in holes between two planks of wood
123 reverend: to be respected (irony) because of age
braggart: vain boaster
128 the grace and person: to the crown and personally
129 Stocking: putting in the stocks
134 colour: complexion, sort
135 away: here
137 fault: offence
138 check: rebuke
purposed: intended
low correction: base means of punishment
139 contemned'st: most despicable
140 pilf'rings: petty theft
trespasses: violations, offences

> • *How does Regan again establish her authority?*

And put upon him such a deal of man,
That worthied him, got praises of the King
For him attempting who was self-subdued;
And, in the fleshment of this dread exploit,   120
Drew on me here again.

KENT   None of these rogues and
cowards
But Ajax is their fool.

CORNWALL   Fetch forth the stocks!
You stubborn ancient knave, you reverend braggart,
We'll teach you.

KENT   Sir, I am too old to learn.
Call not your stocks for me; I serve the King,   125
On whose employment I was sent to you;
You shall do small respect, show too bold malice
Against the grace and person of my master,
Stocking his messenger.

CORNWALL   Fetch forth the stocks!
As I have life and honour, there shall he sit till
noon.   130

REGAN   Till noon! till night, my Lord; and all night too.

KENT   Why, Madam, if I were your father's dog,
You should not use me so.

REGAN   Sir, being his knave, I
will.

CORNWALL   This is a fellow of the self-same colour
Our sister speaks of. Come, bring away the
stocks.   135

[Stocks brought out

GLOUCESTER   Let me beseech your Grace not to do so.
His fault is much, and the good King his master
Will check him for't: your purposed low correction
Is such as basest and contemned'st wretches
For pilf'rings and most common trespasses   140
Are punished with: the King must take it ill,

Regan argues that Goneril will be upset if an attack on her messenger goes unpunished. Kent is put in the stocks. He assures Gloucester that he welcomes the rest. He sleeps.

142 so slightly valued: rated so poorly
143 thus restrained: held in this way
  answer: be answerable for
144 more worse: see note line 99
146 following: carrying out
150 rubbed: impeded (reference to the game of bowls, the rub of the green)
151 watched: gone without sleep
153 may...heels: decline (get holes in his stockings)
154 Give: God give
156 approve...saw: prove the common saying
157–158 Thou...sun: man goes from good to bad (the sun was considered harsh)
159 beacon: sun
  this under globe: earth
161–162 Nothing...misery: those in despair see relief as miraculous
164 obscured course: disguised course of action
164–166 shall find...remedies: (Cordelia) will find time, although she is away from this abnormal situation, to try to put right what is wrong
165 enormous: abnormal
166 o'erwatched: too long without sleep
Stage direction *He sleeps*: Kent remains on stage – possibly curtained off – during the next scene

> • *It is important that there is some hope for the King: that Cordelia is aware of Kent's actions (lines 162–164); and that she means to intervene in Lear's affairs (lines 164–166)*

That he, so slightly valued in his messenger,
Should have him thus restrained.

CORNWALL   I'll answer that.

REGAN   My sister may receive it much more worse
          To have her gentleman abused, assaulted,   145
          For following her affairs. Put in his legs.

                    [KENT *is put in the stocks*

CORNWALL Come, my Lord, away.

                    [*Exeunt all but* GLOUCESTER *and* KENT

GLOUCESTER I am sorry for thee, friend; 'tis the Duke's pleasure,
          Whose disposition, all the world well knows,
          Will not be rubbed nor stopped: I'll entreat
              for thee.   150

KENT   Pray, do not, Sir. I have watched and travelled
              hard;
          Some time I shall sleep out, the rest I'll whistle.
          A good man's fortune may grow out at heels:
          Give you good morrow!

GLOUCESTER The Duke's to blame in this; 'twill be ill taken. 155
                                                      [*Exit*

KENT   Good King, that must approve the common
              saw,
          Thou out of heaven's benediction com'st
          To the warm sun!
          Approach, thou beacon to this under globe,
          That by thy comfortable beams I may   160
          Peruse this letter. Nothing almost sees miracles,
          But misery: I know 'tis from Cordelia,
          Who hath most fortunately been informed
          Of my obscured course; and shall find time
          From this enormous state, seeking to give   165
          Losses their remedies. All weary and o'erwatched,
          Take vantage, heavy eyes, not to behold
          This shameful lodging.
          Fortune, good night; smile once more; turn thy
              wheel!   [*He sleeps*

Edgar describes how he heard himself declared a wanted man, and how he hid from his pursuers. He has no way of escape, so he decides to disguise himself as a filthy, near-naked, mad beggar.

1 **proclaimed**: named an outlaw
2 **by the...tree**: was fortunate to hide in a hollow tree
3 **port**: see Act 2 scene 1 line 79
5 **attend my taking**: wait to capture me
6 **am bethought**: have in mind
most poorest: double superlative – see Act 2 scene 2 lines 99 and 144
8 **penury**: poverty
in contempt of man: with contempt for humanity
10 **elf**: tangle (elves were blamed for knotted hair)
11 **presented**: exposed
outface: defy
13 **proof**: example
14 **Bedlam**: see Act 1 scene 2 line 140
15 **Strike**: stick
mortified: insensible, dead to feeling
16 **wooden pricks**: skewers
rosemary: herb associated with special occasions such as funerals and weddings, believed to dispel evil spirits
17 **object**: sight
low: humble
18 **pelting**: paltry
sheep-cotes: poor shelter for sheep
19 **bans**: curses
20 **Turlygod**: there is no satisfactory explanation for this name
21 **That's...nothing am**: there's some hope for Tom – Edgar has no future

Kent is still in the stocks. Lear, one of his knights and the Fool approach.

1 **they**: Cornwall and Regan

Scene 3

Solitoquy

A wood

Enter EDGAR

EDGAR   I heard myself proclaimed;
And by the happy hollow of a tree
Escaped the hunt. No port is free; no place,
That guard, and most unusual vigilance,
Does not attend my taking. Whiles I may 'scape,   5
I will preserve myself; and am bethought
To take the basest and most poorest shape
That ever penury, in contempt of man,
Brought near to beast; my face I'll grime with filth,
Blanket my loins, elf all my hairs in knots,   10
And with presented nakedness outface
The winds and persecutions of the sky.
The country gives me proof and precedent
Of Bedlam beggars, who, with roaring voices,
Strike in their numbed and mortified bare arms   15
Pins, wooden pricks, nails, sprigs of rosemary;
And with this horrible object, from low farms,
Poor pelting villages, sheep-cotes, and mills,
Sometime with lunatic bans, sometime with
    prayers,
Enforce their charity. Poor Turlygod! poor Tom!   20
That's something yet: Edgar I nothing am.   [*Exit*

Scene 4

Before Gloucester's castle. KENT *in the stocks*

Enter LEAR, FOOL, *and* GENTLEMAN

LEAR   'Tis strange that they should so depart from home,

Lear discovers Kent in the stocks and he is outraged. He refuses to believe that Cornwall and Regan have put him there.

3–4 **no purpose…remove**: no intention to leave
6 **thy pastime**: for amusement
7 **cruel garters**: the stocks round his legs (and a play on words – crewel is a coarse wool)
9–10 **over-lusty at legs**: a wanderer (and a play on words – lust)
10 **nether-stocks**: stocks as stockings
11 **place**: position
12 **To**: as to
20 **Jupiter**: king of the gods
21 **Juno**: Jupiter's wife (association with Cornwall and Regan)
23 **upon respect**: deliberately/to a man to whom respect is due
24 **Resolve…haste**: tell me quickly, but with moderation
26 **Coming from us**: given that you are my messenger

> • *What is the significance of the 'yes'/'no' exchange (lines 14–21)? Why does Lear challenge Kent's version of events?*

	And not send back my messenger.
GENTLEMAN	As I learned,
	The night before there was no purpose in them
	Of this remove.
KENT	Hail to thee, noble master!
LEAR	Ha! 5
	Mak'st thou this shame thy pastime?
KENT	No, my Lord.
FOOL	Ha, ha! he wears cruel garters. Horses are tied by
	the heads, dogs and bears by th'neck, monkeys by
	th'loins, and men by th'legs: when a man's over-
	lusty at legs then he wears wooden nether-stocks. 10
LEAR	What's he that hath so much thy place mistook
	To set thee here?
KENT	It is both he and she,
	Your son and daughter.
LEAR	No.
KENT	Yes. 15
LEAR	No, I say.
KENT	I say, yea.
LEAR	No, no; they would not.
KENT	Yes, yes, they have.
LEAR	By Jupiter, I swear, no. 20
KENT	By Juno, I swear, ay.
LEAR	They durst not do't,
	They could not, would not do't; 'tis worse than murther,
	To do upon respect such violent outrage.
	Resolve me, with all modest haste, which way
	Thou might'st deserve, or they impose, this usage, 25
	Coming from us.
KENT	My Lord, when at their home

Kent gives Lear details of how he comes to be in the stocks.
The Fool implies that Lear has brought this on himself. Lear
goes to find Regan.

27 **commend**: deliver
29 **duty**: respect by
reeking post: steaming messenger
30 **Stewed**: soaked in sweat
32 **spite of intermission**: although he was interrupting my
business
33 **presently**: immediately
34 **meiny**: retinue
40 **Displayed so saucily**: acted insolently
41 **Having...about me**: behaving with honour rather than
discretion
drew: my sword
43 **worth**: derserving
45 **Winter's...that way**: winter's not yet started if the geese are
flying away (reference to the geese flying south before winter
sets in; ie 'the worst is yet to come')
46 **that wear rags**: who are poor
47 **blind**: uncaring, 'blind' to fathers' needs
48 **bear bags**: have money (money-bags)
49 **kind**: considerate
50 **arrant**: downright, out-and-out
51 **Ne'er...key**: never opens the door
52 **dolours**: griefs (because of your daughters); play on words,
dollars
53 **tell**: speak of/count
54 **mother**   55 **Hysterica passio**: two names for the same
indisposition, a feeling of suffocation thought to rise from the
womb – ie hysteria (there is a link here with a sense of
uprising, revolt)
56 **element**: appropriate place

- *Is Kent's version of events leading to his being put in
the stocks strictly accurate?*
- *Is it significant that 'hysterica passio' is an illness
more common in women? Why should Lear be
thinking along these lines when his daughters are on
his mind? What has been his role in bringing them up?*

I did commend your Highness' letters to them,
Ere I was risen from the place that showed
My duty kneeling, came there a reeking post,
Stewed in his haste, half breathless, panting forth 30
From Goneril his mistress salutations;
Delivered letters, spite of intermission,
Which presently they read: on whose contents
They summoned up their meiny, straight took
    horse;
Commanded me to follow, and attend   35
The leisure of their answer; gave me cold looks:
And meeting here the other messenger,
Whose welcome, I perceived, had poisoned mine,
Being the very fellow which of late
Displayed so saucily against your Highness,   40
Having more man than wit about me, drew:
He raised the house with loud and coward cries.
Your son and daughter found this trespass worth
The shame which here it suffers.

FOOL   Winter's not gone yet, if the wild-geese fly that
      way.   45
        Fathers that wear rags
           Do make their children blind,
        But fathers that bear bags
           Shall see their children kind.
        Fortune, that arrant whore,   50
        Ne'er turns the key to th'poor.
    But for all this thou shalt have as many dolours for
    thy daughters as thou canst tell in a year.

LEAR   O! how this mother swells up toward my heart;
    Hysterica passio! down, thou climbing sorrow!   55
    Thy element's below. Where is this daughter?

KENT   With the Earl, Sir; here within.

LEAR   Follow me not; stay here.   [*Exit*

GENTLEMAN   Made you no more offence but what you speak of?

KENT   None.   60

The Fool tells Kent that some of Lear's men have left him since his decline in fortunes. The Fool remains loyal to the King. Lear returns, having been informed that Cornwall and Regan cannot see him because they are tired.

61 chance: does it happen that
62 number: of followers
63 And: if
66–67 We'll...i'th'winter: a reference to Aesop's fable of the ant who stored food in summer because there was none in the winter. Lear's followers will gain nothing by sticking by him in hard times.
67–70 All that...stinking: Even a blind man can recognize failure
69 but can: that cannot
71 wheel: man. (The image of life moving in a circular fashion is repeated in Act 5 scene 3 line 174.)
76 sir: man (servant)
77 follows: does his duty
for form: out of habit
78 pack: pack up
82 The knave...away: the servant who flees is seen, in the end, to be a fool
83 The Fool...perdy: the Fool will stay and, in God's name, prove to be honourable
85 Fool: ie Kent is not dishonourable, not a knave
86 Deny: refuse
87 fetches: tricks
88 images: signs
flying off: desertion
90 quality: nature

- *In lines 70–83 the Fool uses the words knave and Fool in more than one sense. According to him, why should only knaves follow the Fool's advice (lines 74–75)*
- *What has happened to cause Lear's outburst, (lines 86–89?)*

	How chance the King comes with so small a number?
FOOL	And thou hadst been set i'th'stocks for that question, thou'dst well deserved it.
KENT	Why, Fool?

65

FOOL	We'll set thee to school to an ant, to teach thee there's no labouring i'th'winter. All that follow their noses are led by their eyes but blind men; and there's not a nose among twenty but can smell him that's stinking. Let go thy hold when a great wheel runs down a hill, lest it break thy neck with following; but the great one that goes upward, let him draw thee after. When a wise man gives thee better counsel, give me mine again: I would have none but knaves follow it, since a Fool gives it.

70

75

That sir which serves and seeks for gain,
    And follows but for form,
Will pack when it begins to rain,
    And leave thee in the storm.
But I will tarry; the Fool will stay,   80
    And let the wise man fly:
The knave turns Fool that runs away;
    The Fool no knave, perdy.

KENT	Where learned you this, Fool?
FOOL	Not i'th'stocks, Fool.

85

Re-enter LEAR, *with* GLOUCESTER

| LEAR | Deny to speak with me! They are sick! They are weary!
They have travelled all the night! Mere fetches, ay,
The images of revolt and flying off.
Fetch me a better answer. |
|---|---|
| GLOUCESTER | My dear Lord,
You know the fiery quality of the Duke;   90
How unremovable and fixed he is
In his own course. |

Lear's response is confused: in turn he is angry and understanding. But looking again at Kent in the stocks persuades him to act. He sends Gloucester to tell his daughter and son-in-law that he will not be denied.

93 confusion: destruction

100 commands, tends service: commands her service and offers (tenders) his own

102 hot: hot-tempered

104–105 Infirmity doth...bound: illness always causes us to neglect the duties which we have to attend to when we are well

107 forbear: restrain myself

108 fall'n...will: angry with my hastier impulse

109 take: mistake

110 my state: kingly power

112 remotion: keeping remote (out of his way)/being aloof

113 practice: scheming

forth: out of the stocks

115 presently: immediately

116 chamber: bedroom

117 cry...death: kills their sleep

119 my rising heart: see lines 54–55

120 cockney: silly woman

> • *In his heart Lear knows that Cornwall and Regan have snubbed him. Why could he possibly be making excuses for them in lines 103–110? (See also the foot of page 94.)*

LEAR	Vengeance! plague! death! confusion! Fiery! what quality? Why, Gloucester, Gloucester, I'd speak with the Duke of Cornwall and his wife. 95
GLOUCESTER	Well, my good Lord, I have informed them so.
LEAR	Informed them! Dost thou understand me, man?
GLOUCESTER	Ay, my good Lord.

LEAR	The King would speak with Cornwall; the dear
	    father
	Would with his daughter speak, commands, tends
	    service: 100
	Are they informed of this? My breath and blood!
	Fiery! the fiery Duke! Tell the hot Duke that –
	No, but not yet; may be he is not well:
	Infirmity doth still neglect all office
	Whereto our health is bound; we are not
	    ourselves 105
	When Nature, being oppressed, commands the
	    mind
	To suffer with the body. I'll forbear;
	And am fall'n out with my more headier will,
	To take the indisposed and sickly fit
	For the sound man. Death on my state!
	    wherefore 110
	                    [*Looking on* KENT
	Should he sit here? This act persuades me
	That this remotion of the Duke and her
	Is practice only. Give me my servant forth.
	Go tell the Duke and's wife I'd speak with them,
	Now, presently: bid them come forth and hear
	    me, 115
	Or at their chamber-door I'll beat the drum
	Till it cry sleep to death.

GLOUCESTER	I would have all well betwixt you. [*Exit*
LEAR	O me! my heart, my rising heart! but, down!
FOOL	Cry to it, Nuncle, as the cockney did to the eels 120

Gloucester returns with Cornwall and Regan. Lear begins to
complain about Goneril but Regan will not hear criticism of
her sister, whom she claims Lear has misjudged.

121 paste: pastry

121–122 knapped 'em o'th'coxcombs: hit them on the head

123 wantons: rogues

124 buttered his hay: horses will not eat grease – this a reference
to misplaced kindness, like Lear's handing over his kingdom,
bringing trouble

129–130 divorce...adult'ress: consider myself divorced from
your dead mother, letting her lie in the vault an adulteress.
Regan's behaviour would prove that Lear was not her
father.

132 naught: wicked

133 Sharp-toothed: see also Act 1 scene 4 lines 287–288, '*How
sharper than a serpent's tooth...*'
vulture: Prometheus in Greek mythology was tortured by
having a vulture tear at his liver

135 quality: manner

136–138 I have...duty: I hope you undervalue her sense of duty,
rather than she should have shortcomings

141 riots: unruly behaviour

145–146 Nature...confine: you are at the limit of your natural
life

when she put 'em i'th'paste alive; she knapped 'em
o'th'coxcombs with a stick, and cried 'Down,
wantons, down!' 'Twas her brother that, in pure
kindness to his horse, buttered his hay.

Re-enter GLOUCESTER, *with* CORNWALL, REGAN, *and*
SERVANTS

LEAR	Good morrow to you both.
CORNWALL	Hail to your Grace!125 [KENT *is set at liberty*
REGAN	I am glad to see your Highness.

LEAR	Regan, I think you are; I know what reason
	I have to think so: if thou shouldst not be glad,
	I would divorce me from thy mother's tomb,
	Sepulchring an adult'ress. [*To* KENT] O! are you
	    free? 130
	Some other time for that. [*Exit* KENT] Beloved
	    Regan,
	Thy sister's naught: O Regan! she hath tied
	Sharp-toothed unkindness, like a vulture, here.
	                    [*Points to his heart*
	I can scarce speak to thee; thou'lt not believe
	With how depraved a quality – O Regan! 135

REGAN	I pray you, Sir, take patience. I have hope You less know how to value her desert Than she to scant her duty.
LEAR	Say? how is that?
REGAN	I cannot think my sister in the least Would fail her obligation. If, Sir, perchance 140 She have restrained the riots of your followers, 'Tis on such ground, and to such wholesome end, As clears her from all blame.
LEAR	My curses on her!
REGAN	O, Sir! you are old; Nature in you stands on the very verge 145 Of her confine: you should be ruled and led

Regan says Lear is old and he should allow himself to be ruled by those who know what is good for him. She urges Lear to return to Goneril. Lear mocks this suggestion but Regan repeats it. The King curses Goneril again, and assures Regan that she is different from her sister.

147 **discretion...state**: understanding person who knows your condition (a play on words – state also refers to kingdom)
151 **becomes the house**: is appropriate to the household (father–daughter relationship)
153 **Age is unnecessary**: no one wants the aged. (Unnecessary also introduces a key idea which is followed through this scene, culminating in Lear's '*O! reason not the need*' speech, beginning at line 263.)
154 **vouchsafe**: graciously grant
155 **unsightly**: disturbing to see
157 **abated**: deprived
159 **serpent-like**: see note on line 133, page 102
161 **top**: head
young bones: some have suggested that this might refer to an unborn child
162 **taking airs**: infectious vapours
163 **nimble**: swift
165 **fen-sucked**: rising from the fens
166 **fall...her!**: fall on her and cover her in blisters. (There is some variation in the text at this point.)
170 **tender-hefted**: tender-hearted/womanly
174 **scant my sizes**: reduce my allowances
175 **oppose the bolt**: shut the door
177 **offices**: duties
178 **Effects of courtesy**: workings of courtly behaviour

- *Point out the irony of lines 152–154.*
- *Look again at Lear's speech beginning at line 169. Is it a statement of fact, an expression of hope, or a desperate plea?*

By some discretion that discerns your state
Better than you yourself. Therefore I pray you
That to our sister you do make return;
Say you have wronged her.

LEAR   Ask her forgiveness? 150
Do you but mark how this becomes the house:
'Dear daughter, I confess that I am old;
Age is unnecessary: on my knees I beg   [*Kneeling*
That you'll vouchsafe me raiment, bed, and food.'

REGAN   Good sir, no more; these are unsightly tricks.   155
Return you to my sister.

LEAR   [*Rising*]   Never, Regan.
She hath abated me of half my train;
Looked black upon me; struck me with her tongue,
Most serpent-like, upon the very heart.
All the stored vengeances of Heaven fall   160
On her ingrateful top! Strike her young bones,
You taking airs, with lameness!

CORNWALL   Fie, Sir, fie!

LEAR   You nimble lightnings, dart your blinding flames
Into her scornful eyes! Infect her beauty,
You fen-sucked fogs, drawn by the pow'rful sun, 165
To fall and blister her!

REGAN   O the blest Gods! so will you wish on me,
When the rash mood is on.

LEAR   No, Regan, thou shalt never have my curse:
Thy tender-hefted nature shall not give   170
Thee o'er to harshness: her eyes are fierce, but thine
Do comfort and not burn. 'Tis not in thee
To grudge my pleasures, to cut off my train,
To bandy hasty words, to scant my sizes,
And, in conclusion to oppose the bolt   175
Against my coming in: thou better know'st
The offices of nature, bond of childhood,
Effects of courtesy, dues of gratitude;
Thy half o'th'kingdom hast thou not forgot,

Lear is seeking to know who put Kent in the stocks when
Goneril arrives. He asks the gods to help him because he
realises that his daughters are united against him. Goneril
says that an old man's criticism is no proof that she has done
wrong. Cornwall admits to putting Kent in the stocks.

181 Stage direction *Tucket*: personal fanfare, of Goneril this
    time
182 approves: confirms
184 easy-borrowed: shallow/acted
185 Dwells...follows: depends on the changeableness of his
    mistress
187 stocked: put in the stocks
189 sway: power
190 Allow: approve of
191 it: age/authority
    send down...part: step in and act on my behalf
192 this beard: me/old age and authority
195–196 All's not offence...terms so: everything which is
    considered offensive by those who lack judgement, and is
    called offensive by the feeble and old, is not necessarily
    offensive at all
196 sides: of his chest
197 Will...hold?: he expects his body to give way under the strain
    of his inner turmoil
198 disorders: misconduct
199 much less advancement: a worse punishment (not so
    honourable)

> • *In lines 188–191 what assumption about the gods does
> Lear make?*

Wherein I thee endowed.

REGAN   Good sir, to
          th'purpose.   180

LEAR   Who put my man i'th'stocks?   [*Tucket within*

CORNWALL   What trumpet's that?

REGAN   I know't, my sister's: this approves her letter,
          That she would soon be here.

          Enter OSWALD

                              Is your Lady come?

LEAR   This is a slave, whose easy-borrowed pride
          Dwells in the fickle grace of her he follows.   185
          Out, varlet, from my sight!

CORNWALL   What means your
          Grace?

LEAR   Who stocked my servant? Regan, I have good hope
          Thou didst not know on't. Who comes here?

          Enter GONERIL

                                                O
          Heavens
          If you do love old men, if your sweet sway
          Allow obedience, if you yourselves are old,   190
          Make it your cause; send down and take my part!
          [*To* GONERIL] Art not ashamed to look upon this
          beard?
          O Regan! will you take her by the hand?

GONERIL   Why not by th'hand, sir? How have I offended?
          All's not offence that indiscretion finds   195
          And dotage terms so.

LEAR   O sides! you are too tough;
          Will you yet hold? How came my man i'th'stocks?

CORNWALL I set him there, Sir; but his own disorders
          Deserved much less advancement.

Regan suggests that Lear should return to Goneril after dismissing half his men, and then he could come to her at the end of the month, as arranged. Lear says that he would rather live in the wild. He struggles to control his feelings when addressing Goneril. He tells her that he can stay with Regan and keep all his men.

200 being weak, seem so: having no power, act accordingly
204–205 out of that...entertainment: therefore I am unable to provide what is necessary for your reception
207 abjure: reject
208 wage...o'th'air: contend with the open air
210 Necessity's sharp pinch: he knows he has made a lonely and demanding choice
211 hot-blooded: passionate
213 knee: kneel before
squire-like: like a king's young personal attendant
213–214 pension...afoot: beg him to support me
215 sumpter: pack-horse
216 groom: servant
217 I prithee...mad: he knows the fury within him – there is also the crazy/angry ambiguity, and therefore irony, of '*mad*'
223 embossed carbuncle: swollen tumour
224 corrupted: a reference to '*disease*', line 221
chide: argue with
225 Let shame...will: Lear is confident of retribution
226 thunder-bearer: Jupiter
227 high-judging: the supreme judge
Jove: another name for Jupiter
228 Mend: reform, repent

> • *We see Lear experiencing a number of mood changes in lines 217–227. Explain his mood at the following points: lines 217; 218–219; 220; 221–224; and 224–227.*

LEAR	You! did you?
REGAN	I pray you, father, being weak, seem so. 200
	If, till the expiration of your month,
	You will return and sojourn with my sister,
	Dismissing half your train, come then to me:
	I am now from home, and out of that provision
	Which shall be needful for your entertainment. 205
LEAR	Return to her? and fifty men dismissed?
	No, rather I abjure all roofs, and choose
	To wage against the enmity o'th'air;
	To be a comrade with the wolf and owl,
	Necessity's sharp pinch! Return with her! 210
	Why, the hot-blooded France, that dowerless took
	Our youngest born, I could as well be brought
	To knee his throne, and, squire-like, pension beg
	To keep base life afoot. Return with her!
	Persuade me rather to be slave and sumpter 215
	To this detested groom. [*Pointing at* OSWALD
GONERIL	At your choice, Sir.
LEAR	I prithee, daughter, do not make me mad:
	I will not trouble thee, my child; farewell.
	We'll no more meet, no more see one another;
	But yet thou art my flesh, my blood, my daughter; 220
	Or rather a disease that's in my flesh,
	Which I must needs call mine: thou art a boil,
	A plague-sore, or embossed carbuncle,
	In my corrupted blood. But I'll not chide thee;
	Let shame come when it will, I do not call it; 225
	I do not bid the thunder-bearer shoot,
	Nor tell tales of thee to high-judging Jove.
	Mend when thou canst; be better at thy leisure;
	I can be patient; I can stay with Regan,
	I and my hundred knights.
REGAN	Not altogether so; 230

Regan disagrees. She says Lear has taken her by surprise and she is not prepared. Both daughters suggest that Lear does not need his own men at all. Regan says that she will entertain twenty-five only. Lear reminds them of their agreement when he handed over the kingdom. He decides to go back to Goneril because she will allow him fifty men.

233 **mingle...passion**: mix some commonsense with your passionate outbursts
234 **Must be content**: have no choice but to
    and so – : Regan believes that what she is saying is so obvious that there is no point in going on
236 **avouch**: affirm
238 **sith that**: since
    charge and danger: expense and threat to others
241 **Hold amity**: maintain friendship
244 **slack**: neglect
248 **place or notice**: lodging or recognition
249 **all**: everything
250 **Made...depositaries**: put you in charge of my estate, made you trustees
251 **kept a reservation**: made a condition
255 **well-favoured**: good-looking

> • *Lear's judgement of love seems to be linked to material possessions (lines 258–259). In what way does this remind you of Act 1 scene 1?*

	I looked not for you yet, nor am provided	
	For your fit welcome. Give ear, Sir, to my sister;	
	For those that mingle reason with your passion	
	Must be content to think you old, and so –	
	But she knows what she does.	

LEAR   Is this well
                     spoken?   235

REGAN   I dare avouch it, sir: what! fifty followers?
           Is it not well? What should you need of more?
           Yea, or so many, sith that both charge and danger
           Speak 'gainst so great a number? How, in one
               house,
           Should many people, under two commands,   240
           Hold amity? 'Tis hard; almost impossible.

GONERIL   Why might not you, my Lord, receive attendance
           From those that she calls servants, or from mine?

REGAN   Why not, my Lord? If then they chanced to slack ye
           We could control them. If you will come to me, 245
           For now I spy a danger, I entreat you
           To bring but five-and-twenty; to no more
           Will I give place or notice.

LEAR   I gave you all –

REGAN   And in good time you gave it.

LEAR   Made you my guardians, my depositaries,   250
           But kept a reservation to be followed
           With such a number. What! must I come to you
           With five-and-twenty? Regan, said you so?

REGAN   And speak't again, my Lord; no more with me.

LEAR   Those wicked creatures yet do look well-
               favoured   255
           When others are more wicked; not being the worst
           Stands in some rank of praise. [*To* GONERIL] I'll go
               with thee:
           Thy fifty yet doth double five-and-twenty,
           And thou art twice her love.

Goneril tells Lear that a handful of followers will be enough. Regan asks why he should need any at all. Lear begins to argue that man is superior to animals because he has more than basic needs, but, overcome with emotion, he is unable to sustain the argument. Lear promises revenge, and leaves with the knight, Gloucester and the Fool.

261 **To follow**: to be your followers
263 **O!...need**: do not try to calculate need
264 **Are...superfluous**: have something they do not absolutely need
265–266 **Allow...beast's**: if you only allow what is necessary then man is no better than an animal
267–269 **If only...warm**: if you wear clothes for warmth, then you do not need extravagant clothes – which do not keep you warm, anyway
269 **for**: as for
270 **patience**: he says he needs patience, but has he broken off because he has recognized that his own 'needs' – possessions, followers, respect – are the ones that he has just ridiculed his daughters for having?
272 **wretched**: not revered age
274 **fool me...much**: do not make me such a fool
277 **hags**: witches, evil women
283 **Stage direction** *Storm*: the heavens respond to Lear
284 **flaws**: fragments
285 **Or ere**: before
287 **and's**: and his
288 **bestowed**: accommodated
289 **rest**: bed/peace of mind

- *In detail, when and how does Lear's state of mind change during his angry outburst against Goneril and Regan in lines 263–285? (For a reminder, see the foot of page 108.)*
- *What do you notice particularly about the language of lines 278–281?*

GONERIL	Hear me, my Lord.

What need you five-and-twenty, ten, or five,   260
To follow in a house where twice so many
Have a command to tend you?

REGAN   What need one?

LEAR O! reason not the need; our basest beggars
Are in the poorest thing superfluous:
Allow not nature more than nature needs,   265
Man's life is cheap as beast's. Thou art a lady;
If only to go warm were gorgeous,
Why, nature needs not what thou gorgeous wear'st,
Which scarcely keeps thee warm. But, for true
        need, –
You Heavens, give me that patience, patience I
        need! –   270
You see me here, you Gods, a poor old man,
As full of grief as age; wretched in both!
If it be you that stirs these daughters' hearts
Against their father, fool me not so much
To bear it tamely; touch me with noble anger,   275
And let not women's weapons, water-drops,
Stain my man's cheeks! No, you unnatural hags,
I will have such revenges on you both
That all the world shall – I will do such things,
What they are, yet I know not, but they shall be 280
The terrors of the earth. You think I'll weep;
No, I'll not weep:
I have full cause of weeping, [*Storm heard at a
        distance*] but this heart
Shall break into a hundred thousand flaws
Or ere I'll weep. O Fool! I shall go mad.   285
[*Exeunt* LEAR, GLOUCESTER, GENTLEMAN, *and* FOOL

CORNWALL Let us withdraw, 'twill be a storm.

REGAN This house is little: the old man and's people
Cannot be well bestowed.

GONERIL 'Tis his own blame; hath put himself from rest,

Gloucester returns with the news that Lear is preparing to
leave in an extreme fit of anger. He warns that Lear will have
to face an unusually severe storm with little or no shelter.
Goneril tells Gloucester that he should not encourage Lear
to stay; Regan advises locked doors because the 'riotous
knights' might provoke Lear to do anything.

290 **taste**: experience (the results of)
291 **For his particular**: he himself
292 **So am I purposed**: I agree
296 **to horse**: for his horses
297 **give him way**: let him have his own way
   leads himself: makes his own decisions
300 **ruffle**: rage
302–303 **The injuries...schoolmasters**: must learn from the
   harm they do themselves
304 **with**: by
   desperate train: 'riotous knights' (Act 1 scene 3 line 7)
305 **incense**: provoke
306 **have...abused**: listen to bad advice

> • *Do you see any irony in Gloucester's attitude to Lear's
> treatment?*

| | And must needs taste his folly. | 290 |

REGAN   For his particular, I'll receive him gladly,
         But not one follower.

GONERIL   So am I purposed.
         Where is my Lord of Gloucester?

CORNWALL Followed the old man forth. He is returned.

Re-enter GLOUCESTER

GLOUCESTER The King is in high rage.

CORNWALL   Whither is he going? 295

GLOUCESTER He calls to horse; but will I know not whither.

CORNWALL 'Tis best to give him way; he leads himself.

GONERIL My Lord, entreat him by no means to stay.

GLOUCESTER Alack! the night comes on, and the bleak winds
         Do sorely ruffle; for many miles about   300
         There's scarce a bush.

REGAN   O! Sir, to wilful men,
         The injuries that they themselves procure
         Must be their schoolmasters. Shut up your doors;
         He is attended with a desperate train,
         And what they may incense him to, being apt   305
         To have his ear abused, wisdom bids fear.

CORNWALL Shut up your doors, my Lord; 'tis a wild night:
         My Regan counsels well: come out o'th'storm.
                                              [*Exeunt*

CTIVITIES

Keeping track

Scene 1

1 By line 83 Gloucester is saying of Edgar '*I never got him*', and is calling Edmund '*Loyal and natural boy*'. What are your feelings about Gloucester and Edgar at this stage?

Scene 2

2 How does Shakespeare create comedy out of Kent's treatment of Oswald? How does Kent justify his behaviour?

3 How does Kent respond to being put in the stocks, and how is he responsible for the scene's ending on a note of hope?

Scene 3

4 How does Edgar decide to 'preserve himself', and why do you think he chooses that particular method?

Scene 4

5 What is Lear's reaction when he discovers who is responsible for putting Kent in the stocks?

6 Can you justify the argument that the Fool represents Lear's conscience?

7 What is the dramatic irony (see GLOSSARY) of Lear's approach to Regan and Goneril?

8 What arguments do Goneril and Regan use when they confront Lear together? What do you think is the real issue here?

Drama

1 Look at Kent's insulting words to Oswald, beginning Act 2 scene 2 line 13. In pairs, take it in turns to utter these provocative attacks and to be on the receiving end of them.
   • What are appropriate vocal tones and facial expressions?
   • How does Oswald respond?
   • Why does he respond this way – what is his state of mind?

2 We have seen a lot of Cornwall and Regan in public, but what are they like behind closed doors? Do they see eye to eye over most things, or do they argue and fight? Are they fiery, passionate and

determined in their personal relationship; or do they simply share a mutual greed?

Two of your group improvise the couple discussing, in private, the situation at the end of this act. They can be prompted by questions from the rest of the group about what the characters have said and done in the past, to help to present a credible portrayal of Cornwall and Regan.

3 Look at Edgar's speech in Act 2 scene 3. Rehearse this speech as a piece of ensemble work.

Group one:	the words are divided up and spoken from different parts of the room.
Group two:	enact the change that Edgar goes through to become poor Tom.
Group three:	madfolk, mumbling and shouting, culminating in the chant, '*Poor Turlygod! poor Tom!*'
The ending:	all (except one poor Tom) run away leaving poor Tom alone to say weakly, '*Edgar I nothing am.*'

Does this performance help you to understand better how the play works? Might such a treatment help an actor to rehearse the part?

4 Use FORUM THEATRE (see page 273) to examine either: '*O Regan! will you take her by the hand?*' (Act 2 scene 4 line 193) or: '*No, I'll not weep*' (Act 2 scene 4 line 282).

5 If someone dies in strange circumstances a coroner's court has to decide on a verdict.
   • Accidental death means that unusual circumstances were to blame.
   • Death by misadventure means that the death was caused by someone who was behaving legally and who had no intention of causing harm.
   • Death by person or persons unknown is declared when there is evidence of foul play.
   In extreme circumstances the coroner might suggest the person or persons ultimately responsible for the death.

   Imagine that after the end of Act 2, Lear goes off into the storm and is found dead from pneumonia. Set up the room as a coroner's court and select a jury to consider their verdict.

   You will hear evidence from witnesses, including the royal family.
   • The decision will be made after hearing genuine evidence as it appears in the play.
   • A second court can be held in which you might expect certain witnesses not to tell the truth. Will you accept tape

recorded evidence of conversations which took place just
before Lear went off into the storm? Are the tapes genuine,
or have they been tampered with (ie cut, or added to)?

Close study

1 Look again at scene 1.
   • How is Edmund's talent for wickedness and his
     determination to succeed in his scheming emphasized here (lines
     14–76)?
   • In what ways does this scene parallel Act 1 scene 1?
2 The early part of scene 2 provides the audience with some comic
   relief, but it also has a more serious undertone.
   • What serious significance does the scene hold? How is
     this emphasized by Kent's language?
   • What does Cornwall's speech reveal about his character?
     How well suited to Regan do you think he is?
3 Can the developing action of the play be seen as a struggle
   between good and evil characters, or is that too simple? What
   justifications can you find for the 'evil' characters' actions?
      To what extent do the 'good' characters bring their problems on
   themselves?
      Consider these points with especial reference to Edgar and Kent
   in the first two scenes and the Fool and Lear in scene 4.
4 'O! reason not the need...I shall go mad.' (scene 4 lines 263–285)
   • lines 263–266 In what way is the poorest man's life better
     than an animal's?
   • lines 266–269 How, according to Lear, are his daughters
     inconsistent?
   • line 269 'But, for true need,–'   What do you think has flashed
     across his mind at this point?
   • line 270 Why should he need patience – to deal with his daughters
     or with his own thoughts?
   • lines 271–272 What is his attitude here?
   • lines 273–277 Who is he blaming for his daughters' behaviour?
     Where would you place the responsibility?
   • lines 277–282 Is Lear's rage at this point likely to frighten
     his daughters?
   • lines 283–285 What is his attitude now?
   • line 285 'O Fool! I shall go mad.' Is this said to shame his
     daughters; or, because he really believes it: or, perhaps, because he
     really does not know what he is saying?
      If you were an actor in the role of Lear what would the
   language and structure of this speech suggest to you about his

state of mind? How might they affect the way you speak the lines?

Key scene

Lear seeks comfort from Regan: Act 2 scene 4 lines 125–188

Keying it in

1   This encounter comes about as a direct consequence of Lear's confrontation with Goneril in Act 1. He has now arrived at Gloucester's castle in search of Regan and the welcome that he found so lacking in Goneril. However, by the time Lear arrives Regan has already been informed of the situation by her sister's letter.

Look at Act 2 scene 1. The two plots come together here as Regan and Cornwall arrive at Gloucester's castle in an effort to avoid Lear, and Edmund joins forces with them.

• How effective has Goneril's letter been in creating an unfavourable impression of her father (lines 93–94, 97–103)?
• How does the sub-plot, as it develops here, mirror Lear's turning against Cordelia in the main plot (lines 34–84)?
• What is the significance of Cornwall's comments in lines 108–115?

2   Kent arrives at Gloucester's castle ahead of Lear, and after a brief brawl with Oswald he is put in the stocks by Cornwall. Look at Act 2 scene 2. Kent beats Oswald in revenge for his impertinence to Lear.

• What does Cornwall's decision to put Kent in the stocks tell us about his attitude to Lear (lines 125–130)?
• What do you feel about Cornwall's response to Gloucester's intervention (lines 136–143)?
• What is the significance of Regan's comment (lines 144–146)?

3   At the beginning of Act 2 scene 4 Lear and the Fool arrive at Gloucester's castle to find Kent in the stocks.

• What is Lear's initial response (lines 13–26) on hearing who is responsible for this treatment of his servant?
• As the truth begins to dawn on Lear, what is he afraid of (lines 54–56)?
• What thoughts and emotions run through Lear's mind as he is kept waiting to see Regan and Cornwall (lines 86–119)?

The scene itself

4   lines 125–135

- What does Lear feel about the welcome he is given here?
- Lear's '*I would divorce...adult'ress*' (lines 129–130) might lead us to think about his relationships with all his immediate family. Can his instinctive reaction to cut blood-ties be reconciled with his perceived view of 'natural' and 'unnatural' behaviour in others?
- Does Lear's reference to '*Sharp-toothed unkindness*' (line 133) remind you of an earlier comment he made to Goneril? How appropriate is the imagery of Goneril as a bird of prey?

5   lines 136–143

- What has been the nature of Lear's '*O Regan!*' (lines 132, 135)? How, then, does he feel about Regan's response in lines 136–138?
- What tone of voice do you think Regan would adopt in defending her sister (lines 139–143)? What is the significance of Regan's use of '*Sir*' to address her father?

6   lines 144–156

- What attitude does Regan have towards Lear's age?
- How does Lear respond to Regan's suggestion about asking Goneril's forgiveness (lines 148–154)? How should an actor interpret Lear's lines?
- How close is Lear's mock-image of himself to what his daughters really feel about him?
- What is implied by Regan's words in line 155?

7   lines 156–162

- Of what does Lear accuse Goneril?
- How do you interpret Lear's state of mind in lines 160–162?
- What is the implication of Cornwall's interjection in line 162?

8   lines 163–168

- In his continuing curse of Goneril (lines 163–166), is Lear's imagery consistent with that of lines 158–162? Which lines do you find more effective?
- What is the significance of Regan's '*O the blest Gods!*' (line 167)?
- Is Regan justified in her accusation of Lear (lines 167–168)?

9   lines 169–180

- How do you account for the fact that Lear still proclaims Regan's devotion (lines 169–179) even though she has defended her sister's behaviour? That is, is this an example of

dramatic irony (see GLOSSARY) or does Lear appreciate the situation but remain unwilling to acknowledge it?
- In the light of your previous response, what is the significance of Lear's final words in this section, '*Thy half...I thee endowed*' (lines 179–180)?
- How does Lear's vocabulary in this speech compare with that which he used when talking of Goneril?
- What is Regan's attitude to her father's words (line 180)?

10 lines 181–188
- What is the dramatic effect of Goneril's heralded arrival?
- How do you think Regan feels about Goneril's arrival? Why?
- Lear's mind is fixed on the stocking of Kent. Why has this act now assumed a symbolic significance?

Overview

This scene is important because after he has been spurned by Goneril, Lear's hopes now rest with Regan. However, we see in this scene that Regan's attitude is no different from that of her sister. Dramatic tension builds throughout the scene to the arrival of Goneril.
- What changes have you noticed in Lear's state of mind up to the time when Goneril arrives?
- How does Lear behave after Goneril's arrival?
- How far is Lear responsible for his daughters' attitude to him?
- How do you think the two sisters feel about the situation at this point?

Writing

1 Write short descriptions of Gloucester and Cornwall as they appear in this Act. Look particularly at Gloucester's exchange with Edmund in Act 2 scene 1 and his defence of Kent in Act 2 scene 2 lines 136–143; and Cornwall's treatment of Kent in Act 2 scene 2, and Gloucester's comments about Cornwall in the same scene, lines 148–150 and Act 2 scene 4 lines 90–92.

2 Examine how Edmund shows himself in his true colours in this Act. How successful is he in pursuing his plan, and what techniques does he use? Focus on Act 2 scene 2 in particular.

3 Using references from the text to support your ideas, describe Lear's state of mind at the end of the Act. You might find it useful to start by looking at the following references, before finding others for yourself: Act 2 scene 4 lines 21–26, 152–154, 263–285 (see CLOSE STUDY question 4, page 118).

Still in disguise, Kent meets one of Lear's gentlemen on the heath. Kent is told that Lear is wandering the heath in the storm. The King's state of mind is as wild as the weather.

2 **minded**: with a mind
4 **contending with**: struggling against/competing with (in strength of anger)
   fretful elements: angry weather
5–7 **Bids the wind...or cease**: Lear pleads for the water to swallow up the land to bring about an end to the world, or at least a transformation
6 **main**: mainland this could also mean 'sea'; it is not clear
8 **eyeless**: blind
9 **make nothing of**: treat as worthless
10 **his little world of man**: it was a common Elizabethan idea that man was a microcosm – a miniature version of the universe
   out-storm: be more turbulent than
12 **cub-drawn**: sucked dry by cubs
   couch: lie in shelter
14 **unbonneted**: hatless (a hat being a sign of dignity)
15 **what will take all**: anyone/anything wanting to have it, to take everything (the world)
16 **out-jest**: overcome by jesting
17 **heart-strook injuries**: (struck) wounds to the heart
18 **warrant of my note**: strength of my knowledge of you
19 **Commend**: entrust
   dear: important

- *Note the link between weather and emotion (see also Act 2 scene 4 line 283) which will be carried through the next few scenes.*

Act three

Scene 1

A heath
A storm, with thunder and lightning. Enter KENT *and*
a GENTLEMAN, *meeting*

KENT   Who's there, besides foul weather?

GENTLEMAN   One minded like the weather, most unquietly.

KENT   I know you. Where's the King?

GENTLEMAN   Contending with the fretful elements;
Bids the wind blow the earth into the sea,   5
Or swell the curled waters 'bove the main,
That things might change or cease; tears his white
     hair,
Which the impetuous blasts, with eyeless rage,
Catch in their fury, and make nothing of;
Strives in his little world of man to out-storm   10
The to-and-fro-conflicting wind and rain.
This night, wherein the cub-drawn bear would
     couch,
The lion and the belly-pinched wolf
Keep their fur dry, unbonneted he runs,
And bids what will take all.

KENT   But who is with
       him?   15

GENTLEMAN   None but the Fool, who labours to out-jest
His heart-strook injuries.

KENT   Sir, I do know you;
And dare, upon the warrant of my note,
Commend a dear thing to you. There is division,
Although as yet the face of it is covered   20

The rumour of imminent conflict between Albany and Cornwall continues. Kent tells the gentleman that the French army has landed, and Cordelia is with them. He asks the gentleman to trust him, and to go to Dover to report to Cordelia what has happened to Lear. Kent gives him a ring to show Cordelia whom the message is from.

22–25 Who have...state: Albany and Cornwall, like all great men, have in their employment spies for the King of France who know everything about us

22–23 as who...set high: as indeed are all those who are destined for greatness

23 servants...no less: those who appear to be servants
speculations: 'eyes', observers

25 Intelligent: having information

26 snuffs: huffs, fits of indignation
packings: plots

27 rein: play on words, rein/reign
borne: exercised

29 furnishings: external appearances

30 power: army

31 scattered: divided

32 Wise...negligence: aware of our neglect (of security)
secret feet: gained a secret foothold

33–34 at point...banner: about to come out into the open

34 banner: flag

35 my credit: your trust in me

37 making just report: for giving an accurate account

38 unnatural: from his own children
bemadding: maddening

39 plain: complain of

41 assurance: certainty

45 out-wall: exterior appearance

48 fellow: companion/inferior person

52 to effect: in importance

53–55 That, when...other: do that (ie go to Dover) after we have found the King; your job is to go that way, and I'll go this – the first one who sees him, shout to the other

53 pain: task (taking pains)

• *What has been the dramatic purpose of this short scene?*

With mutual cunning, 'twixt Albany and Cornwall;
Who have – as who have not, that their great stars
Throned and set high? – servants, who seem no
    less,
Which are to France the spies and speculations
Intelligent of our state. What hath been seen,   25
Either in snuffs and packings of the Dukes,
Or the hard rein which both of them have borne
Against the old kind King; or something deeper,
Whereof perchance these are but furnishings –
But, true it is, from France there comes a power 30
Into this scattered kingdom; who already,
Wise in our negligence, have secret feet
In some of our best ports, and are at point
To show their open banner. Now to you:
If on my credit you dare build so far   35
To make your speed to Dover, you shall find
Some that will thank you, making just report
Of how unnatural and bemadding sorrow
The King hath cause to plain.
I am a gentleman of blood and breeding,   40
And from some knowledge and assurance offer
This office to you.

GENTLEMAN   I will talk further with you.

KENT   No, do not.
For confirmation that I am much more
Than my out-wall, open this purse, and take   45
What it contains. If you shall see Cordelia, –
As fear not but you shall – show her this ring,
And she will tell you who that fellow is
That yet you do not know. Fie on this storm!
I will go seek the King.   50

GENTLEMAN   Give me your hand. Have you no more to say?

KENT   Few words, but, to effect, more than all yet;
That, when we have found the King, in which your
    pain

54 That: go that
Stage direction *severally*: separately

Lear and the Fool are on another part of the heath. Lear
commands the storm to destroy the earth and bring an end
to mankind. He accepts that the heavens are joined with his
daughters in punishing him.

1 **cheeks**: on old maps winds were indicated by illustrations of
puffing cheeks
2 **cataracts**: waterfalls
hurricanoes: seawater spouts
3 **Till you...cocks!**: he is calling for a second Flood
4 **sulph'rous**: he is talking about lightning; here the suggestion
is of brightness and a burning smell
thought-executing: swift-as-thought (but also the idea that
lightning kills thought)
fires: lightning
5 **Vaunt-couriers**: fore-runners, preparing the way
7 **Strike...o'th'world**: flatten the world
thick rotundity: a suggestion of pregnancy
8 **Crack Nature's moulds**: break nature's pattern
germens: seeds
spill: destroy
10 **court holy-water**: flattery
14 **Rumble thy bellyful!**: addressing the storm
16 **tax**: charge
18 **subscription**: allegiance
21 **servile ministers**: agents, doing what you are told
22 **pernicious**: destructive, wicked
23 **high-engendered battles**: battalions formed in the sky

- *How can the storm be said to reflect a Lear's state of
  mind; b the state of the country?*
- *Comment on Shakespeare's use of onomatopoeia
  (see GLOSSARY) in the first 24 lines of this scene.*

That way, I'll this, he that first lights on him
Holla the other.   55

[*Exeunt severally*

Scene 2

Another part of the heath. Storm still
Enter LEAR *and* FOOL

LEAR   Blow, winds, and crack your cheeks! rage! blow!
           You cataracts and hurricanoes, spout
           Till you have drenched our steeples, drowned the
               cocks!
           You sulph'rous and thought-executing fires,
           Vaunt-couriers of oak-cleaving thunderbolts,   5
           Singe my white head! And thou, all-shaking
               thunder,
           Strike flat the thick rotundity o'th'world!
           Crack Nature's moulds, all germens spill at once
           That makes ingrateful man!

FOOL   O Nuncle, court holy-water in a dry house is   10
           better than this rain-water out o'door. Good
           Nuncle, in, ask thy daughters blessing; here's a
           night pities neither wise men nor Fools.

LEAR   Rumble thy bellyful! Spit, fire! spout, rain!
           Nor rain, wind, thunder, fire, are my daughters: 15
           I tax you not, you elements, with unkindness;
           I never gave you kingdom, called you children,
           You owe me no subscription: then let fall
           Your horrible pleasure; here I stand, your slave,
           A poor, infirm, weak, and despised old man.   20
           But yet I call you servile ministers,
           That will with two pernicious daughters join
           Your high-engendered battles 'gainst a head
           So old and white as this. O, ho! 'tis foul.

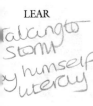

The Fool urges Lear to seek shelter. Kent finds them and says that he has never known such a storm. Lear says that the storm will expose sinners.

26 head-piece: good sense/good covering for his head
27 cod-piece: male garment worn externally over the crotch; here refers to the penis
27–29 The cod-piece...louse: the man who finds a home for his penis before seeking shelter will become a lice-infested beggar
30 So beggars marry many: beggars are more interested in sex than in setting up home
31–33 The man...cry woe: anyone interested in minor things (toe) rather than important ones (heart) will find them just as painful (corn) and disturbing
35–36 For there...glass: it is generally agreed that this does not follow, but it is believed to have been included as a joke with the audience
35–36 made...glass: posed before the mirror
40 grace: King
cod-piece: a Fool (jesters usually had remarkably exaggerated cod-pieces)
44 Gallow...dark: terrify wild beasts
48–49 carry Th'affliction: bear the physical affliction
50 pudder: hubbub
51 their enemies: criminals
53 Unwhipped of: unpunished by
bloody hand: murderer

- *'that's a wise man and a Fool' (lines 40–41) But, Shakespeare asks, which is which?*
- *Note that Kent speaks of the physical effects of the storm, whilst Lear is concerned with the moral implications: the storm will expose sinners.*

FOOL	He that has a house to put's head in has a good 25 head-piece.

    The cod-piece that will house
       Before the head has any,
    The head and he shall louse;
       So beggars marry many.   30
    The man that makes his toe
       What he his heart should make,
    Shall of a corn cry woe,
       And turn his sleep to wake.

	For there was never yet fair woman but she 35 made mouths in a glass.

Enter KENT

LEAR	No, I will be the pattern of all patience; I will say nothing.
KENT	Who's there?
FOOL	Marry, here's grace and a cod-piece, that's a wise 40 man and a Fool.

KENT	Alas! Sir, are you here? things that love night
	Love not such nights as these; the wrathful skies
	Gallow the very wanderers of the dark,
	And make them keep their caves. Since I was
	    man 45
	Such sheets of fire, such bursts of horrid thunder,
	Such groans of roaring wind and rain, I never
	Remember to have heard; man's nature cannot
	    carry
	Th'affliction nor the fear.

LEAR	Let the great Gods,
	That keep this dreadful pudder o'er our heads, 50
	Find out their enemies now. Tremble, thou
	    wretch,
	That hast within thee undivulged crimes,
	Unwhipped of Justice; hide thee, thou bloody
	    hand,

Kent persuades Lear to take shelter in a hut nearby. Lear admits he is feeling the cold, and he is concerned for the Fool. Lear and Kent leave, and the Fool begins to make a prediction about the state of the world.

54 simular of virtue: one who pretends to be virtuous

55 caitiff: wretch

56 under...seeming: behind secret and effective hypocrisy

57 practised on: schemed against
close pent-up guilts: secret, hidden crimes

58 Rive...continents: break open the covering that hides you

58–59 cry...grace: beg for mercy from these terrifying accusers (summoners brought offenders before ecclesiastical courts)

59-60 I am...sinning: Lear claims to be quite unlike the criminals he has just listed

61 hard by: nearby

62 lend: afford

63 hard: cruel. (He refers to Gloucester's castle.)

65 Which: the people in it (Regan, Cornwall, Goneril)
demanding after: asking for

66 to come in: admittance

67 scanted: deliberately insufficient
My wits...turn: Lear seems bewildered to the point of exhaustion

68 Come on, my boy: only now does he seem to realize that the Fool is there

69 straw: hovel, lowly place

70 The art...strange: necessity changes things in strange ways

72–73 I have...thee: what sympathy I have left is for you

74–77 He that...every day: a fool must resign himself to a world which is always against him. (This is another version of the song of Feste in *Twelfth Night*.)

79 a brave...courtezan: a fine night for streetwalkers!

81 are more...matter: talk of virtue but do not practise it

83 nobles are...tutors: fashion-conscious gentlemen dictate to tailors

---

- *'brave night' (line 79) suggests 'brave knight', and the Fool's prophecy is expressed in medieval imagery, commenting on Elizabethan lifestyles. The prophecy is based on rhymes thought to be by Chaucer.*

Thou perjured, and thou simular of virtue
That art incestuous; caitiff, to pieces shake,   55
That under covert and convenient seeming
Has practised on man's life; close pent-up guilts
reflects on Rive your concealing continents, and cry
his behaviour These dreadful summoners grace. I am a man *something from*
More sinned against than sinning. *everyone*

KENT   Alack! bare-
headed!   60
Gracious my Lord, hard by here is a hovel;
Some friendship will it lend you 'gainst the tempest;
Repose you there while I to this hard house, –
More harder than the stones whereof 'tis raised,
Which even but now, demanding after you,   65
Denied me to come in, – return and force
Their scanted courtesy.

LEAR   My wits begin to turn.
How offers Come on, my boy. How dost, my boy? Art cold?
suffer for I am cold myself. Where is this straw, my fellow?
him how The art of our necessities is strange,   70
others And can make vile things precious. Come, your
suffer to hovel.
considers Poor Fool and knave, I have one part in my heart
others feelings That's sorry yet for thee.
of Fool

FOOL   *He that has and a little tiny wit,*
                   With hey, ho, the wind and the rain,   75
                Must make content with his fortunes fit,
                   Though the rain it raineth every day.

LEAR   True, boy. Come, bring us to this hovel.
                                [*Exeunt* LEAR *and* KENT

FOOL   This is a brave night to cool a courtezan.
                I'll speak a prophecy ere I go: 80
                When priests are more in word than matter;
                When brewers mar their malt with water;
                When nobles are their tailors' tutors;

The prophecy is a mixture of what is already happening (in
Elizabethan times) and what will never happen. He ends by
saying that nothing will change in effect.

84 No heretics burned: no one feels strongly about religion
   burned: this also has the meaning of catching venereal disease
88 cut-purses: thieves who mingled with crowds and cut purses
   which were hanging from belts
89 usurers...i'th'field: loan sharks count their money in public
90 bawds and whores: women who profit from vice
91 Albion: Britain
94 That going...feet: feet will be used for walking
95 Merlin: magician at the court of King Arthur, about 1400
   years after Lear's time

> • *What is the point of the Fool's prophecy? How might it
>   be staged?*

In Gloucester's castle, Gloucester tells Edmund that he is
unhappy about the way Lear has been treated. Against the
wishes of Cornwall, Regan and Goneril, Gloucester means to
help the King. There is talk again of the Cornwall/Albany
conflict. Gloucester urges Edmund not to mention the
invasion force.

1–2 unnatural dealing: the behaviour of Goneril and Regan
2 pity: be merciful
5 entreat: plead, speak on his behalf
6 sustain: care for
8 Go to: that's enough
9 a worse matter: the French invasion
11 closet: cabinet
13 home: thoroughly
   already footed: have established a foothold
14 incline to: support
   look: seek
15 privily: secretly
16 of: by

No heretics burned, but wenches' suitors;
When every case in law is right;   85
No squire in debt, nor no poor knight;
When slanders do not live in tongues;
Nor cut-purses come not to throngs;   *nothing will change*
When usurers tell their gold i'th'field;
And bawds and whores do churches build;   90
Then shall the realm of Albion
Come to great confusion:
Then comes the time, who lives to see't,
That going shall be used with feet.
This prophecy Merlin shall make; for I live before
        his time.   95

Scene 3

A room in GLOUCESTER'S *castle*
Enter GLOUCESTER *and* EDMUND, *with lights*

GLOUCESTER Alack, alack! Edmund, I like not this unnatural
                dealing. When I desired their leave that I might pity
says he feels sorry for Lear
                him, they took from me the use of mine own
                house; charged me, on pain of perpetual
                displeasure, neither to speak of him, entreat for   5
                him, or any way sustain him.

EDMUND   Most savage and unnatural!

GLOUCESTER Go to; say you nothing. There is division between
Gloucester confides in Edmund
                the Dukes, and a worse matter than that. I have
                received a letter this night; 'tis dangerous to be   10
                spoken; I have locked the letter in my closet.
                These injuries the King now bears will be revenged
                home; there is part of a power already footed; we
                must incline to the King. I will look him and
                privily relieve him; go you and maintain talk with   15
                the Duke, that my charity be not of him perceived.
                If he ask for me, I am ill and gone to bed. If I die

When Gloucester leaves, Edmund declares that he will tell
Cornwall everything about his father so that he might gain
personal advantage.

20 **toward**: imminent, about to happen
21 **This courtesy**: helping Lear
   forbid: forbidden to
23 **a fair deserving**: deserving of a fair reward

Kent has led Lear to shelter, but Lear does not enter. He says
the storm is nothing compared to his inner turmoil. He
considers his daughters' ingratitude.

 2 **open night**: night in the open
 3 **nature**: human nature
 4 **Wilt break my heart?**: with kindness – which he has not
   experienced recently
 6 **contentious**: battling (reflecting dispute)
 6–9 **Thou think'st...scarce felt**: you are more concerned that
   the storm soaks us; I scarcely feel the rain because of the
   turmoil inside me (see foot of page 128)
11 **free**: free of worries
12 **The body's delicate**: the body feels minor discomforts
12–14 **this tempest...ingratitude!**: my mind is in such a turmoil
   that the only thing in my thoughts and in my heart is the
   ingratitude of my daughters
15 **as**: as if
16 **home**: to the fullest extent

• *Can you explain the imagery of lines 15–16?*

for it, as no less is threatened me, the King, my old
master, must be relieved. There is strange things
toward, Edmund; pray you, be careful.   20

[*Exit*

EDMUND   This courtesy, forbid thee, shall the Duke
         Instantly know; and of that letter too:
         This seems a fair deserving, and must draw me
         That which my father loses; no less than all:
         The younger rises when the old doth fall.   [*Exit* 25

Scene 4

The heath. Before a hovel

Enter LEAR, KENT, *and* FOOL

KENT   Here is the place, my Lord; good my Lord, enter:
         The tyranny of the open night's too rough
         For nature to endure.   [*Storm still*

LEAR   Let me alone.

KENT   Good my Lord, enter here.

LEAR   Wilt break my heart?

KENT   I had rather break mine own. Good my Lord,
                 enter.   5

LEAR   Thou think'st 'tis much that this contentious storm
         Invades us to the skin: so 'tis to thee;
         But where the greater malady is fixed,
         The lesser is scarce felt. Thou'ldst shun a bear;
         But if thy flight lay toward the roaring sea,   10
         Thou'ldst meet the bear i'th'mouth. When the
                 mind's free
         The body's delicate; this tempest in my mind
         Doth from my senses take all feeling else
         Save what beats there – filial ingratitude!
         Is it not as this mouth should tear this hand   15
         For lifting food to't? But I will punish home:

Lear insists that the Fool should enter the shelter first, and then offers a prayer for the poor, regretting that he has done little for them in the past. The Fool rushes out of the hovel, frightened by the appearance of Edgar as Mad Tom.

18 **To shut me out**: (is this an accurate version of Lear's predicament?)

Pour on: (he addresses the storm)

20 **frank**: generous

24–25 **This tempest...more**: this is a contradiction of lines 8–9

26 **houseless poverty**: people who are poor and homeless

27 **pray**: the prayer is for the poor

29 **bide**: endure, put up with

31 **Your looped...raggedness**: clothes full of holes and openings

32 **seasons**: weather conditions

33 **Take physic, Pomp**: let the pompous take medicine to rid them of their pride

35 **shake...them**: distribute superfluous possessions

37 **Fathom**: approximately 1.85 metres. (Edgar is pretending to be a sailor, measuring the depth of water.)

38 **Poor Tom**: see Act 1 scene 2 line 140 and Act 2 scene 3 lines 14–20

39 **spirit**: strange being

43 **grumble**: mutter

45 **Away!**: keep away!

foul fiend: devil

> • *What range of emotions does Lear experience in the first 36 lines of this scene?*

obsessed with meaness of his daughters

No, I will weep no more. In such a night
To shut me out? Pour on; I will endure.
In such a night as this? O Regan, Goneril!
Your old kind father, whose frank heart gave
    all, –   20
O! that way madness lies; let me shun that;
No more of that.

KENT   Good my Lord, enter here.

LEAR   Prithee, go in thyself; seek thine own ease:
This tempest will not give me leave to ponder

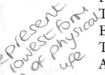

cares other go in first (cares)

On things would hurt me more. But I'll go in.   25
[*To the* FOOL] In, boy; go first. You houseless
    poverty, –
Nay, get thee in. I'll pray, and then I'll sleep.
                          [FOOL *goes in*
Poor naked wretches, whereso'er you are,
That bide the pelting of this pitiless storm,
How shall your houseless heads and unfed sides, 30
Your looped and windowed raggedness, defend you
From seasons such as these? O! I have ta'en

present lowest form of physical life

Too little care of this. Take physic, Pomp;
Expose thyself to feel what wretches feel,
That thou mayst shake the superflux to them, 35
And show the Heavens more just.

EDGAR   [*Within*] Fathom and half, fathom and half!
Poor Tom!   [*The* FOOL *runs out from the hovel*

FOOL   Come not in here, Nuncle; here's a spirit.
Help me! help me!   40

KENT   Give me thy hand. Who's there?

FOOL   A spirit, a spirit: he says his name's poor Tom.

KENT   What art thou that dost grumble there i'th'straw?
Come forth.

Enter EDGAR *disguised as a madman*

EDGAR   Away! the foul fiend follows me! Through the 45

all-teration.

In his feigned madness, Edgar speaks of being tormented by
the devil. Lear sees the bedraggled, near-naked 'Mad Tom' as
a reflection of his own condition, and he is convinced that
ungrateful daughters are responsible.

45–46 Through...cold winds: (this is thought to be a line from
a contemporary song)

46 Humh!: (this could indicate shivering with cold, or it could be
an imitation of the sound of the wind)

46–47 go to...thee: (another catch-phrase, possibly)

48–49 Didst...to this?: (Tom's appearance causes Lear, finally,
to lose his grip on reality)

53 and 54 knives, halters, ratsbane: (the means by which the
devil has tempted him to commit suicide to damn his soul –
knives, ropes and poison)

54 pew: balcony

55–56 to ride...bridges: riding a nervous horse over narrow
bridges

56 course: hunt

57 five wits: five senses/five aspects of the mind – common wit,
imagination, fantasy, estimation and memory

58 O! do de etc: (chattering of teeth, possibly)
Bless: God preserve

59 star-blasting: catching disease under the influence of a planet
taking: infection

61–62 There could...there: he picks at himself, plucking at
lice/the devil

66 reserved: kept

68 plagues: another reference to disease influenced by the planets
pendulous: hanging over us

69 fated: directed by destiny
light: alight

71 Death, traitor!: (for contradicting a king)

71–72 subdued...lowness: brought him so low

74 little mercy...flesh: (reference to thorns sticking in Edgar)

75 Judicious: appropriate

76 pelican daughters: young pelicans were thought to attack
their parents; and it was believed that adult pelicans fed the
young on their own flesh and blood

77 Pillicock: childish word for penis. (Begot and pelican probably
suggest this.)
Pillicock hill: (there was a rhyme beginning 'Pillycock sat on a
hill' to which Shakespeare might be referring)

78 Alow...loo!: (refrain from a song/a hunting cry)

sharp hawthorn blow the cold winds. Humh! go to
thy bed and warm thee.

LEAR Didst thou give all to thy daughters?
And art thou come to this?

— blames his daughters.

EDGAR Who gives any thing to poor Tom? whom the   50
foul fiend hath led through fire and through flame,
through ford and whirlpool, o'er bog and
quagmire; that hath laid knives under his pillow,
and halters in his pew; set ratsbane by his porridge;
made him proud of heart, to ride on a bay   55
trotting-horse over four-inched bridges, to course
his own shadow for a traitor. Bless thy five wits!
Tom's a-cold. O! do de, do de, do de. Bless thee
from whirlwinds, star-blasting, and taking! Do poor
Tom some charity, whom the foul fiend vexes.   60
There could I have him now, and there, and there
again, and there.   [*Storm still*

speaks to show madness

LEAR What! has his daughters brought him to this pass?
Couldst thou save nothing? Would'st thou give 'em
all?   65

daughters madness

FOOL Nay, he reserved a blanket, else we had been all
shamed.

LEAR Now all the plagues that in the pendulous air
Hang fated o'er men's faults light on thy
daughters!   *— repeats*

KENT He hath no daughters, Sir.   70

LEAR Death, traitor! nothing could have subdued nature
To such a lowness but his unkind daughters.
Is it the fashion that discarded fathers
Should have thus little mercy on their flesh?
Judicious punishment! 'twas this flesh begot   75
Those pelican daughters.

EDGAR Pillicock sat on Pillicock hill:
Alow, alow, loo, loo!

FOOL This cold night will turn us all to fools and

sensible sentence.

Edgar tells Lear he has been a serving-man who enjoyed a sensual life. Lear sees him as representing the true nature of man, unspoiled by society. He begins tearing off his own clothes.

81–84 Take heed...array: (Tom's own version of the Commandments)

82 commit: commit adultery

83–84 proud array: fine clothes

86 servingman: servant/lover

87 gloves: favours from his mistress

91 contriving: plotting

93 out-paramoured the Turk: had more women than the Sultan of Turkey has in his harem

93–94 light of ear: ready to listen to gossip

94–95 hog...in prey: beast-like. (The seven deadly sins were often portrayed as animals.)

96–97 Let not...woman: do not let a secret assignation with a woman lead you to think that you are in love

98 plackets: slits in petticoats

99 lenders': moneylenders'

100 through...cold wind: (see lines 45–46)

101 suum...nonny: (a song refrain including wind sounds)

101–102 Dolphin...trot by: (possibly fragments of other songs.) Dolphin could be a horse, or a corruption of Dauphin, the French prince; to link anything French with the 'foul fiend' was popular in Shakespeare's time.
answer: encounter

104 extremity: extreme severity

107 cat no perfume: civet cat, from which perfume was obtained

108 sophisticated: with the trappings of civilization

109 unaccommodated: unfurnished

110 forked: two-legged

111 lendings: clothes borrowed (from the animals)

112 naughty: bad

113 a little fire: (has probably seen Gloucester's torch)

114 old lecher: (preparation for Gloucester's appearance?)

- *Is man no more than this? (line 104) Note that Lear's interpretation of what man really is – without the trappings of civilisation – is based on a deception: Edgar pretends to be something he is not.*

	madmen.	80
EDGAR	Take heed o'th'foul fiend. Obey thy parents; keep thy word justly; swear not; commit not with man's sworn spouse; set not thy sweet heart on proud array. Tom's a-cold.	
LEAR	What hast thou been?	85
EDGAR	A servingman, proud in heart and mind; that curled my hair, wore gloves in my cap, served the lust of my mistress' heart, and did the act of darkness with her; swore as many oaths as I spake words, and broke them in the sweet face of Heaven; one that slept in the contriving of lust, and waked to do it. Wine loved I deeply, dice dearly, and in woman out-paramoured the Turk; false of heart, light of ear, bloody of hand; hog in sloth, fox in stealth, wolf in greediness, dog in madness, lion in prey. Let not the creaking of shoes nor the rustling of silks betray thy poor heart to woman: keep thy foot out of brothels, thy hand out of plackets, thy pen from lenders' books, and defy the foul fiend. Still through the hawthorn blows the cold wind; says suum, mun, hey no nonny. Dolphin my boy, boy; sessa! let him trot by. _[Storm still_	90

95

100
 |
| LEAR | Thou wert better in a grave than to answer with thy uncovered body this extremity of the skies. Is man no more than this? Consider him well. Thou ow'st the worm no silk, the beast no hide, the sheep no wool, the cat no perfume. Ha! here's three on's are sophisticated; thou art the thing itself; unaccommodated man is no more but such a poor, bare, forked animal as thou art. Off, off, you lendings! Come; unbutton here. _[Tearing off his clothes_ | 105

110
 |
| FOOL | Prithee, Nuncle, be contented; 'tis a naughty night to swim in. Now a little fire in a wild field were like an old lecher's heart; a small spark, all the rest on's | |

Gloucester arrives and Edgar fears he will be recognized. He
calls his father a demon, and goes on to exaggerate his
madness with a description of his disgusting diet. Gloucester
is surprised to find Lear with such companions.

116–125 This is...aroint thee!: (Edgar fears recognition)

116 Flibbertigibbet: the name of a demon which Shakespeare
took from a book by Samuel Harsnett, *Declaration of
Egregious Popish Impostures*; more names appear later

116–117 he begins...cock: he works from dusk to dawn

117–118 the web...pin: cataract of the eye. (An eye disease
marked by a film, web, on the eyeball and a small spot like a
pin's head.)

118 squinies: squints

119 white: almost ripe

121 Swithold...old: St Withold walked the wold (open
countryside) three times

122 night-mare...nine-fold: the demon who causes nightmares
and her nine children

123–124 Bid her...plight: tell her to get off the sleeper and
swear (she will do no harm)

125 aroint thee: get thee gone

131 todpole: tadpole
wall-newt: wall-lizard
water: water-newt

132–133 in the fury...rages: when the madness is on him

133 sallets: salads

134 ditch-dog: dead dog thrown in a ditch
mantle: covering (slime)

135 standing: stagnant
tithing: parish

137 three suits...body: (a servant's clothing allowance)

139 deer: animals in general

139–140 But mice...year: (an adaptation of lines from a popular
story)

141 follower: familiar spirit
Smulkin: another demon (Harsnett)

144–145 Modo, Mahu: different names for the leader of the
spirits (Harsnett)

146–147 Our flesh...gets it: (is there something familiar about
Mad Tom's voice which sets Gloucester thinking on these
lines?)

146 flesh and blood: children

147 hate what gets it: hate their parents

body cold. Look! here comes a walking fire.   115

Enter GLOUCESTER, *with a torch*

EDGAR   This is the foul Flibbertigibbet: he begins at curfew,
and walks till the first cock; he gives the web
and the pin, squinies the eye, and makes the hare-
lip; mildews the white wheat, and hurts the poor
creature of earth.   120
  Swithold footed thrice the old;
  He met the night-mare, and her nine-fold;
   Bid her alight,
   And her troth plight,
  And aroint thee, witch, aroint thee!   125

KENT   How fares your Grace?

LEAR   What's he?

KENT   Who's there? What is't you seek?

GLOUCESTER   What are you there? Your names?

EDGAR   Poor Tom; that eats the swimming frog, the   130
toad, the todpole, the wall-newt, and the water;
that in the fury of his heart, when the foul fiend
rages, eats cow-dung for sallets; swallows the old rat
and the ditch-dog; drinks the green mantle of the
standing pool; who is whipped from tithing to   135
tithing, and stock-punished, and imprisoned; who
hath had three suits to his back, six shirts to his body,

  Horse to ride, and weapons to wear,
  But mice and rats and such small deer,
  Have been Tom's food for seven long year.   140

Beware my follower. Peace, Smulkin! peace,
thou fiend!

GLOUCESTER   What! hath your Grace no better company?

EDGAR   The Prince of Darkness is a gentleman; Modo he's
called, and Mahu.   145

GLOUCESTER   Our flesh and blood, my lord, is grown so vile,
That it doth hate what gets it.

Gloucester has come to take Lear back, despite the wishes of
Goneril and Regan. Lear says he first wants a word with
Mad Tom. Gloucester is not surprised at Lear's condition
because his own son's behaviour has affected him so much.
Gloucester tries to usher Tom into the hovel, and Lear
suggests that they all go in together.

148 **Poor Tom's a-cold**: he is Tom o'Bedlam, having no
connection with Gloucester
149 **suffer**: allow me
151 **injunction**: order
155 **philosopher**: one who understands nature or science
156 **What is...thunder?**: perhaps he is thinking of his own views,
expressed in Act 3 scene 2
158 **learned Theban**: wise man from the Greek city of Thebes.
(The reference is not clear.)
159 **study**: subject
160 **prevent**: avoid
162 **Importune**: urge
168 **outlawed...my blood**: made an outlaw (Act 2 scene 1 lines
59–62)/disowned by me (Act 2 scene 1 lines 77 and 82–84)
169 **lately**: recently
172 **I do...Grace**: he tries to get Lear away from Edgar
O! cry...Sir: I beg your pardon

> • *Note that Gloucester's reference to Kent, lines 164–165,*
> *reminds us that Edgar is not the only person in*
> *disguise.*

EDGAR	Poor Tom's a-cold.
GLOUCESTER	Go in with me. My duty cannot suffer
	T'obey in all your daughters' hard commands: 150
	Though their injunction be to bar my doors,
	And let this tyrannous night take hold upon you,
	Yet I have ventured to come seek you out
	And bring you where both fire and food is ready.
LEAR	First let me talk with this philosopher. 155
	What is the cause of thunder?
KENT	Good my Lord, take his offer; go into th'house.
LEAR	I'll talk a word with this same learned Theban.
	What is your study?
EDGAR	How to prevent the fiend, and to kill vermin. 160
LEAR	Let me ask you one word in private.
KENT	Importune him once more to go, my Lord;
	His wits begin t'unsettle.
GLOUCESTER	Canst thou blame him?
	[Storm still
	His daughters seek his death. Ah! that good
	Kent;
	He said it would be thus, poor banished man! 165
	Thou say'st the king grows mad; I'll tell thee,
	friend,
	I am almost mad myself. I had a son,
	Now outlawed from my blood; he sought my life,
	But lately, very late; I loved him, friend,
	No father his son dearer; true to tell thee, 170
	The grief hath crazed my wits. What a night's this!
	I do beseech your Grace, –
LEAR	O! cry you mercy, Sir:
	Noble philosopher, your company.
EDGAR	Tom's a-cold.
GLOUCESTER	In, fellow, there, into th'hovel: keep thee warm. 175
LEAR	Come, let's in all.

They decide to take Mad Tom back with them.

178 **sooth**: humour
183 **Child...came**: (again a fragment from another work)
    Child: candidate for a knighthood
    dark tower: (possibly Gloucester's castle)
184 **His word was still**: his motto was always
184–185 **Fie, foh...man**: (reference to the story, *Jack the Giant-Killer*, now *Jack and the Beanstalk*)

Edmund has told Cornwall about Gloucester's admissions of Act 3 scene 3. He claims to regret being the one to convey the news. Edmund is declared Earl of Gloucester by Cornwall.

2–3 **How, my lord...think of**: I am somewhat concerned, my lord Cornwall, about what people will think of me because my patriotism is stronger than my family loyalty
5 **made him seek his**: made Edgar seek Gloucester's
6–7 **but a...himself**: Edgar was provoked, but one has to be basically evil to contemplate patricide
8–9 **repent to be just**: regret that I am loyal to the state
10–11 **approves...France**: proves he is a spy for France
16 **True or...Gloucester**: whether or not the French have landed, Gloucester is a traitor and must die; you will succeed to his title

> • *I will have my revenge (line 1) – on whom, and why?*
> *Are you clear about Edmund's latest piece of villainy?*

KENT   This way, my Lord.

LEAR   With him;
I will keep still with my philosopher.

KENT   Good my Lord, soothe him; let him take the fellow.

GLOUCESTER Take him you on.

KENT   Sirrah, come on; go along with us.   180

LEAR   Come, good Athenian.

GLOUCESTER No words, no words: hush.

EDGAR   *Child Rowland to the dark tower came,*
His word was still: Fie, foh, and fum,
I smell the blood of a British man. —   185

[*Exeunt*

Scene 5

A room in GLOUCESTER'S *castle*
Enter CORNWALL *and* EDMUND

CORNWALL   I will have my revenge ere I depart his house.

EDMUND   How, my lord, I may be censured, that nature thus
gives way to loyalty, something fears me to think of.

CORNWALL   I now perceive it was not altogether your brother's
evil disposition made him seek his   5
death; but a provoking merit, set a-work by a
reproveable badness in himself.

EDMUND   How malicious is my fortune, that I must repent to
be just! This is the letter he spoke of, which
approves him an intelligent party to the   10
advantages of France. O Heavens! that this treason
were not, or not I the detector!

CORNWALL   Go with me to the Duchess.

EDMUND   If the matter of this paper be certain, you have
mighty business in hand.   15

CORNWALL   True or false, it hath made thee Earl of Gloucester.

Edmund again claims to be acting through loyalty to the state, although torn by family ties.

18 our apprehension: to be arrested on my orders
19 comforting: assisting
20 stuff...fully: increase Cornwall's suspicion
21 persever: (emphasis on the second syllable) persevere
22 blood: family loyalty

Gloucester and Kent arrive at a cottage on Gloucester's estate. Gloucester leaves to seek more means of making the place comfortable. The Fool is concerned with the madness, real and assumed, which he sees around him.

2 piece out: add to
6 Frateretto: name of another Harsnett demon (frateretto means little brother)
   Nero: amongst his other crimes, Nero was guilty of matricide and was condemned to hell
7 Lake of Darkness: sometimes referred to as the bottomless pit of hell; another suggestion is that Nero actually visited the Alcyonian Lake, through which – in Greek mythology – Dionysus went to hell
   innocent: addressing the Fool
10 gentleman or a yeoman?: both were landowners – the gentleman lived off the income from his land, whilst the yeoman had to work his land for a living
11 A King, a King!: he confesses his own madness; as King he was the ultimate landowner
13–14 for he's...before him: it's a crazy father who hands everything over to his child (or children)
15 a thousand...spits: a thousand attackers (devils?) with red-hot weapons. (Lear imagines Goneril and Regan suffering the torments of hell.)
16 hizzing: hissing
17 foul fiend: devil (sitting on his back?)
18–19 He's mad...oath: a list of unlikely circumstances

Seek out where thy father is, that he may be ready
for our apprehension.

EDMUND [*Aside*] If I find him comforting the King, it will
stuff his suspicion more fully. [*Aloud*] I will   20
persever in my course of loyalty, though the conflict
be sore between that and my blood.

CORNWALL I will lay trust upon thee; and thou shalt find a
dearer father in my love.   [*Exeunt*

Scene 6

A chamber in a farmhouse adjoining the castle
Enter GLOUCESTER *and* KENT

GLOUCESTER Here is better than the open air; take it thankfully.
I will piece out the comfort with what addition I
can: I will not be long from you.

KENT All the power of his wits have given way to his
impatience. The Gods reward your kindness!   5
                              [*Exit* GLOUCESTER

Enter LEAR, EDGAR, *and* FOOL

EDGAR Frateretto calls me, and tells me Nero is an angler
in the Lake of Darkness. Pray, innocent, and beware
the foul fiend.

FOOL Prithee, Nuncle, tell me whether a madman be a
gentleman or a yeoman?   10

LEAR A King, a King!

FOOL No; he's a yeoman that has a gentleman to his son;
for he's a mad yeoman that sees his son a
gentleman before him.

LEAR To have a thousand with red burning spits   15
Come hizzing in upon 'em –

EDGAR The foul fiend bites my back.

FOOL He's mad that trusts in the tameness of a wolf, a

Lear decides to stage the mock trial of his daughters. He 'appoints' Edgar and the Fool as judges of the case. Goneril is first to be tried. Lear addresses a stool.

20 arraign them straight: bring them to trial immediately
22 justicer: judge
  sapient: wise
24 he: Lear/foul fiend
24–25 Wants thou...trial: (possibly) do you want witnesses?
25 madam: Goneril or Regan
26 Come o'er...to me: (line from a love song)
  bourn: stream
27–29 Her boat...to thee!: (the Fool completes the song – obscenely)
27 Her boat...leak: (reference to sexual disease)
30–31 the voice...nightingale: (referring to the Fool's voice)
31 Hoppedance: (another Harsnett demon)
32 white: unsmoked
  Croak: rumble (as a belly)
  black angel: fiend
34 amazed: dumbfounded (much stronger than today's meaning)
36 evidence: the witnesses against them
37 robed: (a reference to Tom's blanket)
37 and 38 justice, equity: (the Courts of Justice and the Courts of Equity were parts of the English legal system – Edgar and the Fool are therefore representing both courts)
38 yoke-fellow: partner
39 Bench...side: join him on the bench
  o'th'commission: a justice of the peace
42–45 Sleepest...no harm: (this song seems to be an early version of *Little Boy Blue*. An analogy can be made of Lear as the shepherd, his daughters the sheep and his land the corn)
44 minikin: delicate/shrill
46 Purr: (reference to a witch's familiar, with Purr as a sound or the name of the cat)

- *Do you think Shakespeare might be commenting on contemporary justice when he has two madmen and a Fool sitting in judgement?*
- *The voices of Lear, Edgar and the Fool, separately pursuing themes of betrayal, possession by devils and injustice, together create a moving experience.*

horse's health, a boy's love, or a whore's oath.

LEAR It shall be done; I will arraign them straight. 20
[*To* EDGAR] Come, sit thou here, most learned
justicer; [*To the* FOOL] Thou, sapient sir, sit here.
Now, you she foxes!

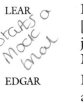

Starts a Mock trial

Edgar, fool are Judges

EDGAR Look where he stands and glares! Want'st thou eyes
at trial, madam? 25
Come o'er the bourn, Bessy, to me, –

FOOL [*Sings*] *Her boat hath a leak,*
And she must not speak;
Why she dares not come over to thee!

EDGAR The foul fiend haunts poor Tom in the voice of 30
a nightingale. Hoppedance cries in Tom's belly
for two white herring. Croak not, black angel; I
have no food for thee.

devil

KENT How do you, sir? Stand you not so amazed:
Will you lie down and rest upon the cushions? 35

Kent to Calm Lear down

LEAR I'll see their trial first. Bring in their evidence.
[*To* EDGAR] Thou robed man of justice, take thy
place;
[*To the* FOOL] And thou, his yoke-fellow of equity,
Bench by his side. [*To* KENT] You are
o'th'commission,
Sit you too. 40

EDGAR Let us deal justly.
Sleepest or wakest thou, jolly shepherd?
Thy sheep be in the corn;
And for one blast of thy minikin mouth,
Thy sheep shall take no harm. 45
Purr, the cat is grey.

LEAR Arraign her first; 'tis Goneril. I here take my oath
before this honourable assembly, she kicked the
poor King her father.

FOOL Come hither, mistress. Is your name Goneril? 50

LEAR She cannot deny it.

She is a stool cannot deny it

Lear introduces Regan, another stool, to the court. Edgar and the Fool are moved by Lear's madness and they humour his fantasy. Kent urges Lear to rest.

52 Cry you mercy: excuse me
　　joint: jointed (skilfully made)
53 another: Regan
　　warped looks: twisted features
54 What store...made on: what stuff she is made of
55 fire: torches
55–56 Corruption...'scape?: the court is corrupt – the judge has let the prisoner escape
57 five wits: (see Act 3 scene 4 line 57)
61 mar my counterfeiting: spoil my acting
62–63 The little...at me: see what I have come to – even little lapdogs bark at me
64 throw...at them: (possibly) move his head aggressively towards them
　　Avaunt: be off
65 or, or: either, or
68 brach: bitch
　　lym: bloodhound
69 bobtail tike: short-tailed cur
　　trundle-tail: longtailed (tail trundling behind)
72 hatch: bottom half of a divided door
73 Do de, de, de: (see Act 3 scene 4 line 58)
　　Sessa: (as in Act 3 scene 4 line 102, an encouragement to move forward)
　　wakes: parish celebrations
74 thy horn is dry: your drinking horn is empty
75 anatomize: dissect
76 breeds: grows
77 hard hearts: (a reference to 'horn', line 74)
　　You, sir: Edgar
78 entertain: engage
80 Persian: (ie exotic)
　　changed: reference to the laws of the Medes and the Persians which were unchangeable
82 draw the curtains: (Lear imagines a four-poster bed)
83 We'll go...i'th'morning: rest is more important than food
84 And I'll...noon: (the Fool's last words of the play show him 'playing the Fool' by following up Lear's suggestion; there is also a reference to death in the prime of life)

FOOL   Cry you mercy, I took you for a joint-stool.

LEAR   And here's another, whose warped looks proclaim
What store her heart is made on. Stop her there!
Arms, arms, sword, fire! Corruption in the
    place!   55
False justicer, why hast thou let her 'scape?

EDGAR   Bless thy five wits!

KENT   O pity! Sir, where is the patience now
That you so oft have boasted to retain?

EDGAR   [Aside] My tears begin to take his part so much,   60
They mar my counterfeiting.

LEAR   The little dogs and all,
Tray, Blanch, and Sweetheart, see, they bark at me.

EDGAR   Tom will throw his head at them. Avaunt, you curs!
    Be thy mouth or black or white,   65
    Tooth that poisons if it bite;
    Mastiff, greyhound, mongrel grim,
    Hound or spaniel, brach or lym;
    Or bobtail tike or trundle-tail;
    Tom will make him weep and wail: 70
    For, with throwing thus my head,
    Dogs leaped the hatch, and all are fled.
Do de, de, de. Sessa! Come, march to wakes and
fairs and market-towns. Poor Tom, thy horn is dry.

LEAR   Then let them anatomize Regan, see what   75
breeds about her heart. Is there any cause in nature
that make these hard hearts? [To EDGAR] You, sir, I
entertain for one of my hundred; only I do not like
the fashion of your garments: you will say they are
Persian; but let them be changed.   80

KENT   Now, good my Lord, lie here and rest awhile.

LEAR   Make no noise, make no noise; draw the curtains:
so, so. We'll go to supper i'th'morning.

FOOL   And I'll go to bed at noon.

Gloucester returns with the news that the king is in danger
and he suggests that Kent should take him to Dover. It is
imperative that they leave at once. Edgar is left to compare
his condition with that of Lear: he says he has been treated
by his father as Lear's daughters treated him.

88 upon: against
89 litter: a means of transport, a curtained 'stretcher'
90 drive: the litter is horse-drawn
94 Stand in assured loss: are sure to be forfeit
Take up: get the King
95–96 that will...conduct: I will take you to get supplies
97 balmed...sinews: soothed your shattered nerves
98–99 Which...cure: will be hard to cure if it is not convenient
to let you rest
101 betters: superiors
our woes: troubles such as we have
102 We scarcely...foes: our suffering seems much less
103 alone: on his own
104 free: carefree
happy shows: joyful sights
106 When grief...fellowship: when suffering is shared and can
be endured with others
107 portable: bearable
109 He childed...fathered: his children treated him as my father
treated me
110 Mark...noises: pay attention to what is happening in the
world of important people
bewray: reveal

- *How would you respond to criticism that Edgar and Kent
  are in close proximity to relatives and/or friends for
  some time in this scene, and yet their disguises are
  unchallenged. Can this be justified dramatically?*

Re-enter GLOUCESTER

GLOUCESTER Come hither, friend: where is the King my
     master?   85

KENT   Here, Sir, but trouble him not, his wits are gone.

GLOUCESTER Good friend, I prithee, take him in thy arms;
     I have o'erheard a plot of death upon him.
     There is a litter ready; lay him in't,
     And drive toward Dover, friend, where thou shalt
      meet   90
     Both welcome and protection. Take up thy master:
     If thou should'st dally half an hour, his life,
     With thine, and all that offer to defend him,
     Stand in assured loss. Take up, take up;
     And follow me, that will to some provision 95
     Give thee quick conduct.

KENT   Oppressed nature sleeps.
     This rest might yet have balmed thy broken sinews
     Which, if convenience will not allow,
     Stand in hard cure. [*To the* FOOL] Come, help to
      bear thy master;
     Thou must not stay behind.

GLOUCESTER   Come, come, away. 100
     [*Exeunt* KENT, GLOUCESTER, *and the* FOOL,
          bearing off the KING

EDGAR   When we our betters see bearing our woes,
     We scarcely think our miseries our foes.
     Who alone suffers, suffers most i'th'mind,
     Leaving free things and happy shows behind;
     But then the mind much sufferance doth
      o'erskip,   105
     When grief hath mates, and bearing fellowship.
     How light and portable my pain seems now,
     When that which makes me bend makes the king
      bow;
     He childed as I fathered! Tom, away!
     Mark the high noises, and thyself bewray 110

110–112 **thyself bewray...reconciles thee**: reveal yourself when
you have proved that you have integrity, at which time
the false criticisms which have made you an outlaw will be
withdrawn and you will be reconciled with your father
113 **What will hap more**: whatever else happens
114 **Lurk**: hide

Cornwall insists that Albany is informed immediately of the
French invasion, and he orders the capture of Gloucester.
Regan demands the hanging of Gloucester: Goneril says his
eyes should be put out. Cornwall addresses Edmund as '*Lord
of Gloucester*', and asks him to take Goneril home so that he
will not have to witness his father's punishment.

1 **Post speedily**: hurry
2 **this letter**: Gloucester's letter, taken by Edmund
7 **sister**: Goneril
9 **the Duke**: of Albany
10 **festinate**: speedy
11 **posts**: messengers
   intelligent: full of information
12–13 **my Lord of Gloucester**: Edmund
16 **his**: Lear's
17 **questrists**: seekers
18 **the Lord's dependants**: Gloucester's followers

> • *In what ways has Gloucester caused offence to
>   Cornwall?*
> • *Does the language of Cornwall's response to the sisters'
>   demands (lines 6–13) suggest what he has in mind?*

When false opinion, whose wrong thoughts defile
  thee,
In thy just proof repeals and reconciles thee.
What will hap more to-night, safe 'scape the King!
Lurk, lurk.   [*Exit*

Scene

no guilt or regret

A room in GLOUCESTER'S *castle*
Enter CORNWALL, REGAN, GONERIL, EDMUND, *and*
SERVANTS

CORNWALL [*To* GONERIL] Post speedily to my Lord your
husband; show him this letter: the army of France is
landed. Seek out the traitor Gloucester.
                        [*Exeunt some of the* SERVANTS

REGAN Hang him instantly.

GONERIL Pluck out his eyes.   5

CORNWALL Leave him to my displeasure. Edmund, keep you
our sister company: the revenges we are bound to
take upon your traitorous father are not fit for your
beholding. Advise the Duke, where you are going,
to a most festinate preparation: we are bound to 10
the like. Our posts shall be swift and intelligent
betwixt us. Farewell, dear sister; farewell, my Lord
of Gloucester.

Enter OSWALD

How now! where's the King?

OSWALD My Lord of Gloucester hath conveyed him
  hence: 15
Some five or six and thirty of his knights,
Hot questrists after him, met him at gate;
Who, with some other of the Lord's dependants,
Are gone with him toward Dover, where they boast
To have well-armed friends.

*don't want
Edmund to
see.*

*that Gloucester
Lear has
escaped*

Cornwall regrets that Gloucester cannot be condemned to
death without a trial. Gloucester is brought before Cornwall.
He is surprised that, as host, he should be treated so harshly.
He denies being a traitor. Regan insults him by plucking his
beard.

23 Pinion: bind his arms
24 upon his life: a death sentence
25–27 yet our power...not control: my power (and hence,
    responsibility) will give way to (bow before) my anger; people
    will be critical but they will not be able to do anything about it
28 Ingrateful: ungrateful (to Cornwall)
    fox: sly (in his dealings with Lear)
29 corky: dry, withered
33 Unmerciful: merciless
    none: no traitor
Stage direction *plucks his beard*: an extreme insult
37 white: the hairs of his beard; Regan is mocking, showing that
    she has no respect for age
    Naughty: wicked
39 quicken: come to life
40 my hospitable favours: the kindnesses of your host
41 ruffle thus: treat with this outrage

> • *What is the significance of Regan's showing contempt for
>   Gloucester's age (line 37)?*

CORNWALL	Get horses for your mistress. 20
GONERIL	Farewell, sweet Lord, and sister.
CORNWALL	Edmund, farewell. [*Exeunt* GONERIL, EDMUND, *and* OSWALD

tie him up

Go seek the traitor Gloucester,
Pinion him like a thief, bring him before us.
[*Exeunt other* SERVANTS
Though well we may not pass upon his life
Without the form of justice, yet our power 25
Shall do a court'sy to our wrath, which men
May blame but not control. Who's there? The
traitor?

Re-enter SERVANTS, *with* GLOUCESTER *prisoner*

REGAN	Ingrateful fox! 'tis he.
CORNWALL	Bind fast his corky arms.

Gloucester's me

GLOUCESTER	What means your Graces? Good my friends, consider 30

They are staying at Gloucester's

You are my guests: do me no foul play, friends.

CORNWALL	Bind him, I say. [SERVANTS *bind him*
REGAN	Hard, hard. O filthy traitor!
GLOUCESTER	Unmerciful lady as you are, I'm none.
CORNWALL	To this chair bind him. Villain, thou shalt find – [REGAN *plucks his beard*
GLOUCESTER	By the kind Gods, 'tis most ignobly done 35 To pluck me by the beard.
REGAN	So white, and such a traitor!
GLOUCESTER	Naughty lady, These hairs, which thou dost ravish from my chin, Will quicken, and accuse thee: I am your host: With robbers' hands my hospitable favours 40 You should not ruffle thus. What will you do?
CORNWALL	Come, sir, what letters had you late from France?

Gloucester is accused of being in league with the French. He
admits that he helped Lear to escape to Dover, and he
condemns Regan and Goneril for their treatment of Lear.
Cornwall tears out one of Gloucester's eyes.

43 Be simple-answered: give a straight answer
44 confederacy: conspiracy
45 footed: landed
46 lunatic: but she does not know his state of mind!
47 guessingly set down: written without certain knowledge
51 at peril: under the threat of punishment
53 I am...course: like the bear tied to the stake in bear-baiting so
that the dogs can be set on him, he is being attacked and he
has to see it through
56 anointed: part of the coronation ceremony is the anointing of
the monarch
57 Rash: slash (as with a boar's tusk)
59 buoyed: risen
quenched...fires: put out the stars
60 holp: helped
61 dearn: dire
62 turn the key: let them in
63 All cruels else subscribe: all other cruel creatures can show
compassion (but not you!)
64 winged: divine, heavenly
67 will think: hopes
live...old: ie not struck down prematurely by the wrath of the
gods

• *Can you explain the awful irony and inevitability about
line 55? (You might look again at lines 4, 5, and 24–25.)*

Accused of helping french.

REGAN   Be simple-answered, for we know the truth.

CORNWALL   And what confederacy have you with the traitors
             Late footed in the kingdom?

REGAN   To whose hands   45
             You have sent the lunatic King: speak.

GLOUCESTER   I have a letter guessingly set down,

rdelia   Which came from one that's of a neutral heart,
             And not from one opposed.

CORNWALL   Cunning.

REGAN   And false.

CORNWALL   Where hast thou sent the King?

GLOUCESTER   To Dover.   50

REGAN   Wherefore to Dover? Wast thou not charged at peril –

CORNWALL   Wherefore to Dover? Let him answer that.

GLOUCESTER   I am tied to th'stake, and I must stand the course.

REGAN   Wherefore to Dover?   *repeatingon*

GLOUCESTER   Because I would not see

uwultreat Thy cruel nails pluck out his poor old eyes;   55   *imagery of*
mbad so   Nor thy fierce sister in his anointed flesh   *animal*
et him   Rash boarish fangs. The sea, with such a storm
scape   As his bare head in hell-black night endured,
             Would have buoyed up, and quenched the stelled
                 fires;
             Yet, poor old heart, he holp the heavens to rain. 60
             If wolves had at thy gate howled that dearn time,
             Thou should'st have said 'Good porter, turn the
                 key.'
             All cruels else subscribe: but I shall see
             The winged vengeance overtake such children.

CORNWALL   See't shalt thou never. Fellows, hold the chair.   65
             Upon these eyes of thine I'll set my foot.

GLOUCESTER   He that will think to live till he be old,
             Give me some help! O cruel! O you Gods!

*I believe in
justice in
Heaven*

Regan urges Cornwall to put out Gloucester's remaining eye.
One of Cornwall's servants tries to intervene, and he and
Cornwall fight. Regan kills the servant from behind. Totally
blinded, Gloucester calls for Edmund, to be told that
Edmund has betrayed him. Gloucester is turned out of his
own castle to fend for himself.

69 mock another: make the other look odd
74–75 If you...shake it: if you were a man I'd fight you
76 villain: villein or serf meaning (approximately) slave
77 the chance of anger: risk the outcome of an angry encounter
78 A peasant...thus!: having the gall to oppose us!
80 mischief on: injury done to
84 sparks of nature: fire of family feeling
85 quit: avenge
87 overture: disclosure
89 abused: wronged
90 prosper him: take care of him, see that he does well
92 How look you?: how are you?
93 hurt: wound
94 slave: dead servant
95 apace: fast

> • *Gloucester has been savagely blinded. He is told that the
> son he has come to trust has betrayed him. What do lines
> 89–90 tell us about the character of this man?*

pull other eye out

REGAN   One side will mock another; th'other too.

CORNWALL   If you see vengeance, –

1ST SERVANT   Hold your hand, my Lord.   70
mes to oucesters defence
               I have served you ever since I was a child,
               But better service have I never done you
               Than now to bid you hold.

REGAN – *kills servent*   How now, you dog!

1ST SERVANT   If you did wear a beard upon your chin
               I'd shake it on this quarrel.

REGAN   What do you mean? 75

CORNWALL   My villain!   [*They draw and fight*

1ST SERVANT   Nay then, come on, and take the chance of anger.

REGAN   Give me thy sword. A peasant stand up thus!
                          [*Takes a sword and runs at him behind*

1ST SERVANT   O! I am slain. My Lord, you have one eye left
               To see some mischief on him. Oh!   [*Dies*   80

CORNWALL   Lest it see more, prevent it. Out, vile jelly!
               Where is thy lustre now?

GLOUCESTER   All dark and comfortless. Where's my son Edmund?
               Edmund, enkindle all the sparks of nature
               To quit this horrid act.

REGAN   Out, treacherous villain! 85
Us him dmund etrayed him
               Thou call'st on him that hates thee; it was he
               That made the overture of thy treasons to us,
               Who is too good to pity thee.

GLOUCESTER   O my follies! Then Edgar was abused.
               Kind Gods, forgive me that, and prosper him!   90

REGAN   Go thrust him out at gates, and let him smell
               His way to Dover.   [*Exit one with* GLOUCESTER
                          How is't, my Lord. How look
               you?

CORNWALL   I have received a hurt. Follow me, Lady.
gan aues hurt to die
               Turn out that eyeless villain; throw this slave
               Upon the dunghill. Regan, I bleed apace: 95

The injured Cornwall goes to seek treatment. Gloucester's servants intend to get Tom o'Bedlam to look after their master.

96 Untimely: at the wrong time (the French have landed)

97–98 I'll never...to good: men will not be encouraged to hold moral values if Cornwall is successful

99 meet...death: die in the normal way

100 Women...monsters: because they will not fear divine retribution

101 Bedlam: Poor Tom (Edgar)

102 would: wants to go

102–103 his roguish...thing: because he is a vagabond and a madman he will not be made to answer for it

104 flax...eggs: believed to be soothing for injured eyes

Untimely comes this hurt. Give me your arm.

[*Exit* CORNWALL, *led by* REGAN

2ND SERVANT I'll never care what wickedness I do
If this man come to good.

3RD SERVANT   If she live long,
And in the end meet the old course of death,
Women will all turn monsters.   100

2ND SERVANT Let's follow the old Earl, and get the Bedlam
To lead him where he would: his roguish madness
Allows itself to any thing.

3RD SERVANT Go thou; I'll fetch some flax and whites of eggs
To apply to his bleeding face. Now, heaven
help him!   105

[*Exeunt severally*

Do anything to help Cornwall
go to help Gloucester

paras - Lear has Gloucester, Kent
         Gloucester has servants.

know Tom+ Gloucester will be re-united

CTIVITIES

Keeping track

Scene 1

1   This is a scene which keeps us informed about the prevailing political and international situation. What do we learn of the current state of affairs?

Scene 2

2   What does the Fool see as his duty to Lear, and how effective is he in carrying it out in this scene?

Scene 3

3   What reasons does Gloucester give for going out in search of the King? What does this reveal about him?
4   '*Most savage and unnatural!*' is Edmund's response to Gloucester's news (line 7). What is significant about this?

Scene 4

5   What does Lear learn from his encounter with Edgar here?
6   What ironies arise from characters' true identities being disguised in this scene?

Scene 5

7   How does Edmund deceive Cornwall as well as his own father?
8   Why does Edmund hope to find Gloucester comforting the King (line 19)?

Scene 6

9   In what ways does Gloucester help the King, and how does this affect his own position?

Scene 7

10 For what reasons might Regan and Cornwall be accused of sheer heartlessness in this scene?
11 How does Gloucester speak to Regan and Cornwall when he is first brought before them? How do his speech and his manner change when they challenge him about sending Lear to Dover?

12 How is Cornwall injured?

Drama

1 The startling imagery of Act 3 enables Shakespeare to build a rollercoaster of emotional power climaxing in the blinding of Gloucester. As the effect is created from the accumulation of horrors and madness it is only possible to get a real feel of this act through producing the whole thing. However, it might be possible to begin to feel its power by working as an ensemble on one section.

Look at the mock court in Act 3 scene 6 lines 35–77. You will need to represent the three principal characters, although this could be more than one actor per part. You will have to try to capture the different layers of madness, humour and despair that are involved. The rest of the class can become Tom and Lear's demons; there is a lot of detailed animal imagery. (You might also include the five fiends which are described in Act 4 scene 1 lines 58–62.)

As well as saying the actual words, the ensemble will fill the air with noises and random words and phrases from the text. The three characters will be surrounded by these demons, seeing them in every corner; every object will be become alive and frightening.

2 In a modern version of the play what would the set for the heath (scenes 1, 2 and 4) be like? As set designers, prepare drawings and diagrams for your 'director' to consider. The 'nature' image is very important.

Could this scene be transferred to an urban setting; perhaps a derelict area inhabited by drug-crazed down-and-outs?

3 The blinding of Gloucester in Act 3 scene 7 is one of the most horrific scenes in the theatre. Many critics have considered it so horrible as to be unperformable. Remembering that today's audience is less likely to be easily shocked or frightened, how would you, as directors, stage this scene?

As for the climax, how would you actually demonstrate the plucking out of the eyes? Often Gloucester has his back to the audience for this, but how else might it be presented?

4 Regan's behaviour in the final scene has been described as inhuman. How does an actress prepare for this part?

Is the act of killing a servant an instinctive, animal-like, protective response to the wounding of her mate, or is this just the culmination of her blood-lust?

In pairs rehearse the moment when she stabs the servant. Try a variety of approaches to see which seems the most horrific.

How would a contemporary 'blood-and-guts' film director tackle this scene? Try to make it as physically violent as possible – without hurting each other. Show your version to the rest of the class and decide which is the most awful.

Hotseat Regan afterwards, the interviewers playing different roles – psychiatrists, police interrogators and reporters, for instance.

Close study

1   Examine Lear's contributions to the first 60 lines of scene 2. How does the style of his language reflect his own experiences and emotions, and connect them with the storm raging about him?
    Look at examples of:
    • vocabulary (for example, lines 4–6)
    • sentence structures and rhythms (for example, lines 14–20)
    • sound effects (for example lines 1–3).

2   In scenes 4 and 6 we see Lear who is becoming mad, the Fool who is employed to 'act the fool' and who must disguise his meaning in 'madness', and Edgar who is pretending to be mad. What criteria might we use to recognize 'madness' in the way people speak?
    To help you, look at the following examples of speeches from each of the three characters, and for each example answer the questions below.
    • Lear: scene 4 lines 48–49 and scene 6 lines 47–49
    • the Fool: scene 4 lines 107–109 and scene 6 lines 12–14
    • Edgar: scene 4 lines 55–57 and 77 and scene 6 lines 6–8
    To what extent do the words of each show:
    a   awareness of what is going on at the present moment
    b   knowledge of Lear's predicament
    c   wisdom or good sense
    d   coherent use of language?
    To what extent do they show a lack of these things?
    Find further examples for each character.

3   What is the purpose of the 'mock trial' in scene 6? Some editors suggest that the play would be improved without it. Do you agree?
    What would be lost from Lear's journey through the play if the trial were omitted?

4   Why do you think the Fool does not appear again after scene 6? What does his last line, 'And I'll go to bed at noon' (line 84), suggest to you?

5   In scene 7, what does the language of Regan and Cornwall convey about their characters? Look, for example, at lines 23–29; 65–66; 81–82; 91–95.

6   Compare the language of the scenes inside Gloucester's castle (scenes 3, 5, 7) with those which take place on the heath (4, 6).

What is the dramatic effect of the contrast and alternation between the two? Look at Edmund's words in scene 3 lines 21–22, and scene 5 lines 19–22, in relation to the 'mad' talk of Lear, the Fool and Edgar; and compare scene 4 lines 149–154, 164–173 and scene 6 lines 62–84 with scene 7.

7 How far is it possible to link Gloucester with those matters concerning 'good' and 'evil' characters which you considered in CLOSE STUDY question 3, Act 2 page 118?

8 Have you noticed any connection between the incidents in Act 3 and Lear's speech beginning '*O! reason not the need*' (Act 2 scene 4 lines 263–285)?

Key scene

Lear meets Edgar on the heath: Act 3 scene 4 lines 1–111

Keying it in

1 This encounter presents the climax of the storm scene and shows the full extent of Lear's madness. The situation building up to this encounter begins in Act 3 scene 1, where we see the storm develop before we actually see Lear.
   • Look at Act 3 scene 1 lines 4–14. What impression of Lear does the gentleman give?
   • Make a note of the specific images he uses to create this impression.
   • What is Kent's function in this scene?

2 We next see the entry of Lear as the storm rages. Read again Act 3 scene 2.
   • Compare and contrast the images that Lear uses in lines 1–9.
   • Examine Lear's changing view of the gods in lines 14–24 and 49–60. What is the significance of his words here?

The scene itself

3 **lines 1–5**
   • What impression do you get of Lear here?
   • What is the significance of his question '*Wilt break my heart?*' (line 4)?

4 **lines 6–22**
   • How would you describe Lear's state of mind in this speech?
   • What is the effect of the image of the mouth tearing at the hand that feeds it (lines 15–16)?

J.M.C.
ENGLISH

• What effect does the line structure create in lines 14–22?

5 **lines 23–36**
   • Do you detect a change in tone in Lear's lines here? How has his viewpoint changed?
   • How does this contrast with the earlier viewpoint that Lear expressed?
   • What does his attitude to the Fool show here?
   • How important is the vocabulary in this section? (Note words such as '*naked*', '*houseless*', '*unfed*', '*looped and windowed raggedness.*')

6 **lines 37–62**
   • What effect does '*Poor Tom*' have on the Fool?
   • What is his effect on Lear, and why does Lear ask about daughters (lines 48–49)?
   • Is the speech of '*Poor Tom*' simply babble, or does it have a purpose and significance?

7 **lines 63–80**
   • Look at Lear's response to Kent's comment that Edgar has no daughters (lines 68–72). How do these lines show the insight that Lear has developed?
   • Do you understand why Lear describes Goneril and Regan as '*pelican daughters*' (line 76)?

8 **lines 81–99**
   • Edgar invents a false identity for himself here. What are the features of this identity? Why does he create it?
   • Do you think there is any significance in Edgar's choosing a false serving man for his false identity?
   • Why do you think Edgar seems particularly obsessed with lust in this speech?

9 **lines 99–111**
   • How does Lear's speech mark another stage in his developing 'understanding'?
   • How does this passage relate to the play as a whole and the theme of 'nothing'?
   • Imagery based on clothing is used at various points in the play. To what effect is it used here?

Overview

This scene is important as it traces the onslaught of Lear's madness as the storm rages but, at the same time, it marks a new level of understanding for Lear. In one sense his 'madness' is enabling him to see

more clearly. The scene is followed by the arrival of Gloucester.
• How does Gloucester form the focus of various layers of irony in the remainder of Act 3 scene 4?
• How does the closing sequence of the scene make clear the parallels between Lear and Gloucester?

Writing

1 '*Our flesh and blood, my lord, is grown so vile,*
   That it doth hate what gets it.' (Act 3 scene 4 lines 146–147)
      Gloucester has become aware of the connection between his own situation and that of the King. Examine the ways in which this statement is true and false when applied to the parent/child relationships in each family and show, in as many ways as possible, how the two plots are parallel.
2 Is Lear's madness brought on by the actions of his daughters, or is it just a natural progression for an already unstable personality who, Regan suggests, has '*ever but slenderly known himself*'? (Your notes on WRITING, question 3, Act 1, will be useful.)
3 In Act 3 scene 7 we see quite a marked change in the stance Gloucester takes to those around him. From being a courtier who is eager to stay on the right side of everyone in authority, he becomes a man who makes a stand for what he believes to be right. Do you find this change of character convincing?
   Consider:
   • on what occasions he has seemed to be obsequious
   • how, when and why he begins to change
   • how far he is prepared to go.
4 In his encounter with Edgar as Poor Tom, Lear begins to see human life and his own position differently. What does he learn from the experience?
      You might begin by looking again at Act 3 scene 4 lines 23–76 and Act 3 scene 4 lines 103–111.

Edgar reflects that he is in such a poor position that things can only improve. He recognizes Gloucester, led by a servant. Gloucester urges the servant to leave him for his own safety. The servant is reluctant to leave him in his blindness, but Gloucester says that he could not see when he had eyes.

1–2 **Yet better...worst**: it is better to be despised ('contemned') and know it, than – the worst thing of all – to be flattered by people who secretly despise you

3 **most dejected...Fortune**: the person who is worst off, hardest hit by fate

4 **esperance**: hope
fear: of something worse about to happen

5–6 **The lamentable...laughter**: it is bound to be sad when you are doing well and changes occur; when you are at the bottom, change can only mean improvement

7 **unsubstantial**: lacking substance (in physical and material sense)

8–9 **The wretch...thy blasts**: the elements have brought me to this, and I have nothing more to fear from them

8 **worst**: also line 6 – repetition for emphasis

9 **Owes**: if he had been driven to this condition by debt he would still have repayments to make

10 **poorly led**: led like a poor man. (Other versions of the text at this point are poorly eyed – with eyes in a poor state; and parti-eyed – eyes of two colours, red and white.)

10–12 **World...to age**: it is because life is hateful at times that we are prepared to grow old and die

12 **good Lord**: addressing Gloucester

16 **comforts**: efforts to comfort me

18 **I have no way**: I am not going anywhere (life holds nothing for me)

19 **stumbled**: made mistakes

20–21 **Our means...commodities**: our possessions make us feel falsely secure; while our deficiencies might prove to be advantages

22 **food**: object ie what he concentrated on, fed on
abused: deceived

23 **in my touch**: by touching you

Act four

Scene 1

The heath

Enter EDGAR — shows compassion.

EDGAR
Yet better thus, and known to be contemned,
Than, still contemned and flattered, to be worst.
The lowest and most dejected thing of Fortune
Stands still in esperance, lives not in fear:
The lamentable change is from the best;   5
The worst returns to laughter. Welcome, then,
Thou unsubstantial air that I embrace:
The wretch that thou hast blown unto the worst
Owes nothing to thy blasts. But who comes here?

Enter GLOUCESTER, *led by an* OLD MAN

My father, poorly led? World, world, O world!   10
But that thy strange mutations make us hate thee,
Life would not yield to age.

OLD MAN   O my good Lord!
I have been your tenant, and your father's tenant,
These fourscore years.

GLOUCESTER Away, get thee away; good friend, be gone: 15
Thy comforts can do me no good at all;
Thee they may hurt.

OLD MAN   You cannot see your way.

GLOUCESTER I have no way, and therefore want no eyes;
I stumbled when I saw. Full oft 'tis seen,
Our means secure us, and our mere defects   20
Prove our commodities. Oh! dear son Edgar,
The food of thy abused father's wrath;
Might I but live to see thee in my touch,

Edgar realizes that he has been wrong in thinking that things could not get worse. Gloucester remembers that when he met a man such as Mad Tom in the storm, Edgar came to his mind. He tells his servant to bring clothes for Tom, who will lead him towards Dover.

25 Who is't...worst': see lines 2–6
27–28 the worst...worst': whilst we still have reason we cannot be at our lowest ebb
31 reason: mental power
33 a man a worm: a Biblical reference, *Job 25 verse 6* – 'How much less man, that is a worm! And the son of man, which is a worm!'
36–37 As flies...sport: the gods seem to be playing with us, as boys play maliciously with flies
37 this: a number of possibilities here – father's injuries/change of attitude to him/the attack on the gods)
38 Bad is...sorrow: it is a bad business to clown about with someone so sorrowful
39 Ang'ring...others: it annoys everyone because it is inappropriate
43 I'th'way: along the road
ancient: of long-standing
46 'Tis the times' plague: it is a disease of the time madmen lead the blind. (This could also refer to rulers leading their unseeing, unaware subjects.)

- *Look again at lines 36–37.*
  How much is the condition of Edgar and Gloucester really due to the gods, and how much to human influence?
  In what sense is Gloucester's comment ironic?

I'd say I had eyes again.

OLD MAN   How now! Who's there?

EDGAR   [*Aside*] O Gods! Who is't can say 'I am at the
       worst'?   25
       I am worse than e'er I was.

OLD MAN   'Tis poor mad Tom.

EDGAR   [*Aside*] And worse I may be yet; the worst is not
       So long as we can say 'This is the worst.'

OLD MAN   Fellow, where goest?

GLOUCESTER   Is it a beggar-man?

OLD MAN   Madman and beggar too.   30

GLOUCESTER   He has some reason, else he could not beg.
       I'th'last night's storm I such a fellow saw,
       Which made me think a man a worm. My son
       Came then into my mind; and yet my mind
       Was then scarce friends with him. I have heard
          more since: 35
       As flies to wanton boys, are we to th'Gods;
       They kill us for their sport.

EDGAR   [*Aside*]   How should this be?
       Bad is the trade that must play fool to sorrow,
       Ang'ring itself and others. [*Aloud*] Bless thee,
          master!

GLOUCESTER   Is that the naked fellow?

OLD MAN   Ay, my Lord.   40

GLOUCESTER   Then, prithee, get thee away. If, for my sake,
       Thou wilt o'ertake us, hence a mile or twain,
       I'th'way toward Dover, do it for ancient love;
       And bring some covering for this naked soul,
       Which I'll entreat to lead me.

OLD MAN   Alack, sir! he is
       mad.   45

GLOUCESTER   'Tis the times' plague, when madmen lead the
       blind.

Edgar thinks about revealing his identity, but does not do
so. Gloucester asks him to lead him to Dover. There he
intends to alleviate Tom's misery and ask for no further help
from him.

47 do thy pleasure: do as you wish (He feels unable to give
orders.)
49 'parel: apparel, clothing
50 Come on't what will: whatever might happen to me as a
result (Such an act will be treason.)
51 daub it further: plaster it (put on the pretence) any more
55 horse-way: bridle path
56 Poor Tom...wits: the fiends frighten Tom wherever he goes
**59–61 Obidicut, Hoberdidance, Mahu, Modo,
Flibbertigibbet**: demons from Harsnett, again
61 mopping and mowing: making faces
62 since possesses...waiting-women: since leaving me has taken
over servants (who constantly pose before their mistresses'
mirrors)
64–65 thou whom...strokes: you whom the blows of fate have
brought so low that you will accept anything
66 happier: by having a companion – see Act 3 scene 6 lines
105–106
deal so still: share out miseries always
67 superfluous...man: man who has too much and satisfies his
appetites
68 slaves your ordinance: treats your law with scorn (ie treats it
like a slave)
68 see: understand (misery)
69 feel: have compassion
70 distribution: sharing out
73 bending: overhanging
74 fearfully: personification – the cliff is frightened of the drop
confined deep: the sea shut in by cliffs
76 repair: remedy

> • *Does this scene tell us more about Gloucester's character
> or reinforce what we already know about him?*

	Do as I bid thee, or rather do thy pleasure;
	Above the rest, be gone.
OLD MAN	I'll bring him the best 'parel that I have,
	Come on't what will. [*Exit*
GLOUCESTER	Sirrah, naked fellow, – 50
EDGAR	Poor Tom's a-cold. [*Aside*] I cannot daub it further.
GLOUCESTER	Come hither, fellow.
EDGAR	[*Aside*] And yet I must. Bless thy sweet eyes, they
	bleed.
GLOUCESTER	Know'st thou the way to Dover?
EDGAR	Both stile and gate, horse-way and foot-path. 55
	Poor Tom hath been scared out of his good wits:
	bless thee, good man's son, from the foul fiend!
	Five fiends have been in poor Tom at once; as
	Obidicut, of lust; Hoberdidance, prince of
	dumbness; Mahu, of stealing; Modo, of murder; 60
	Flibbertigibbet, of mopping and mowing; who
	since possesses chambermaids and waiting-women.
	So, bless thee, master!
GLOUCESTER	Here, take this purse, thou whom the heav'ns'
	plagues
	Have humbled to all strokes: that I am wretched 65
	Makes thee the happier: Heavens, deal so still!
	Let the superfluous and lust-dieted man,
	That slaves your ordinance, that will not see
	Because he does not feel, feel your power quickly;
	So distribution should undo excess, 70
	And each man have enough. Dost thou know
	Dover?
EDGAR	Ay, master.
GLOUCESTER	There is a cliff, whose high and bending head
	Looks fearfully in the confined deep;
	Bring me but to the very brim of it, 75
	And I'll repair the misery thou dost bear
	With something rich about me; from that place

Goneril and Edmund arrive at Albany's palace. Apparently they have discussed becoming lovers. They are told that Albany's reactions to recent events are not what they expected. Goneril says her husband is a coward. She tells Edmund to return to the Duke of Cornwall and help with his army.

1 **Welcome**: to my palace
 mild: is this an insight into Albany's character?
2 **met...way**: come out to meet us
8 **sot**: fool
9 **turned...out**: got things the wrong way round
11 **What like, offensive**: he takes exception to news that he should approve of
12 **cowish**: cowardly
13 **undertake**: take action
 not feel wrongs: ignore insults
14 **tie...answer**: require a response
14–15 **Our wishes...effects**: what we spoke of on the way here (uniting in love) may become real
15 **brother**: the Duke of Cornwall
16 **musters**: gatherings of troops
 powers: army
17 **arms**: symbols, coats of arms
 distaff: originally a stick used in spinning wool, and hence representative of the domestic, female role

I shall no leading need.

EDGAR   Give me thy arm:
Poor Tom shall lead thee.   [*Exeunt*

Scene 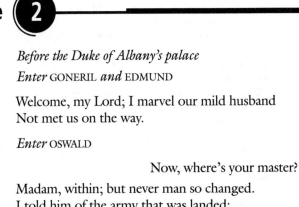 2

Before the Duke of Albany's palace
Enter GONERIL *and* EDMUND

GONERIL   Welcome, my Lord; I marvel our mild husband
Not met us on the way.

Enter OSWALD

                              Now, where's your master?

OSWALD   Madam, within; but never man so changed.
I told him of the army that was landed;
He smiled at it: I told him you were coming;   5
His answer was 'The worse': of Gloucester's
    treachery,
And of the loyal service of his son,
When I informed him, then he called me sot,
And told me I had turned the wrong side out:
What most he should dislike seems pleasant to
    him;   10
What like, offensive.

GONERIL   [*To* EDMUND]   Then shall you go no further.
It is the cowish terror of his spirit
That dares not undertake; he'll not feel wrongs
Which tie him to an answer. Our wishes on the
    way
May prove effects. Back, Edmund, to my
    brother;   15
Hasten his musters and conduct his powers:
I must change arms at home, and give the distaff
Into my husband's hands. This trusty servant

Goneril and Edmund part like lovers, their conversation filled with sexual innuendo. Albany enters to tell Goneril, bluntly, that she and Regan have treated Lear inhumanely.

19 like: likely
20 in your own behalf: thinking of yourself
21–28 A mistress's...bed: a risqué, teasing conversation – oblique references to a sexual relationship
21 mistress: woman who gives orders/lover
23 stretch thy spirits: give you hope/excite you sexually
24 Conceive: think about this/take part in conception
25 death: after-life/(metaphorically) orgasm
27 services: duties/sexual favours
28 bed: rightful place/scene of consummation
29 I have...whistle: so you have condescended to meet me. (Variation on the proverb – It is a poor dog that is not worth the whistling.)
31 fear: distrust
disposition: character
32 contemns it origin: scorns its source (ie Lear)
33 Cannot...itself: is unpredictable
34 sliver and disbranch: tear herself away
35 material sap: origins (see line 32)
36 deadly use: burn (as dead wood)
37 the text is foolish: your sermon makes no sense
39 Filths...themselves: to the filthy all tastes filthy
42 head-lugged: pulled by the head (and therefore in a bad temper)
43 madded: driven mad

> • *We last saw Albany in Act 1 scene 4. Was there any indication then that he would respond to his wife's actions in this way?*

Shall pass between us; ere long you are like to hear,
If you dare venture in your own behalf,   20
A mistress's command. Wear this; spare speech;
                                        [*Giving a favour*
Decline your head: this kiss, if it durst speak,
Would stretch thy spirits up into the air.
Conceive, and fare thee well.

EDMUND   Yours in the ranks of death.

GONERIL   My most dear
            Gloucester!   25
                                        [*Exit* EDMUND
Oh! the difference of man and man.
To thee a woman's services are due:
A fool usurps my bed.

OSWALD   Madam, here comes my
            Lord.   [*Exit*

Enter ALBANY

GONERIL   I have been worth the whistle.

ALBANY   O Goneril!
            You are not worth the dust which the rude wind 30
            Blows in your face. I fear your disposition.
            That nature, which contemns it origin,
            Cannot be bordered certain in itself;
            She that herself will sliver and disbranch
            From her material sap, perforce must wither   35
            And come to deadly use.

GONERIL   No more; the text is foolish.

ALBANY   Wisdom and goodness to the vile seem vile;
            Filths savour but themselves. What have you done?
            Tigers, not daughters, what have you performed? 40
            A father, and a gracious aged man,
            Whose reverence even the head-lugged bear would
                lick,
            Most barbarous, most degenerate! have you
                madded.

Albany says that behaviour such as Goneril's will lead to
chaos and the fall of civilization. She accuses him of
cowardice, and of having the wrong priority. She says he
should be preparing to defend his kingdom from the French.
News arrives of Cornwall's death from the wound he
received in the fight with his servant.

44 my good brother: Cornwall
   suffer: allow

45 A man...benefited!: human, noble, in Lear's debt (three
reasons to act humanely)

46 visible: manifest, in visible form

47 vilde offences: vile offenders

48 come: happen that

49–50 Humanity...deep: the ultimate disorder of the survival of
the fittest, and cannibalism

50 milk-livered: cowardly (milk – not blood – in the liver)

51 That bear'st...wrongs: see lines 13–4

52–53 Who hast...suffering: you do not know when to retaliate
and when to endure

54–55 Fools...mischief: only fools pity those who are punished
before they have committed their crime

56 noiseless: no noise of war (drums)

57 helm: helmet
   state: realm
   threat: threaten

58 moral: moralizing

59 See: look at

60–61 Proper...woman: the deformity of twisted features is
more horrible in a woman than in the devil because they are
appropriate to him

62 changed: transformed
   self-covered: concealing your femininity

63 Be-monster...feature: do not appear like a monster
   Were't my fitness: if it were proper for me

64 blood: passion

65 apt: ready

66 howe'er: however much

68 Marry: by the Virgin Mary
   your manhood: you talk of your manhood!
   mew!: the sound of a cat – implying weakness

Could my good brother suffer you to do it?
A man, a prince, by him so benefited!   45
If that the heavens do not their visible spirits
Send quickly down to tame these vilde offences,
It will come,
Humanity must perforce prey on itself,
Like monsters of the deep.

GONERIL   Milk-livered man!   50
That bear'st a cheek for blows, a head for wrongs;
Who hast not in thy brows an eye discerning
Thine honour from thy suffering; that not know'st
Fools do those villains pity who are punished
Ere they have done their mischief. Where's thy
        drum;   55
France spreads his banners in our noiseless land,
With plumed helm thy state begins to threat,
Whil'st thou, a moral fool, sits still, and cries
'Alack! why does he so?'

ALBANY   See thyself, devil!
Proper deformity shows not in the fiend   60
So horrid as in woman.

GONERIL   O vain fool!

ALBANY   Thou changed and self-covered thing, for shame,
Be-monster not thy feature. Were't my fitness
To let these hands obey my blood,
They are apt enough to dislocate and tear   65
Thy flesh and bones; howe'er thou art a fiend,
A woman's shape doth shield thee.

GONERIL   Marry, your manhood – mew!

Enter a MESSENGER

ALBANY   What news?

MESSENGER   O! my good Lord, the Duke of Cornwall's dead; 70
Slain by his servant, going to put out
The other eye of Gloucester.

Albany is shocked by the news of Gloucester, and considers
Cornwall's death fitting retribution. Goneril is given a letter
which a messenger has brought from Regan. She is worried
that Regan, now a widow, might come between her and
Edmund. Albany intends to avenge Gloucester.

73 **bred**: raised
   thrilled with remorse: excited by compassion
74 **bending**: directing
75 **To**: against
76 **amongst them**: between them they
78 **Hath...after**: has drawn him to his death after the servant
79 **justicers**: judges (see lines 46–47); ie the gods
   nether crimes: crimes here below
80 **venge**: avenge
85–86 **May all...hateful life**: it could be that all that my fantasy
   has built up (concerning Edmund) will come to nothing in my
   hated life (hateful because she herself is still married)
87 **tart**: bitter
90 **back**: on his way back

- *Is Albany a likely hero? Is he going to be a force to be*
  reckoned with, or is he as weak as his wife suggests?
- *There is an argument that the play is improved if most of*
  the Albany–Goneril confrontation is cut. How might this
  affect the answers to the questions about Albany (above)?

ALBANY	Gloucester's eyes!
MESSENGER	A servant that he bred, thrilled with remorse,
	Opposed against the act, bending his sword
	To his great master; who, thereat enraged, 75
	Flew on him, and amongst them felled him dead;
	But not without that harmful stroke, which since
	Hath plucked him after.
ALBANY	This shows you are above,
	You justicers, that these our nether crimes
	So speedily can venge! But, O poor Gloucester! 80
	Lost he his other eye?
MESSENGER	Both, both, my Lord.
	This letter, Madam, craves a speedy answer;
	'Tis from your sister. [*Presents a letter*
GONERIL	[*Aside*] One way I like this well;
	But being widow, and my Gloucester with her,
	May all the building in my fancy pluck 85
	Upon my hateful life: another way,
	The news is not so tart. [*Aloud*] I'll read, and
	answer. [*Exit*
ALBANY	Where was his son when they did take his eyes?
MESSENGER	Come with my Lady hither.
ALBANY	He is not here.
MESSENGER	No, my good Lord; I met him back again. 90
ALBANY	Knows he the wickedness?
MESSENGER	Ay, my good Lord; 'twas he informed against him,
	And quit the house on purpose that their
	punishment
	Might have the freer course.
ALBANY	Gloucester, I live
	To thank thee for the love thou show'dst the
	king, 95
	And to revenge thine eyes. Come hither, friend:
	Tell me what more thou know'st. [*Exeunt*

At Dover, Cordelia has received news of her father with
sorrow, but with great self-control.

1–2 Why...no reason?: Shakespeare's audience would not be
sympathetic to a French king fighting on English soil

3–4 Something...thought of: he had some unfinished business
in France which he had forgotten about. (See note on lines
1–2, above; this puts a different complexion on the situation in
that the forces supporting Lear are now led by Cordelia.)

4 imports: portends

7 general: in charge (over all)

9 pierce: move
the queen: Cordelia

12 trilled: trickled

13–15 it seemed...o'er her: with difficulty she controlled her
emotion

16–17 patience...goodliest: self-control and grief competed as
to which should represent her most accurately

19 like, a better way: similar, but after a better fashion
smilets: little smiles

23 a rarity most beloved: much sought-after

24 If all...become it: if it made everyone so attractive

> • *Act 4 scene 3 is not in the folio. Can you make out an
> argument for cutting, or retaining, it?*

Scene  3

The French camp near Dover
Enter KENT *and a* GENTLEMAN

KENT   Why the King of France is so suddenly gone back
              know you no reason?

GENTLEMAN   Something he left imperfect in the state, which
              since his coming forth is thought of; which imports
              to the kingdom so much fear and danger that his   5
              personal return was most required and necessary.

KENT   Who hath he left behind him general?

GENTLEMAN   The Marshal of France, Monsieur La Far.

KENT   Did your letters pierce the queen to any
              demonstration of grief?   10

GENTLEMAN   Ay, sir; she took them, read them in my presence;
              And now and then an ample tear trilled down
              Her delicate cheek; it seemed she was a queen
              Over her passion; who, most rebel-like,
              Sought to be king o'er her.

KENT   O! then it moved
              her.   15

GENTLEMAN   Not to a rage; patience and sorrow strove
              Who should express her goodliest. You have seen
              Sunshine and rain at once; her smiles and tears
              Were like, a better way; those happy smilets
              That played on her ripe lip seemed not to know   20
              What guests were in her eyes; which parted thence,
              As pearls from diamonds dropped. In brief,
              Sorrow would be a rarity most beloved,
              If all could so become it.

KENT   Made she no verbal
              question?

Cordelia has been outraged by her sisters' behaviour towards
Lear. Lear himself is in Dover, but he cannot bring himself
to see Cordelia because he is so ashamed of his treatment of
her. The armies of Albany and Cornwall are reported to be
moving south.

25 **heaved**: uttered with difficulty
29 **Let pity not believe it!'**: pity cannot exist!
   There: at that point
31 **clamour moistened**: drowned her exclamations with tears
33 **conditions**: characters
34 **Else...make**: otherwise the same husband and wife
35 **issues**: children
37 **the King**: of France
39 **sometime**: sometimes
   in his better tune: when in better spirits
40 **What we are come about**: why we are here
42 **sovereign**: dominant
   elbows him: keeps him back
43 **stripped**: tore
   turned her: turned her out
44 **To foreign casualties**: to take her chances abroad
45 **dog-hearted**: pitiless
49 **afoot**: on the move
51 **Some dear cause**: an important matter

> • *Cordelia is not present here, nor has she been since Act 1
> scene 1. How does the vocabulary of this scene convince
> the audience that she is a character of heroic
> proportions?*

GENTLEMAN	Faith, once or twice she heaved the name of
	'father' 25
	Pantingly forth, as if it pressed her heart;
	Cried 'Sisters! sisters! Shame of ladies! sisters!
	Kent! father! sisters! What? i'th'storm! i'th'night?
	Let pity not believe it!' There she shook
	The holy water from her heavenly eyes, 30
	And clamour moistened, then away she started
	To deal with grief alone.

KENT   It is the stars,
The stars above us, govern our conditions;
Else one self mate and make could not beget
Such different issues. You spoke not with her
since?   35

GENTLEMAN   No.

KENT   Was this before the king returned?

GENTLEMAN   No, since.

KENT   Well, sir, the poor distressed Lear's i'th'town;
Who sometime, in his better tune, remembers
What we are come about, and by no means   40
Will yield to see his daughter.

GENTLEMAN   Why, good sir?

KENT   A sovereign shame so elbows him: his own
unkindness,
That stripped her from his benediction, turned her
To foreign casualties, gave her dear rights
To his dog-hearted daughters, these things sting   45
His mind so venomously that burning shame
Detains him from Cordelia.

GENTLEMAN   Alack! poor gentleman.

KENT   Of Albany's and Cornwall's powers you heard not?

GENTLEMAN   'Tis so, they are afoot.

KENT   Well, sir, I'll bring you to our master Lear,   50
And leave you to attend him. Some dear cause

52 **wrap me up**: engage my attention
53 **aright**: as Kent
54 **Lending...acquaintance**: knowing me

Cordelia says Lear has been seen with a circlet of wild flowers in his hair. She orders a search for her father, and promises a rich reward for anyone who can cure his madness. A doctor says Lear needs lots of rest. Cordelia fears that he might take his own life.

2 **vexed**: stormy
3–5 **Crowned...weeds**: all the named flowers are bitter or poisonous
3 **fumiter**: fumitory
  furrow-weeds: weeds growing in the furrows of ploughed land
4 **hardocks**: hoar dock, possibly, or burdock
  hemlock: poisonous weed
  cuckoo-flowers: cuckoo pint
5 **Darnel**: a type of wild grass
  idle: worthless
6 **sustaining**: life-sustaining
  century: one hundred men
7 **high-grown field**: indicating late summer
8 **What...wisdom**: what can science do
  bereaved: that has been taken away, stolen
10 **helps**: cures
  outward worth: wealth
12 **Our foster-nurse...repose**: rest is Nature's way of healing
13 **that to provoke in him**: to bring about repose
14 **simples operative**: effective herbs
15 **anguish**: pain, suffering
16 **unpublished virtues**: unknown medicinal plants
17 **Spring with**: grow quickly from the effect of
  aidant and remediate: beneficial and curative
19 **rage**: frenzy
  dissolve: take away
20 **wants...lead it**: lacks the reason to govern it

Will in concealment wrap me up awhile;
When I am known aright, you shall not grieve
Lending me this acquaintance. I pray you,
Go along with me.   [*Exeunt*   55

Scene 4

The same
Enter, with drum and colours, CORDELIA, DOCTOR,
and SOLDIERS

CORDELIA   Alack! 'tis he: why, he was met even now
As mad as the vexed sea; singing aloud;
Crowned with rank fumiter and furrow-weeds,
With hardocks, hemlock, nettles, cuckoo-flowers,
Darnel, and all the idle weeds that grow   5
In our sustaining corn. A century send forth;
Search every acre in the high-grown field,
And bring him to our eye.   [*Exit an* OFFICER
                            What can man's

   wisdom
In the restoring his bereaved sense?
He that helps him take all my outward worth.   10

DOCTOR   There is means, Madam;
Our foster-nurse of nature is repose,
The which he lacks; that to provoke in him,
Are many simples operative, whose power
Will close the eye of anguish.

CORDELIA   All blessed secrets, 15
All you unpublished virtues of the earth,
Spring with my tears! be aidant and remediate
In the good man's distress! Seek, seek for him,
Lest his ungoverned rage dissolve the life
That wants the means to lead it.

Enter a MESSENGER

Cordelia makes it clear that the French are not interested in conquest; that her husband has reacted to Cordelia's feelings for her father.

22 preparation: prepared army
24 It is...about: a Biblical reference, *Luke 2 verse 49* – 'Wist ye not that I must be about my father's business.'
25 France: King of France
26 importuned: demanding
27 blown: inflated with pride (a Biblical reference, *I Corinthians 13 verses 4–8*, which include the words 'love...is not puffed up')

Regan is suspicious of a letter from Goneril to Edmund. After delivering Goneril's message to Cornwall, Edmund has gone off, Regan believes, to end Gloucester's misery by killing him.

2 with much ado: after much bother (Albany is not happy to be involved)
4 Lord Edmund...at home?: they have obviously spoken of this before
6 import: be the significance of, mean
8 is posted: has ridden
serious matter: important business (in contrast with the trivial nature of the letter)
9 ignorance: naivety, lack of awareness
12 In pity of his misery: irony!
13 nighted: darkened/benighted, bewildered
descry: discover

MESSENGER   News, Madam; 20
The British powers are marching hitherward.

CORDELIA   'Tis known before; our preparation stands
In expectation of them. O dear father!
It is thy business that I go about;
Therefore great France   25
My mourning and importuned tears hath pitied.
No blown ambition doth our arms incite,
But love, dear love, and our aged father's right.
Soon may I hear and see him!   [*Exeunt*

Scene 5

A room in Gloucester's castle
Enter REGAN *and* OSWALD

REGAN   But are my brother's powers set forth?

OSWALD   Ay, Madam.

REGAN   Himself in person there?

OSWALD   Madam, with much ado:
Your sister is the better soldier.

REGAN   Lord Edmund spake not with your Lord at home?

OSWALD   No, Madam.   5

REGAN   What might import my sister's letter to him?

OSWALD   I know not, Lady.

REGAN   Faith, he is posted hence on serious matter.
It was great ignorance, Gloucester's eyes being out,
To let him live; where he arrives he moves   10
All hearts against us. Edmund, I think, is gone,
In pity of his misery, to dispatch
His nighted life; moreover, to descry
The strength o'th'enemy.

OSWALD   I must needs after him, Madam, with my letter.   15

REGAN   Our troops set forth to-morrow; stay with us,

Regan wants to open the letter to Edmund. She suspects that
Goneril and Edmund are lovers, but points out to Oswald
that, as a widow, she is more eligible for Edmund and she
hints that they have an understanding. Regan gives Oswald a
token to hand to Edmund, and reminds him that killing
Gloucester would bring benefits.

18 **charged my duty**: made me give a solemn undertaking
20 **Transport**: convey
   Belike: perhaps
21 **I'll love thee much**: I'll be grateful
25 **strange oeilliads**: surprising loving glances
   speaking looks: looks which spoke volumes
26 **of her bosom**: in her confidence
28 **I speak in understanding**: I know what I am talking about
29 **take this note**: to pay attention
30 **talked**: come to an understanding
31 **convenient**: fitting
32 **gather**: assume
33 **this**: probably a token, a favour, or, possibly, a letter
34 **thus much**: about it
35 **desire her...to her**: tell her to be sensible about it
38 **Preferment**: promotion
   cuts him off: kills him
40 **What...follow**: whose side I am on

> • *Do you get an impression here of how the rumours might
> have started – or flourished – about the
> Albany/Cornwall conflict?*

The ways are dangerous.

OSWALD   I may not, Madam;
My Lady charged my duty in this business.

REGAN   Why should she write to Edmund? Might not you
Transport her purposes by word? Belike,   20
Some things – I know not what. I'll love thee
    much,
Let me unseal the letter.

OSWALD   Madam, I had rather –

REGAN   I know your Lady does not love her husband;
I am sure of that: and at her late being here
She gave strange œilliads and most speaking
    looks   25
To noble Edmund. I know you are of her bosom.

OSWALD   I, Madam!

REGAN   I speak in understanding: y'are, I know't:
Therefore I do advise you, take this note:
My Lord is dead; Edmund and I have talked   30
And more convenient is he for my hand
Than for your Lady's. You may gather more.
If you do find him, pray you give him this,
And when your mistress hears thus much from you,
I pray desire her call her wisdom to her: 35
So, fare you well.
If you do chance to hear of that blind traitor,
Preferment falls on him that cuts him off.

OSWALD   Would I could meet him, Madam: I should show
What party I do follow.

REGAN   Fare thee well.   40
                                              [*Exeunt*

Edgar suspects Gloucester's motive for wanting to go to the
cliff top, so in a field near Dover he tells him that they are
overlooking the sea. He describes the 'sight' far below.

  1 **that same hill**: the hill we talked about
  6 **By your eyes' anguish**: because of the pain in your eyes
  7-8 **Methinks...didst**: Edgar is now speaking in verse, having
     abandoned the role of Poor Tom – see notes at the foot of this
     page and page 198
  9 **You're much deceived**: (Gloucester is about to be!)
  11–24 **Come on...headlong**: the language of these lines
     sometimes misleads the audience into believing that Edgar is
     indeed where he claims to be
  13 **choughs**: red-legged birds of the crow family, common to to
     sea-cliffs
  15 **sampire**: samphire – a seaside herb used in pickles
  18 **anchoring bark**: anchored ship
  19 **cock**: dinghy (ship's boat)
  21 **unnumbered idle pebble**: innumerable shifting pebbles

> • *Note in this scene how Edgar tries to unsettle Gloucester*
> *and keep him off-balance, so that he is not quite sure*
> *what is happening and has to rely on Edgar's version of*
> *events.*

Scene  6

The country near Dover
Enter GLOUCESTER *and* EDGAR *dressed like a peasant*

GLOUCESTER When shall I come to th'top of that same hill?

EDGAR You do climb up it now; look how we labour.

GLOUCESTER Methinks the ground is even.

EDGAR   Horrible steep:
Hark! do you hear the sea?

GLOUCESTER   No, truly.

EDGAR Why, then your other senses grow imperfect   5
By your eyes' anguish.

GLOUCESTER   So may it be, indeed.
Methinks thy voice is altered, and thou speak'st
In better phrase and matter than thou didst.

EDGAR You're much deceived; in nothing am I changed
But in my garments.

GLOUCESTER   Methinks you're better
spoken.   10

EDGAR Come on, sir; here's the place: stand still. How
    fearful
And dizzy 'tis to cast one's eyes so low!
The crows and choughs that wing the midway air
Show scarce so gross as beetles; half way down
Hangs one that gathers sampire, dreadful trade!   15
Methinks he seems no bigger than his head.
The fishermen that walk upon the beach
Appear like mice, and yond tall anchoring bark
Diminished to her cock, her cock a buoy
Almost too small for sight. The murmuring
    surge,   20
That on th'unnumbered idle pebble chafes,

Gloucester gives Edgar a jewel as payment for his help, and tells him to leave. Gloucester then prays, before throwing himself forward off the cliff, as he believes. For a moment Edgar is worried that the shock will have killed his father anyway.

23–24 Lest...headlong: in case dizziness causes me – and the eyes which fail me – to fall
27 upright: vertically (never mind forward!)
28 another purse: see Act 4 scene 1 line 64
29–30 fairies...with thee!: may the fairies and gods see that your good fortune multiplies
32 With all my heart: I shall fare well where I am going
36 Shake...off: rationally end my pain
37–38 fall To quarrel with: begin to rebel against
38 opposeless: irresistible
39 snuff: smouldering wick
    loathed part of nature: hateful old age
41 Gone: consider me gone
42–44 And yet...theft: it might be that delusion can kill when one is so willing to die
42 conceit: imagination
44 Yields: consents
    where he thought: at the top of the cliff
45 By this...past: by this time thinking would have been over
47 pass indeed: die in reality
49 gossamer: cobwebs

- *It can be argued that Edgar has dropped all pretence of Poor Tom in this scene. On the other hand it might be said that Poor Tom only disappears on line 32, because although Gloucester comments on a changed tone of voice and manner of speaking, he never suggests that someone has taken Tom's place. Which side of the argument do you tend to favour? (You must bear in mind, of course, that both men have more important things to think about, and that can effect their behaviour and responses.)*
- *From line 46, Edgar is pretending to be someone else. Why does he still think it unwise to reveal his true identity?*

Cannot be heard so high. I'll look no more,
Lest my brain turn, and the deficient sight
Topple down headlong.

GLOUCESTER   Set me where you stand.

EDGAR   Give me your hand; you are now within a foot   25
Of th'extreme verge: for all beneath the moon
Would I not leap upright.

GLOUCESTER   Let go my hand.
Here, friend, 's another purse; in it a jewel
Well worth a poor man's taking: fairies and Gods
Prosper it with thee! Go thou further off;   30
Bid me farewell, and let me hear thee going.

EDGAR   Now fare ye well, good sir.

GLOUCESTER   With all my heart.

EDGAR   [*Aside*] Why I do trifle thus with his despair
Is done to cure it.

GLOUCESTER   [*Kneeling*]   O you mighty Gods!
This world I do renounce, and in your sights   35
Shake patiently my great affliction off;
If I could bear it longer, and not fall
To quarrel with your great opposeless wills,
My snuff and loathed part of nature should
Burn itself out. If Edgar live, O, bless him!   40
Now, fellow, fare thee well.

EDGAR   Gone, sir: farewell.
                [GLOUCESTER *throws himself forward and falls*
And yet I know not how conceit may rob
The treasury of life when life itself
Yields to the theft; had he been where he thought
By this had thought been past. Alive or dead?   45
Ho, you sir! friend! Hear you, sir! speak!
Thus might he pass indeed; yet he revives.
What are you, sir?

GLOUCESTER   Away, and let me die.

EDGAR   Hadst thou been aught but gossamer, feathers, air,

Edgar pretends to come across Gloucester at the bottom of
the cliff. He declares how surprised he is that anyone should
survive such a fall. He says that the figure who left
Gloucester on the cliff-top looked to him like a devil, and he
tells Gloucester that the gods must be watching over him.

50 **precipitating**: dropping
51 **shivered**: shattered
52 **Hast heavy substance**: are made of flesh
53 **at each**: one on top of the other
54 **fell**: fallen
57 **bourn**: boundary
58 **Look**: pretends not to know that Gloucester is blind
   a-height: on high
   shrill-gorged: shrill-throated, -voiced
62–64 **'Twas yet...proud will**: there was a time (Ancient Rome)
   when suicide was regarded by some as a noble way of
   escaping tyranny
63 **beguile**: trick
65 **Feel you**: do you have any feeling in
69–72 **As I...fiend**: Edgar's deception – see line 9 and the
   footnote on page 194 – is an attempt to revitalize Gloucester,
   lifting his spirits by making him believe that he has survived
   not only the fall, but also an encounter with the devil
71 **whelked**: twisted spirally
   enridged: ridged with waves
72 **happy father**: fortunate old man
73 **clearest**: purest
73–74 **who make...impossibilities**: who are honoured by man
   because they do what men cannot do
75 **remember**: remember myself, pull myself together
76–77 **Affliction...die**: until affliction realizes I have stood
   enough and lets me die

> • *Gloucester refers to the Roman attitude to suicide
> (lines 62–64) but does that apply in his case? Could he
> be said to be acting in a cowardly way? Ought he to
> have been concentrating on putting things right for
> Edgar?*

So many fathom down precipitating, 50
Thou'dst shivered like an egg; but thou dost
   breathe,
Hast heavy substance, bleed'st not, speak'st, art
   sound.
Ten masts at each make not the altitude
Which thou hast perpendicularly fell:
Thy life's a miracle. Speak yet again. 55

GLOUCESTER   But have I fall'n or no?

EDGAR   From the dread summit of this chalky bourn.
Look up a-height: the shrill-gorged lark so far
Cannot be seen or heard: do but look up.

GLOUCESTER   Alack! I have no eyes. 60
Is wretchedness deprived that benefit
To end itself by death? 'Twas yet some comfort,
When misery could beguile the tyrant's rage,
And frustrate his proud will.

EDGAR   Give me your arm:
Up: so; how is't? Feel you your legs? You stand. 65

GLOUCESTER   Too well, too well.

EDGAR   This is above all strangeness.
Upon the crown o'th'cliff what thing was that
Which parted from you?

GLOUCESTER   A poor unfortunate
   beggar.

EDGAR   As I stood here below methought his eyes
Were two full moons; he had a thousand noses, 70
Horns whelked and waved like the enridged sea:
It was some fiend; therefore, thou happy father,
Think that the clearest Gods, who make them
   honours
Of men's impossibilities, have preserved thee.

GLOUCESTER   I do remember now; henceforth I'll bear 75
Affliction till it do cry out itself
'Enough, enough,' and die. That thing you speak
   of

The sight of Lear in his crown of weeds, talking to himself, is heart-rending for Edgar. Gloucester recognizes the King's voice, but Gloucester's beard sets Lear on a train of thought about his daughters' insincerity.

80 free: happy

81–82 The safer...thus: a man in his right mind would never go around dressed like that/Gloucester's new resolve will not stand finding Lear like this

83 coining: making counterfeit money

85 side-piercing: heart-rending

86 Nature's...respect: the true king cannot be copied, unlike his image on a coin

87 press-money: money paid to a recruit

88 crow-keeper: farmer's boy
draw me...yard: pull the bow back the full length of the arrow. (Cloth was measured from the outstretched arm to the nose.)

90 do't: catch it
gauntlet: glove, thrown down as a challenge

90–91 I'll prove...giant: I'll justify myself against anyone, even a giant

91 brown bills: halberdiers. (A halberd was a weapon, a combination of spear and axe, which was painted brown to prevent rust.)

92 clout: target
hewgh!: the sound of an arrow in flight
word: password. (He has become aware of the presence of other people.)

93 marjoram: a herb thought to cure diseases of the brain

96 Goneril: Gloucester probably kneels, reminding Lear of Goneril's flattery

97 like a dog: as a dog fawns on his master

97–98 I had...there: said I was old and wise much too soon

98–99 To say...'no' to: to agree with

100 no good divinity: against the teaching of the *Bible*. (There are several references in the *Bible* to 'yea' and 'nay'.)

103 'em: the flatterers

105 ague-proof: fever-proof

106 trick: individual intonation

	I took it for a man; often 'twould say 'The Fiend, the Fiend': he led me to that place.
EDGAR	Bear free and patient thoughts. But who comes here? 80

Enter LEAR, *fantastically dressed with wild flowers*

	The safer sense will ne'er accommodate His master thus.
LEAR	No, they cannot touch me for coining; I am the king himself.
EDGAR	O thou side-piercing sight! 85
LEAR	Nature's above art in that respect. There's your press-money. That fellow handles his bow like a crow-keeper: draw me a clothier's yard. Look, look! a mouse. Peace, peace! this piece of toasted cheese will do't. There's my gauntlet; I'll prove it on a 90 giant. Bring up the brown bills. O! well flown bird; i'th'clout, i'th'clout: hewgh! Give the word.
EDGAR	Sweet marjoram.
LEAR	Pass.
GLOUCESTER	I know that voice. 95
LEAR	Ha! Goneril, with a white beard! They flattered me like a dog, and told me I had the white hairs in my beard ere the black ones were there. To say 'ay' and 'no' to every thing that I said! 'Ay' and 'no' too was no good divinity. When the rain came 100 to wet me once and the wind to make me chatter, when the thunder would not peace at my bidding, there I found 'em, there I smelt 'em out. Go to, they are not men o'their words: they told me I was every thing; 'tis a lie, I am not ague-proof. 105
GLOUCESTER	The trick of that voice I do well remember: Is't not the King?
LEAR	Ay, every inch a king: When I do stare, see how the subject quakes.

As if somehow aware of whom he is addressing, Lear talks of
adultery and Edmund. He says that women are animals
sexually. Gloucester recognizes Lear's madness. Lear asks
Gloucester to read a challenge he has written.

109 cause: charge against you

113 Does lecher: lusts

115 kinder: (literally) more naturally child-like; 'kinder' is the
German word for 'children'

116 Luxury: lechery

117 I lack soldiers: an increased population would mean a bigger
army

simp'ring dame: goody-goody woman

118 Whose face...snow: whose face indicates sexual frigidity
(coldness between her forks)

forks: legs

119 minces: makes a show of

120 pleasure's name: the very name of pleasure

121 The fitchew: the polecat (prostitute)

soiled: full of rich grass and raring to go

123 Down...Centaurs: from the waist down they are beasts

Centaur: half man, half horse

125 girdle: waist

inherit: possess

128 consumption: destruction by fire

fie...pah!: he is disgusted by his own references to female
sexuality

129 civet: perfume (from the civet cat)

apothecary: chemist

130 sweeten: to sweeten (against the sulphurous stench)

131 thee: Gloucester

132 mortality: human life – and death

133 O ruined...Nature!: microcosm, man representing the
greater universe

great world: macrocosm

134 so wear...naught: in this way decay to nothing

135 squiny: squint

136 blind Cupid: Cupid is often pictured blindfold - it was also
the sign of a brothel. (For a moment Lear seems somehow
aware of who Gloucester is, what has happened to his eyes
and the reason – his infidelity – for it.)

137 challenge: see line 90

139 I would...report: I would not believe this if I were told it

I pardon that man's life. What was thy cause?
Adultery?   110
Thou shalt not die: die for adultery! No:
The wren goes to't, and the small gilded fly
Does lecher in my sight.
Let copulation thrive; for Gloucester's bastard son
Was kinder to his father than my daughters   115
Got 'tween the lawful sheets. To't, Luxury,
      pell-mell!
For I lack soldiers. Behold yond simp'ring dame,
Whose face between her forks presages snow;
That minces virtue, and does shake the head
To hear of pleasure's name;   120
The fitchew nor the soiled horse goes to't
With a more riotous appetite.
Down from the waist they are Centaurs,
Though women all above:
But to the girdle do the Gods inherit,   125
Beneath is all the fiend's: there's hell, there's
      darkness,
There is the sulphurous pit – burning, scalding,
Stench, consumption; fie, fie, fie! pah, pah!
Give me an ounce of civet, good apothecary,
To sweeten my imagination.   130
There's money for thee.

GLOUCESTER   O! let me kiss that hand.

LEAR   Let me wipe it first; it smells of mortality.

GLOUCESTER O ruined piece of Nature! This great world
Shall so wear out to naught. Dost thou know me?

LEAR   I remember thine eyes well enough. Dost thou
      squiny at me?   135
No, do thy worst, blind Cupid; I'll not love.
Read thou this challenge; mark but the penning of
      it.

GLOUCESTER Were all thy letters suns, I could not see.

EDGAR   [*Aside*] I would not take this from report; it is,

When Gloucester says that he has no eyes, Lear says that that
should not stop him from seeing how things are: that justice
is only available to the rich and influential. Lear suggests that
glass eyes would make Gloucester like a politician – he could
pretend to see things he did not.

142 **case of eyes**: eye sockets
143 **are you...me?**: is that what you mean?
145 **heavy case**: bad way
     in a light: empty, lightweight
147 **feelingly**: keenly/by my sense of feeling
148 **What! art mad?**: Lear takes Gloucester to mean he does not
     understand
150 **rails upon**: rebukes
     simple: humble
150–151 **Hark...ear**: a whisper in the ear (bribery)
151 **handy-dandy**: children's game – guess which hand it is in
155 **creature**: human being
156 **image**: symbol
158 **beadle**: parish constable
159 **lash that whore**: whipping was a punishment for whores
160 **in that kind**: for that purpose
161 **The usurer...cozener**: the loan shark punishes the petty
     trickster
162 **Thorough...appear**: the vices of the poor are evident,
     however small
     Thorough: through
163 **Robes...gowns**: still thinking of judges
     Plate: cover (as armour/gold plate)
164 **hurtless**: without hurting
166 **None...say, none**: everyone is a sinner so no one has the
     right to accuse anyone else
     able 'em: vouch for them
167 **Take that of me**: believe me
168 **glass: false, or...glass eyes**: spectacles. (In either case the
     'seeing' will be pretence.)
169 **scurvy politician**: vile trickster

	And my heart breaks at it.	140
LEAR	Read.	
GLOUCESTER	What! with the case of eyes?	
LEAR	O, ho! are you there with me? No eyes in your head, nor no money in your purse? Your eyes are in a heavy case, your purse in a light: yet you see how this world goes.	145
GLOUCESTER	I see it feelingly.	
LEAR	What! art mad? A man may see how this world goes with no eyes. Look with thine ears: see how yond justice rails upon yond simple thief. Hark, in thine ear: change places, and, handy-dandy, which is the justice, which is the thief? Thou hast seen a farmer's dog bark at a beggar?	150
GLOUCESTER	Ay, Sir.	
LEAR	And the creature run from the cur? There thou might'st behold	155

The great image of Authority:
A dog's obeyed in office.
Thou rascal beadle, hold thy bloody hand!
Why dost thou lash that whore? Strip thine own back;
Thou hotly lusts to use her in that kind   160
For which thou whipp'st her. The usurer hangs the cozener.
Thorough tattered clothes small vices do appear;
Robes and furred gowns hide all. Plate sin with gold,
And the strong lance of justice hurtless breaks;
Arm it in rags, a pigmy's straw does pierce it.   165
None does offend, none, I say, none; I'll able 'em:
Take that of me, my friend, who have the power
To seal th'accuser's lips. Get thee glass eyes;
And, like a scurvy politician, seem
To see the things thou dost not. Now, now, now, now;   170

Edgar says that Lear's words combine truth and nonsense.
Lear admits to recognizing Gloucester. His mind is diverted
by thoughts of revenge on his sons-in-law. Cordelia's men
find Lear and want to take him back with them. He runs off.

172 **matter and impertinency**: sense and nonsense
176 **hither**: into the world
178 **wawl**: wail
180 **that**: because
181 **great stage of fools**: life being a performance on stage is a
 recurring Shakespearean theme
 block: (several possibilities occur, each linked with other
 parts of this speech) executioner's block from the idea of
 stage scaffolding/mounting-block connected with
 'horse'/cobbler's block connected with 'shoe'/milliner's
 block connected with 'felt' (as in hat)
182 **delicate stratagem**: neat scheme
182–183 **shoe...felt**: to make them quiet
183 **in proof**: to the test
184 **son-in-laws**: Cornwall and Albany
189 **The natural...Fortune**: the simpleton, the plaything of
 fortune
191 **cut to th'brains**: implies physical and mental wounds
192 **seconds**: supporters
193 **man of salt**: man of tears
195 **die**: lose life (as Act 4 scene 2 line 25; link with 'bridegroom')
 bravely: courageously/smartly dressed
196 **smug**: well turned out
199 **Then...in't**: it's not over yet
200 **Sa, sa, sa, sa**: a hunting cry

> • *Would you agree that Lear seems more sensitive and
> sensible in his madness than he ever was when sane?*

Pull off my boots; harder, harder; so.

EDGAR [*Aside*] O! matter and impertinency mixed;
Reason in madness.

LEAR If thou wilt weep my fortunes, take my eyes;
I know thee well enough; thy name is
    Gloucester;   175
Thou must be patient; we came crying hither:
Thou know'st the first time that we smell the air
We wawl and cry. I will preach to thee: mark.

GLOUCESTER Alack, alack the day!

LEAR When we are born, we cry that we are come   180
To this great stage of fools. This' a good block!
It were a delicate stratagem to shoe
A troop of horse with felt; I'll put't in proof,
And when I have stol'n upon these son-in-laws,
Then, kill, kill, kill, kill, kill, kill!   185

Enter a GENTLEMAN, *with* ATTENDANTS

GENTLEMAN O! here he is; lay hand upon him. Sir,
Your most dear daughter –

LEAR No rescue? What! a prisoner? I am even
The natural fool of Fortune. Use me well;
You shall have ransom. Let me have surgeons;   190
I am cut to th'brains.

GENTLEMAN   You shall have any thing.

LEAR No seconds? all myself?
Why this would make a man a man of salt,
To use his eyes for garden water-pots,
Ay, and laying autumn's dust. I will die bravely, 195
Like a smug bridegroom. What! I will be jovial:
Come, come; I am a king, masters, know you that?

GENTLEMAN You are a royal one, and we obey you.

LEAR Then there's life in't. Come and you get it, you
shall get it by running. Sa, sa, sa, sa.   200
             [*Exit running.* ATTENDANTS *follow*

Edgar is told that the battle between the British and the
French is about to begin. Gloucester is aware of Cordelia's
efforts to help her father. He asks the gods not to let him be
tempted to commit suicide. Edgar still does not reveal his
true identity.

203 **redeems nature**: re-establishes natural affection:
    general curse: universal affliction
204 **twain**: Goneril and Regan
205 **gentle**: honourable
    speed: may you prosper
206 **toward**: imminent
207 **sure**: certain
    vulgar: generally known
208 **Which...sound**: who has ears
210 **speedy**: advancing rapidly
    descry: sighting, catching sight of
210–211 **the main...thought**: the sighting of the main force is
    expected any hour now
212 **on special cause**: for a particular reason
215 **my worser spirit**: the evil side of my nature
216 **father**: old man. (Edgar is still unwilling to reveal himself.)
218 **tame**: submissive
219 **by the art...sorrows**: taught by the sufferings I have
    experienced
220 **pregnant**: susceptible
221 **biding**: place to stay
222 **bounty**: generous goodness
    benison: blessing
223 **To boot, and boot!**: reward you in addition (to my thanks)

GENTLEMAN	A sight most pitiful in the meanest wretch,
	Past speaking of in a King! Thou hast one
	daughter,
	Who redeems nature from the general curse
	Which twain have brought her to.
EDGAR	Hail, gentle sir!
GENTLEMAN	Sir, speed you: what's your
	will? 205
EDGAR	Do you hear aught, sir, of a battle toward?
GENTLEMAN	Most sure and vulgar; every one hears that,
	Which can distinguish sound.
EDGAR	But, by your favour,
	How near's the other army?
GENTLEMAN	Near, and on speedy foot; the main descry 210
	Stands on the hourly thought.
EDGAR	I thank you, sir:
	that's all.
GENTLEMAN	Though that the Queen on special cause is here,
	Her army is moved on.
EDGAR	I thank you sir.
	[*Exit* GENTLEMAN
GLOUCESTER	You ever-gentle Gods, take my breath from me:
	Let not my worser spirit tempt me again 215
	To die before you please!
EDGAR	Well pray you, father.
GLOUCESTER	Now, good sir, what are you?
EDGAR	A most poor man, made tame to Fortune's blows;
	Who, by the art of known and feeling sorrows,
	Am pregnant to good pity. Give me your hand, 220
	I'll lead you to some biding.
GLOUCESTER	Hearty thanks:
	The bounty and the benison of Heaven
	To boot, and boot!

Oswald arrives, intent on killing Gloucester and claiming his
reward. Edgar, posing as a country bumpkin, tells Oswald to
keep his distance. Oswald ignores the warning and Edgar
intervenes and kills him. The dying Oswald asks Edgar to
deliver letters to Edmund.

223 **proclaimed prize!**: outlaw with a price on his head!
    Most happy!: I am in luck!
224 **framed**: made
226 **Briefly thyself remember**: quickly say your last prayer
227 **friendly**: because he wants to die
228 **peasant**: this gives Edgar the idea for the style of his response
229 **published**: proclaimed
230–231 **th'infection...thee**: you are infected with his
    misfortune (death)
232 **Chill**: I'll
    vurther 'casion: further occasion (better cause)
234 **your gait**: on your way
    volk: folk
235–236 **And 'chud...life**: if I could have been killed by
    swaggering talk
236–237 **'twould not...vortnight**: I should have been dead a
    fortnight ago
238 **che vor' ye**: I warrant you
    ise: I shall
    costard: apple (head)
239 **ballow**: cudgel
240 **dunghill**: dunghill-born, low fellow
241 **pick your teeth**: knock your teeth out
241–242 **no matter...foins**: I don't care about your rapier
    thrusts
243 **Villain**: serf
247 **Upon**: among
249 **serviceable**: fussily attentive, officious
251 **badness**: a bad person

> • *Look at Edgar's final speech on this page. To what extent
> has Oswald shown himself to be the personification of evil?*

Enter OSWALD

OSWALD   A proclaimed prize! Most
          happy!
          That eyeless head of thine was first framed flesh
          To raise my fortunes. Thou old unhappy traitor, 225
          Briefly thyself remember: the sword is out
          That must destroy thee.

GLOUCESTER   Now let thy friendly hand
          Put strength enough to't.   [EDGAR *interposes*

OSWALD   Wherefore, bold peasant
          Dar'st thou support a published traitor? Hence;
          Lest that th'infection of his fortune take   230
          Like hold on thee. Let go his arm.

EDGAR   Chill not let go, zir, without vurther 'casion.

OSWALD   Let go, slave, or thou di'st.

EDGAR   Good gentleman, go your gait, and let poor volk
          pass. And 'chud ha' bin zwaggered out of my   235
          life, 'twould not ha' bin zo long as 'tis by a
          vortnight. Nay, come not near th'old man; keep
          out, che vor' ye, or ise try whither your costard or
          my ballow be the harder. Chill be plain with you.

OSWALD   Out, dunghill!   240

EDGAR   Chill pick your teeth, zir. Come; no matter vor
          your foins. [*They fight, and* EDGAR *knocks him down*

OSWALD   Slave, thou hast slain me. Villain, take my purse.
          If ever thou wilt thrive, bury my body;
          And give the letters which thou find'st about
              me   245
          To Edmund Earl of Gloucester; seek him out
          Upon the British party: O! untimely death.
          Death!   [*Dies*

EDGAR   I know thee well: a serviceable villain;
          As duteous to the vices of thy mistress   250
          As badness would desire.

Edgar reads a letter from Goneril to Edmund, urging him to
kill Albany and become her husband. Edgar intends that
Albany should see the letter. Gloucester says he could bear
his sorrows better if he were mad. Edgar leads him off
towards the French camp.

255 **deathsman**: executioner
256 **Leave, gentle wax**: by your leave (he breaks the seal)
    manners, blame us not: we shall not be accused of bad
    manners
257 **To know...hearts**: we torture enemies for information
258 **Their papers**: to rip their letters
259 **reciprocal**: mutual
260 **cut him off**: murder Albany
261 **will want not**: determination is not lacking
261–262 **fruitfully offered**: plentiful
262 **There is nothing done**: nothing will have been achieved
265 **supply the place**: fill his place
    for your labour: as a reward for your work/for love-making
266 **so I would say**: as I should like to say
268 **indistinguished...will!**: immeasurable range of woman's lust
270 **in the sands**: Edgar is speaking for his father's benefit; they
    are not on the beach, of course
271 **rake**: cover
    post unsanctified: unholy messenger
272 **in the mature time**: at the right time
273 **ungracious paper**: wicked letter
274 **death-practised Duke**: Albany, whose death is plotted
276 **stiff**: unyielding
    vile: wicked (will not give way to insanity)
277 **ingenious**: conscious
278 **distract**: mad
280–281 **And woes...themselves**: sorrows would be forgotten in
    insane illusions
283 **bestow**: lodge

> • *Can you suggest what should be done about Oswald's body?*
> *A corpse is usually manhandled from the stage at the end*
> *of a scene but that is not possible here. Do you have any*
> *ideas?*

GLOUCESTER   What! is he dead?

EDGAR   Sit you down, father; rest you.
               Let's see these pockets: the letters that he speaks of
               May be my friends. He's dead; I am only sorry
               He had no other deathsman. Let us see: 255
               Leave, gentle wax; and, manners, blame us not:
               To know our enemies' minds, we rip their hearts;
               Their papers is more lawful.   [*Reads*

                   Let our reciprocal vows be remembered. You have
               many opportunities to cut him off; if your   260
               will want not, time and place will be fruitfully
               offered. There is nothing done if he return the
               conqueror; then am I the prisoner, and his bed my
               gaol; from the loathed warmth whereof deliver me,
               and supply the place for your labour.   265
                   Your wife, so I would say –
                       Affectionate servant, GONERIL.
               O indistinguished space of woman's will!
               A plot upon her virtuous husband's life,
               And the exchange my brother! Here, in the
                   sands,   270
               Thee I'll rake up, the post unsanctified
               Of murtherous lechers; and in the mature time
               With this ungracious paper strike the sight
               Of the death-practised Duke. For him 'tis well
               That of thy death and business I can tell.   275

GLOUCESTER   The King is mad: how stiff is my vile sense
               That I stand up, and have ingenious feeling
               Of my huge sorrows! Better I were distract:
               So should my thoughts be severed from my griefs,
               And woes by wrong imaginations lose   280
               The knowledge of themselves.   [*Drum afar off*

EDGAR   Give me your hand:
               Far off, methinks, I hear the beaten drum.
               Come, father, I'll bestow you with a friend.
                                                           [*Exeunt*

Cordelia thanks Kent profusely for his services to her father.
Kent asks her to let him remain incognito for a while. The
doctor tells Cordelia that Lear is sleeping well, and Cordelia
prays that he will be cured. She agrees to the doctor's
suggestion that it is time to wake Lear.

3 **every measure fail me**: every action will be inadequate

4 **To be...o'er-paid**: that you recognize my efforts is more than
I deserve

5–6 **All my...but so**: I have told you the simple truth, without
addition nor omission but just as things happened

6 **suited**: dressed

7 **weeds**: clothes

9 **Yet...intent**: to reveal myself now would be sooner than I
intended

10 **My boon I make it**: I ask for this favour

11 **Till time...meet**: until I judge the circumstances to be right

15 **breach**: breakdown

16 **jarring**: discordant
wind up: bring into tune (by tightening the strings)

17 **child-changed**: changed by his children/changed to a child
again

20 **I'th'sway...will**: using your own judgement
arrayed: dressed fittingly

Scene  7

A tent in the French camp

Enter CORDELIA, KENT, DOCTOR, *and* GENTLEMAN

CORDELIA	O thou good Kent! how shall I live and work To match thy goodness? My life will be too short, And every measure fail me.
KENT	To be acknowledged, Madam, is o'er-paid. All my reports go with the modest truth, 5 No more nor clipped, but so.
CORDELIA	Be better suited: These weeds are memories of those worser hours: I prithee, put them off.
KENT	Pardon, dear Madam; Yet to be known shortens my made intent: My boon I make it that you know me not 10 Till time and I think meet.
CORDELIA	Then be't so, my good Lord. [*To the* DOCTOR] How does the King?
DOCTOR	Madam, sleeps still.
CORDELIA	O you kind Gods, Cure this great breach in his abused nature! 15 Th'untuned and jarring senses, O! wind up Of this child-changed father.
DOCTOR	So please your Majesty That we may wake the King? he hath slept long.
CORDELIA	Be governed by your knowledge, and proceed I'th'sway of your own will. Is he arrayed? 20

Enter LEAR *in a chair carried by* SERVANTS

GENTLEMAN	Ay, Madam, in the heaviness of sleep

Cordelia cannot believe that her sisters could have treated anyone as they have done, let alone their own father. When Lear wakes he seems not to recognize Cordelia. She believes he has not been cured.

23 by: near
24 I doubt...temperance: I am sure he will be calm
Stage direction *Music*: in the Elizabethan theatre the sound effect of music was often used as part of the process of mental healing; indeed, many therapists today are convinced of its restorative powers
29 in thy reverence: against thy revered person
30 white flakes: snowy hair
31 challenge: demand
32 warring: fighting, bitterly opposed
33 deep dread-bolted thunder: deep voiced with dreaded thunderbolts
35 cross: fork
perdu: guard or sentry in the most dangerous position (from the French word for 'lost')
36 thin helm: head with thin hair
38 fain: willing, content
40 short and musty straw: the worst sort of bed
42 all: together
44 royal Lord, Majesty: when he was asleep she thought of him as 'father'
45–48 You do...molten lead: Lear believes he is experiencing life after death and he is in hell – '*wheel of fire*', '*molten lead*' – whilst Cordelia is an angel in heaven
47 that: so that
50 far wide: wandering

> • *What is to be said in favour of the 'rogues forlorn'(line 39)? How can Cordelia have mis-read the situation so badly?*

	We put fresh garments on him.	
DOCTOR	Be by, good Madam, when we do awake him;	
	I doubt not of his temperance.	
CORDELIA	Very well. [*Music*	
DOCTOR	Please you, draw near. Louder the music there!	25
CORDELIA	O my dear father! Restoration hang	
	Thy medicine on my lips, and let this kiss	
	Repair those violent harms that my two sisters	
	Have in thy reverence made!	
KENT	Kind and dear	
	Princess!	
CORDELIA	Had you not been their father, these white flakes	30
	Did challenge pity of them. Was this a face	
	To be opposed against the warring winds?	
	To stand against the deep dread-bolted thunder?	
	In the most terrible and nimble stroke	
	Of quick, cross lightning? to watch – poor	
	perdu! –	35
	With this thin helm? Mine enemy's dog,	
	Though he had bit me, should have stood that night	
	Against my fire. And wast thou fain, poor father,	
	To hovel thee with swine and rogues forlorn,	
	In short and musty straw? Alack, alack!	40
	'Tis wonder that thy life and wits at once	
	Had not concluded all. He wakes; speak to him.	
DOCTOR	Madam, do you; 'tis fittest.	
CORDELIA	How does my royal Lord? How fares your Majesty?	
LEAR	You do me wrong to take me out o'th'grave;	45
	Thou art a soul in bliss; but I am bound	
	Upon a wheel of fire, that mine own tears	
	Do scald like molten lead.	
CORDELIA	Sir, do you know me?	
LEAR	You are a spirit, I know; where did you die?	
CORDELIA	Still, still, far wide.	50

Cordelia is relieved when Lear does recognize her. He says that she has cause to hate him, and if she has poison for him he will take it. The doctor says that Lear is improved.

53 abused: deluded
54 thus: in this state of mind
60 fond: silly
61 Fourscore...or less: a strange mixture of precision and approximation
64 this man: Kent
65 mainly: entirely
71 Be your tears wet?: are you really crying?
73 do not: cannot
77 abuse: deceive
　　rage: frenzy

DOCTOR	He's scarce awake; let him alone awhile.
LEAR	Where have I been? Where am I? Fair daylight?
	I am mightily abused. I should e'en die with pity
	To see another thus. I know not what to say.
	I will not swear these are my hands: let's see; 55
	I feel this pin prick. Would I were assured
	Of my condition!
CORDELIA	O! look upon me, Sir,
	And hold your hand in benediction o'er me.
	No, Sir, you must not kneel.
LEAR	Pray, do not mock
	me:
	I am a very foolish fond old man, 60
	Fourscore and upward, not an hour more or less;
	And, to deal plainly,
	I fear I am not in my perfect mind.
	Methinks I should know you and know this man;
	Yet I am doubtful: for I am mainly ignorant 65
	What place this is, and all the skill I have
	Remembers not these garments; nor I know not
	Where I did lodge last night. Do not laugh at me;
	For, as I am a man, I think this lady
	To be my child Cordelia.
CORDELIA	And so I am, I am. 70
LEAR	Be your tears wet? Yes, faith. I pray, weep not:
	If you have poison for me, I will drink it.
	I know you do not love me; for your sisters
	Have, as I do remember, done me wrong:
	You have some cause, they have not.
CORDELIA	No cause, no cause. 75
LEAR	Am I in France?
KENT	In your own kingdom, Sir.
LEAR	Do not abuse me.
DOCTOR	Be comforted, good Madam; the great rage,

The doctor goes on to say that Lear needs time to make a full recovery. Lear begs Cordelia's forgiveness. Rumours are circulating that Edgar and Kent are in Germany. The battle is imminent.

80 make him...lost: fill in the gaps in his memory
82 further settling: he has settled a little more
83 walk: withdraw
85 Holds it true: is it confirmed
88 conductor: leader
92 Report is changeable: rumour varies
　　look about: be wary
93 powers of the kingdom: British forces
94 arbitrement: decisive encounter
96 My point...wrought: my purpose in life and life's end will be thoroughly worked out. (The battle is going to be absolutely crucial for my future.)
98 Or...or: either...or

	You see, is killed in him: and yet it is danger	
	To make him even o'er the time he has lost.	80
	Desire him to go in; trouble him no more	
	Till further settling.	
CORDELIA	Will't please your Highness walk?	
LEAR	You must bear with me.	
	Pray you now, forget and forgive: I am old and foolish.	

[Exeunt LEAR, CORDELIA, DOCTOR, and
ATTENDANTS

GENTLEMAN	Holds it true, sir, that the Duke of Cornwall was so slain?	85
KENT	Most certain, sir.	
GENTLEMAN	Who is conductor of his people?	
KENT	As 'tis said, the bastard son of Gloucester.	
GENTLEMAN	They say Edgar, his banished son, is with the Earl of Kent in Germany.	90
KENT	Report is changeable. 'Tis time to look about; the powers of the kingdom approach apace.	
GENTLEMAN	The arbitrement is like to be bloody. Fare you well, sir.	95

[Exit

KENT	My point and period will be throughly wrought,	
	Or well or ill, as this day's battle's fought.	*[Exit*

ACTIVITIES

Keeping track

Scene 1

1 • What view of his own position does Edgar hold at the opening of this scene?
   • How and why does he revise this opinion?

Scene 2

2 How does Goneril respond to the news of Cornwall's death (lines 83–87)? Why does she react in this way?

Scene 3

3 Bearing in mind his earlier treatment of her, why does Lear refuse to see Cordelia although she is nearby?

Scene 4

4 What are Cordelia's feelings about her father at this point?

Scene 5

5 Why does Regan regret not killing Gloucester?
6 What are Regan's plans for Edmund?

Scene 6

7 At the beginning of the scene, Gloucester is determined upon suicide; by line 75 he has decided that, after all, he will bear:
   '*Affliction till it do cry out itself*
   "Enough, enough," and die.'
   How exactly has Edgar brought about this change?
8 What is the significance of the letter which Oswald is carrying?

Scene 7

9 How would you describe Lear's condition when he wakes to see Cordelia?
10 What emotions does Cordelia show here? Remember that not only is she responding to her father's condition, but she is also thinking of how he came to be like that.

Drama

1 It is perhaps difficult in our cynical times to believe in a genuinely good man who is not a simpleton. Look at Edgar's opening speech in Act 4. Hotseat volunteers to see if they can sustain the role as Edgar. The questioners will subject the volunteers to the sort of aggressive interrogation popular with some radio and television interviewers. The underlying cynicism will be concerned with 'what's in it for him?'

2 In threes, rehearse the exchanges between Goneril and Albany in Act 4 scene 2 lines 29–68. One person acts as director. When you have practised, present your version to the rest of the class for their comments. They could also adopt the roles of embarrassed attendants.

Show these portraits to the class for comment and discussion.

3 Use FORUM THEATRE (see page 273) to examine the moment when Regan says to Oswald, '*I'll love thee much, Let me unseal the letter.*' (Act 4 scene 5 lines 21–22).

What is she promising? Has she any idea of what is in the letter? Why does Oswald not let her see the letter?

4 Look again at Lear's speeches of Act 4 scene 6 lines 148–185 (see CLOSE STUDY question 7, page 226). Working in small groups, imagine that you are doctors preparing evidence to convince a court that Lear is not insane and that indeed, in some respects, he is more aware of reality than many of his contemporaries. Look particularly at what he has to say about the nature of criminality.

Make your declaration to the 'court'.

5 The exchange between Lear and Cordelia, Act 4 scene 7 lines 30–84, is extremely moving. Can you suggest ways in which this might be staged appropriately?

Close study

1 '*I have no way, and therefore want no eyes;*
I stumbled when I saw.' (Act 4 scene 1 lines 18–20)
Gloucester tells us that he made mistakes when he still had his eyes, but hints that he 'sees' some things better now that he has lost them.

What new understandings does he reveal in Act 4 scene 1 lines 18–24; 31–37; 46; and 64–71?

2 '*Wisdom and goodness to the vile seem vile;*' (Act 4 scene 2 line 38)
• What do you notice about the language and imagery Albany uses to denounce his wife in Act 4 scene 2 lines 29–67?
• In the same dialogue, how many times does Goneril use the word fool or foolish when referring to her husband?
What actual qualities seem to be associated with her idea of a fool?

3 In Act 4 scene 3 lines 11–32, a gentleman describes Cordelia's reactions and emotions on learning of her father's plight. What do you notice about the vocabulary and imagery he uses?

4 Moments of painful dramatic irony (where the audience have knowledge which is denied the characters on the stage) are a feature of this play. Often, characters witness events or overhear remarks about themselves, or concerning matters close to them, and remain unrecognized, either because they are disguised or because the speaker is blind or mad.

For instance, the following examples are of concern to Edgar: Act 4 scene 1 lines 21–4 and 33–37; Act 4 scene 6 lines 114–116. Try to find other examples from Act 4, and elsewhere in the play. What is the effect of such moments for the audience, do you think?

5 Gloucester's suicide attempt at the beginning of Act 4 scene 6 is a part of the play which is difficult to stage convincingly. Look at the scene up to line 80 and decide what the difficulties are, and how they might be overcome. Gloucester's 'suicide' sometimes raises a laugh in an audience. Does it matter if it appears comic? Is it, perhaps, meant to be so? (See also KEY SCENE, opposite.)

6 How does Lear come to be wandering around on his own in Act 4 scene 6 when he was previously being so carefully looked after by Kent?

7 'Ay, every inch a king....kill, kill, kill!' (scene 6 lines 107–185) Lear presents an ugly image of society's depravity and causes us to reflect on humanity's responsibilities.
- What attitude do we see in Lear at Gloucester's mention of his title (lines 107–109)?
- How often does Lear swing from speaking of matters which relate to himself personally to talking of immorality in general terms (lines 109–117)?
- Why might Lear be obsessed at this point with the behaviour of women (lines 117–128)?
  How does he link women's attitude to sex with that of nature and the supernatural?
- How do we know that Lear sees himself as being above this universal corruption (lines 128–130)?
- How do we know that Gloucester 'sees' Lear as representative of the depraved world (lines 131–134)?
- Why is Edgar in despair (lines 134–140)?
  - What examples of public corruption does Lear give (lines 141–161)?
  - Why does it seem strange that a king is complaining of injustice in these terms (lines 162–171)?
  - Is there some nonsense in what Lear has said (lines 172–173)?
  - How is Lear's reference to crying related to the human condition,

and to his own situation in particular (lines 174–185)?
    What is his mood at line 185? How have his thoughts progressed
    to this change of heart?
  8 Are there any differences between the sort of thing Lear says
    when speaking in verse in Act 4 scene 6, and what he says when
    speaking in prose?
  9 The storm is over, the Fool has gone, and in this scene Edgar
    drops the pretence of Mad Tom. How might all these be said to be
    embodied by the person of Lear himself, and contained and reflected
    in what he says?
 10 Look closely at Lear's language when he first wakes in scene 7
    (lines 45–75). How would you describe it? What response will this
    draw from an audience and why? Compare his style of speech here
    with his opening words (Act 1 scene 1, beginning at line 35) and
    with examples of his 'mad' speech (for example, Act 3 scene 2 lines
    1–24).
    In what ways are they different?
 11 How do Cordelia's words in Act 4 scene 7 lines 26–42, and her
    responses to Lear's words which follow (for example, lines 70, 75)
    build our sympathy for Lear; and what do they add to our
    impressions of her?

Key scene

The 'suicide scene': Act 4 scene 6 lines 1–80

Keying it in

  1 This is an important scene that begins to draw together the Lear and
    Gloucester plots. The scene slows the pace of the action after the
    frantic storm scene but there is no abating in terms of emotional
    intensity. We see here the regeneration of Gloucester in which he
    breaks through his despair with the guidance of Edgar in the guise of
    'Poor Tom'. Until now Edgar has taken a rather passive role in the
    action but, in the build-up to this scene, he starts to take a more active
    part.
      Look at Act 4 scene 1.
    • What impression of life is given by Edgar in lines 10–12, 25–26,
      27–28, 51?
    • Do you see any link here with the impression created in Act 3?
    • Look at Gloucester's state of mind in this scene as a whole. Does his
      attitude to humanity in general, and to Edgar in particular, seem to
      have changed from his feelings as seen earlier in the play?
  2 There are faint signs that a regenerative process is underway here, and
    the interludes presented by scenes 3 and 4 serve to reinforce this
    impression.

- In what ways is the feeling confirmed to some extent in:
  a scene 3
  b scene 4?
- Although we see now that help is on the way, Lear's troubles are still far from over. How are we reminded of this in scene 4?

The scene itself

3 lines 1–24
- How is Gloucester right when he tells Edgar, '*thou speak'st/ In better phrase and matter than thou didst*' (lines 7–8)?
- Look at lines 11–24. How does Shakespeare achieve a vivid impression of height here through his use of visual language?
- It is important that Edgar convinces Gloucester of the height while at the same time letting the audience know that he is pretending. Think of ways in which this could be achieved on the stage.

4 lines 25–41
- What is the purpose of Edgar's aside (lines 32–33)?
- How do you think Edgar's 'trifling' with Gloucester's '*despair Is done to cure it*'?
- Describe Gloucester's state of mind just before he tries to kill himself.
- Does he have any positive thoughts in his despair?

5 lines 42–64
- How does Gloucester's state of mind change immediately after the 'fall'?
- How do Edgar's words help to dispel Gloucester's despair?
- How does his vivid use of language once again help him to keep up his illusion?

6 lines 65–80
- What is the effect on Gloucester of Edgar's urging him to:
  '*Think that the clearest Gods, who make them honours Of men's impossibilities, have preserved thee*'?
- How successful have Edgar's attempts been to restore and regenerate his father's spirits?

Overview

The regeneration of Gloucester is immediately contrasted with the continuing madness of Lear who enters at this point. However, although we can see that Lear still has some way to go, there is very much a sense that his recovery process is underway, preparing for this to materialize in the next scene.

• What effect does the presence of Lear have on the remaining part of Act 4 scene 6? Are there any signs that he is moving towards greater self-knowledge?
• What are the similarities of, and the differences between, the regeneration of Gloucester in Scene 6 and that of Lear in scene 7?

Writing

1 '...they told me I was every thing; 'tis a lie, I am not ague-proof.'
With particular reference to Act 4 scene 6 lines 96–171, discuss what Lear learns in the play about what it means to be king and have authority. You will need to think about:
  • Lear's behaviour and intentions at the start of the play
  • the consequence of his actions regarding his status and influence
  • his expectations of other people
  • the reality of how others regard – and treat – him
  • the warnings (including Act 1 scene 4 lines 156–161) which he ignores
  • the outcome.

2 '...to deal plainly...'
In what ways is the theme of dealing, or speaking, plainly central to King Lear? You might wish to think about:
  • characters who 'deal plainly'
  • characters who use simple language, when and where and with what consequences
  • characters who act deceitfully
  • characters who use complex language, when and where and with what consequences.
You might also want to use Lear as an example of the use of language reflecting status and state of mind.

3 Lear's awakening in Act 4 is almost like a rebirth after his descent into madness. Looking closely at the language he uses and what other characters report about him, explain how his mental state deteriorates in Acts 1–3, and how he re-emerges with a new understanding in Act 4.

In the British camp Edmund complains that Albany cannot
decide on a plan of action. Regan asks Edmund about his
relationship with Goneril.

1 **Know of...hold**: find out from the Duke of Albany if he intends
   to carry out his most recent plan
2 **advised**: persuaded
3 **full of alteration**: keeps changing his mind
4 **self-reproving**: conscience-stricken
   constant pleasure: fixed decision
5 **Our sister's man**: Oswald
   miscarried: come to harm
6 **doubted**: feared
7 **intend**: mean to confer
8 **but then**: even if it is unpleasant
9 **honoured**: honourable
10–11 **But have...place?**: have you not behaved like a husband
   with her?
10 **my brother**: Duke of Albany
11 **forfended**: forbidden
12 **doubtful**: fearful
12–13 **been conjunct And bosomed**: coupled and been intimate
13 **as far as we call hers**: in the fullest sense
15 **I never...her**: I shall not allow her (to come between us)
16 **familiar**: intimate
   Fear me not: do not worry about me on that account

Act five

Scene 1

The British camp near Dover
Enter, with drum and colours, EDMUND, REGAN,
OFFICERS, SOLDIERS, *and Others*

EDMUND   Know of the Duke if his last purpose hold,
Or whether since he is advised by aught
To change the course; he's full of alteration
And self-reproving; bring his constant pleasure.
                    [*To an* OFFICER, *who goes out*

REGAN   Our sister's man is certainly miscarried.   5

EDMUND   'Tis to be doubted, Madam.

REGAN   Now, sweet Lord,
You know the goodness I intend upon you:
Tell me, but truly, but then speak the truth,
Do you not love my sister?

EDMUND   In honoured love.

REGAN   But have you never found my brother's way   10
To the forfended place?

EDMUND   That thought abuses you.

REGAN   I am doubtful that you have been conjunct
And bosomed with her, as far as we call hers.

EDMUND   No, by mine honour, Madam.

REGAN   I never shall ensure her: dear my Lord,   15
Be not familiar with her.

EDMUND   Fear me not.
She and the Duke her husband!

Enter, with drum and colours, ALBANY, GONERIL,
and SOLDIERS

Goneril is more concerned about Regan's influence on
Edmund than on the outcome of the coming battle, and
Regan does not want to let Goneril out of her sight, being
unwilling to give her the chance to speak privately with
Edmund. Edgar arrives as Poor Tom and gives Albany the
letter which he took from Oswald; he says the contents will
be proved true.

20 **be-met**: met
22 **rigour of our state**: harshness of our rule
23 **honest**: fighting a just cause
24 **valiant**: brave
   For: as for
25 **touches**: concerns
   France: the King of France
26–27 **Not bolds...oppose**: not because the King of France
   supports Lear and others, who oppose us with just grievances
   (Note that it is suspected that at least two lines are missing
   from the text prior to line 26 making interpretation difficult.)
27 **heavy causes**: weighty reasons
28 **Sir, you speak nobly**: said with heavy sarcasm
   Why...reasoned: What is the point (of talking about the
   justice of our cause)?
30 **particular broils**: private quarrels
31–32 **Let's then...proceeding**: let us decide with our
   experienced soldiers what to do next
33 **presently**: immediately
34 **us**: me (royal plural)
36 **convenient**: fitting
37 **O, ho!...riddle**: I see what your game is
39 **I'll overtake you**: I'll catch up with you
40 **letter**: from Goneril to Edmund, taken from Oswald's body
43 **champion**: honourable person who will speak for me

> • *Edgar has a good opportunity to reveal his identity to
> Albany here, but he does not do so. Is he wise to keep his
> disguise intact at this stage?*

GONERIL	[*Aside*] I had rather lose the battle than that sister Should loosen him and me.
ALBANY	Our very loving sister, well be-met. 20 Sir, this I hear; the King is come to his daughter, With others whom the rigour of our state Forced to cry out. Where I could not be honest, I never yet was valiant: for this business, It touches us, as France invades our land, 25 Not bolds the King, with others, whom, I fear, Most just and heavy causes make oppose.
EDMUND	Sir, you speak nobly.
REGAN	Why is this reasoned?
GONERIL	Combine together 'gainst the enemy; For these domestic and particular broils 30 Are not the question here.
ALBANY	Let's then determine With th'ancient of war on our proceeding.
EDMUND	I shall attend you presently at your tent.
REGAN	Sister, you'll go with us?
GONERIL	No. 35
REGAN	'Tis most convenient; pray go with us.
GONERIL	[*Aside*] O, ho! I know the riddle. I will go.

As they are going out enter EDGAR, *disguised*

EDGAR	If e'er your grace had speech with man so poor, Hear me one word.

ALBANY	I'll overtake you.
	[*Exeunt* EDMUND, REGAN, GONERIL, OFFICERS,
	             SOLDIERS, *and* ATTENDANTS
	             Speak.

EDGAR	Before you fight the battle, ope this letter. 40 If you have victory, let the trumpet sound For him that brought it: wretched though I seem, I can produce a champion that will prove

Albany says he will read the letter. Edmund's promises to
both Goneril and Regan have left him with a problem. He
says Albany is a useful figurehead for the battle, but
afterwards Goneril must find a way to get rid of him. When
this happens Lear and Cordelia will also suffer.

44 avouched: declared
   miscarry: come to misfortune, lose
46 machination: evil plotting
48 When time shall serve: when you are ready
50 o'erlook: scrutinize
51 powers: forces
52 Here: he hands over a note
53 diligent discovery: careful reconnaissance
54 greet the time: address the situation
56 jealous: suspicious
61 my side: of the bargain with Goneril
63 countenance: authority
64 devise: arrange
65 taking off: killing
68 Shall never see his pardon: they shall never know about
   Albany's intention to pardon them (because he will be dead)
   state: position
69 Stands: depends
   debate: talk about it

> • *How do lines 55–69 sum up what we already know
>   about Edmund? Do we learn anything new about him
>   here?*

	What is avouched there. If you miscarry,	
	Your business of the world hath so an end,	45
	And machination ceases. Fortune love you!	

ALBANY   Stay till I have read the letter.

EDGAR   I was forbid it.
          When time shall serve, let but the herald cry,
          And I'll appear again.

ALBANY   Why, fare thee well:
          I will o'erlook thy paper.   [*Exit* EDGAR   50

          Re-enter EDMUND

EDMUND   The enemy's in view; draw up your powers.
          Here is the guess of their true strength and forces
          By diligent discovery; but your haste
          Is now urged on you.

ALBANY   We will greet the time. [*Exit*

EDMUND   To both these sisters have I sworn my love;   55
          Each jealous of the other, as the stung
          Are of the adder. Which of them shall I take?
          Both? one? or neither? Neither can be enjoyed
          If both remain alive: to take the widow
          Exasperates, makes mad her sister Goneril;   60
          And hardly shall I carry out my side,
          Her husband being alive. Now then, we'll use
          His countenance for the battle; which being done,
          Let her who would be rid of him devise
          His speedy taking off. As for the mercy   65
          Which he intends to Lear and to Cordelia,
          The battle done, and they within our power,
          Shall never see his pardon; for my state
          Stands on me to defend, not to debate.   [*Exit*

The French army is beaten and Lear and Cordelia have been captured. Gloucester, once again in despair, is taken out of harm's way by Edgar.

1 **father**: old man
2 **good host**: one who shelters you
3–4 **If ever...comfort**: dramatic irony, referring to Edgar's revealing his true identity
6 **ta'en**: captured
8 **a man...even here**: I might as well die here
9–10 **Men must...hither**: like birth, death is something that man has to struggle through
11 **Ripeness is all**: (a link with rot) going at the right time is the important thing

Edmund escorts the prisoners, Cordelia and Lear.

1 **good guard**: keep a strict guard
2 **their greater pleasures**: the wishes of those in greater authority

Scene 2

A field between the two camps

Alarum within. Enter, with drum and colours, LEAR,
CORDELIA, *and their* FORCES; *and exeunt*

Enter EDGAR *and* GLOUCESTER

EDGAR   Here, father, take the shadow of this tree
For your good host; pray that the right may thrive.
If ever I return to you again, *reveal identy if he*
I'll bring you comfort.   *comes back*

GLOUCESTER   Grace go with you, sir!

                                   [*Exit* EDGAR

Alarum; afterwards a retreat. Re-enter EDGAR

EDGAR   Away, old man! give me thy hand: away!   5
King Lear hath lost, he and his daughter ta'en.
Give me thy hand; come on.

GLOUCESTER   No further, sir; a man may rot even here.

EDGAR   What! in ill thoughts again? Men must endure
Their going hence, even as their coming hither: 10
Ripeness is all. Come on.

GLOUCESTER   And that's true too.

                                   [*Exeunt*

Scene 3

The British camp near Dover
Enter, in conquest, with drum and colours, EDMUND,
LEAR *and* CORDELIA, PRISONERS; OFFICERS,
SOLDIERS, *etc*

EDMUND   Some officers take them away: good guard,
Until their greater pleasures first be known

Lear looks forward to sharing a happy life with Cordelia in
prison. When they have been led away, Edmund gives a
written instruction to one of the officers, promising him
further advancement if he follows orders.

3 **censure**: pass judgement on
4 **meaning**: intention
6 **out-frown...frown**: withstand what unkind Fate throws at us
9 **cage**: birdcage/prison
10–11 **When thou...forgiveness**: mutual forgiveness
13 **gilded butterflies**: dandified courtiers. (Gilded means covered
with gold.)
13–14 **poor rogues...news**: gossiping courtiers who are mere
idlers
15 **who's in, who's out**: who's in favour or out of favour
16 **take upon's**: claim to understand
17 **wear out**: outlast
18 **packs and sects**: groups and parties
19 **That ebb...th'moon**: come and go monthly/whose senses are
governed by the moon (lunatics)
20 **sacrifices**: (as we are) offering up our lives to the gods
21 **throw incense**: ie show approval
22–23 **He that...foxes**: ie no human can part us now
22 **brand**: burning torch
23 **fire us...foxes**: foxes were smoked out
24 **good years**: (it is probable – see '*devour...starved*' – that this
is a reference to the story of Pharaoh's dream in *Genesis,
Chapter 41*, when seven thin ears of corn devoured seven fat
ears, signifying famine following prosperity. Here Lear predicts
that the prosperity of their enemies will be followed by their
downfall.)
fell: skin
25 **starved**: dead
29 **advanced**: promoted
31 **noble fortunes**: becoming a nobleman
32 **Are as the time is**: have to adapt to different situations

> • *Is it ominous that Cordelia speaks in rhyming couplets,
> (lines 3–6)?*

That are to censure them.

CORDELIA   We are not the first
Who, with best meaning, have incurred the worst.
For thee, oppressed King, I am cast down;   5
Myself could else out-frown false Fortune's frown.
Shall we not see these daughters and these sisters?

LEAR   No, no, no, no! Come, let's away to prison;
We two alone will sing like birds i'th'cage:
When thou dost ask me blessing, I'll kneel
    down,   10
And ask of thee forgiveness: so we'll live,
And pray, and sing, and tell old tales, and laugh
At gilded butterflies, and hear poor rogues
Talk of court news; and we'll talk with them too,
Who loses and who wins; who's in, who's out;   15
And take upon's the mystery of things,
As if we were Gods' spies: and we'll wear out,
In a walled prison, packs and sects of great ones
That ebb and flow by th'moon.

EDMUND   Take them away.

LEAR   Upon such sacrifices, my Cordelia,   20
The Gods themselves throw incense. Have I caught
    thee?
He that parts us shall bring a brand from heaven,
And fire us hence like foxes. Wipe thine eyes;
The good years shall devour them, flesh and fell,
Ere they shall make us weep: we'll see 'em starved
    first.   25
Come.   [*Exeunt* LEAR *and* CORDELIA, *guarded*

EDMUND   Come hither, captain; hark.
Take thou this note;   [*Giving a paper*
                    Go follow them to prison.
One step I have advanced thee; if thou dost
As this instructs thee, thou dost make thy way   30
To noble fortunes; know thou this, that men
Are as the time is; to be tender-minded

The instruction is to be carried out immediately and without question. Albany enters and congratulates Edmund on the victory. He asks that Lear and Cordelia should be handed over to him. Edmund says the prisoners are safe and it would be better for Albany to see them later. Albany is not pleased.

33 Does not...sword: is not appropriate for a soldier (one who wears a sword)
employment: service
34 Will not bear question: is not open to discussion
35 thrive: get on in life
36 About: get on with
write: call yourself
37 carry: arrange
39 I cannot...oats: I am not a horse (ie I do not want to do ill-paid labouring jobs; I am meant for better things.)
41 valiant strain: the bravery of your ancestors
43 opposites: opponents
45 their merits: what they deserve
46 equally: justly
48 retention: confinement
49 Whose: the King's
title: king/right to land
50 To pluck...bosom: win the hearts of the common people
51 impressed lances: conscripted soldiers
in our eyes: towards (against) us. (We are reminded of Gloucester – by extension this line could mean that the lances will take out the eyes which have a vision of how things will be in the future.)
54 at further space: even later, if you like
55 session: hearing
55–60 At this time...fitter place: he is playing for time by suggesting that Lear and Cordelia will not get a fair hearing
57 quarrels: causes
heat: passion
60 fitter: more appropriate
61 subject: subordinate

- *Why is Edmund so confident (lines 46–60) when facing the most powerful man in the country? What are his feelings for – and about – Albany?*

	Does not become a sword; thy great employment	
	Will not bear question; either say thou'lt do't,	
	Or thrive by other means.	
OFFICER	I'll do't, my Lord.	35
EDMUND	About it; and write happy when th'hast done.	
	Mark, – I say, instantly, and carry it so	
	As I have set it down.	
OFFICER	I cannot draw a cart nor eat dried oats;	
	If it be man's work I'll do't. *[Exit*	40

Flourish. Enter ALBANY, GONERIL, REGAN, OFFICERS, *and* SOLDIERS

ALBANY	Sir, you have showed to-day your valiant strain,	
	And Fortune led you well; you have the captives	
	Who were the opposites of this day's strife;	
	I do require them of you, so to use them	
	As we shall find their merits and our safety	45
	May equally determine.	
EDMUND	Sir, I thought it fit	
	To send the old and miserable King	
	To some retention and appointed guard;	
	Whose age had charms in it, whose title more,	
	To pluck the common bosom on his side,	50
	And turn our impressed lances in our eyes	
	Which do command them. With him I sent the Queen;	
	My reason all the same; and they are ready	
	To-morrow, or at further space, t'appear	
	Where you shall hold your session. At this time	55
	We sweat and bleed; the friend hath lost his friend,	
	And the best quarrels, in the heat, are cursed	
	By those that feel their sharpness;	
	The question of Cordelia and her father	
	Requires a fitter place.	
ALBANY	Sir, by your patience,	60
	I hold you but a subject of this war,	

Despite not feeling well, Regan argues on Edmund's behalf, and says he will be her husband. Albany arrests Edmund and Goneril for treason, and tells Regan that Edmund is already promised in marriage to Goneril.

62 we: royal plural
   list: wish
63 Methinks...demanded: you might have consulted me
65 Bore...person: led Cornwall's army
66 immediacy: closeness ie as direct representative
67 hot: enthusiastic
68–69 In his own...addition: he has brought more honour on himself by his actions, than has been accorded him by the titles you have given him
69 In my rights: on my behalf
70 compeers: equals
71 the most: most clearly shown
72 Jesters...prophets: many a true word is spoken in jest
73 That eye...a-squint: you have mis-read the signs (ie you are fooling yourself)
75 From...stomach: with a flood of anger
75–79 General...master: Regan surrenders, like a fortress, to Edmund
76 patrimony: heritage
79 enjoy: in sexual terms, usually associated with men – this shows Regan as a commanding figure
80 let-alone: prohibition
   good will: consent
81 Half-blooded fellow: bastard
82 Let the drum strike: sound the drum for combat
   prove...thine: by defending it in combat
83 hear reason: he tries to calm the situation
84 in thy attaint: a accused with you; b sharing your dishonour
85 gilded: superficially attractive
87 sub-contracted: promised, engaged (a second contract since she is already married)

> • *What do Goneril's interventions (lines 67–69, 72–73, 79) show us about her feelings for Regan, Edmund and Albany?*

	Not as a brother.	
REGAN	That's as we list to grace him;	
	Methinks our pleasure might have been demanded,	
	Ere you had spoke so far. He led our powers,	
	Bore the commission of my place and person;	65
	The which immediacy may well stand up,	
	And call itself your brother.	
GONERIL	Not so hot;	
	In his own grace he doth exalt himself	
	More than in your addition.	
REGAN	In my rights,	
	By me invested, he compeers the best.	70
ALBANY	That were the most, if he should husband you.	
REGAN	Jesters do oft prove prophets.	
GONERIL	Holla, holla!	
	That eye that told you so looked but a-squint.	
REGAN	Lady, I am not well; else I should answer	
	From a full-flowing stomach. General,	75
	Take thou my soldiers, prisoners, patrimony;	
	Dispose of them, of me; the walls are thine;	
	Witness the world, that I create thee here	
	My lord and master.	
GONERIL	Mean you to enjoy him?	
ALBANY	The let-alone lies not in your good will.	80
EDMUND	Nor in thine, Lord.	
ALBANY	Half-blooded fellow, yes.	
REGAN	[*To* EDMUND] Let the drum strike, and prove my title thine.	
ALBANY	Stay yet; hear reason. Edmund, I arrest thee	
	On capital treason; and, in thy attaint,	
	This gilded serpent. [*Pointing to* GONERIL	
	For your claim, fair sister,	85
	I bar it in the interest of my wife;	
	'Tis she is sub-contracted to this lord,	

Albany orders the trumpet be sounded for anyone to come forward to prove Edmund's treason in combat. He says he will fight Edmund himself if no-one responds. He tells Edmund that he will receive no outside help since his army has dispersed. Regan is increasingly sick and has to be led away.

88   **banes**: banns
89   **make...to me**: he is the only one free to marry!
90   **bespoke**: promised
      interlude: little play, a farce, a diversion (literally, between important events)
93   **heinous**: infamous
      manifest: blatant
94   **make it**: make it good
95   **in nothing**: in no respect
97   **medicine**: poison
98   **What**: whatever (rank)
99   **villain-like**: like a slave
101 **On him...not?**: on anyone at all
      maintain: justify
103 **thy single virtue**: your own valour, bravery (you are on your own!)
104 **levied**: enlisted
104–105 **have in my name...discharge**: I have paid them off
110 **quality or degree**: high standing
111 **lists**: registers

> • *Can you add to your observations about Goneril (page 242) from her two brief interjections here?*

	And I, her husband, contradict your banes.	
	If you will marry, make your loves to me,	
	My lady is bespoke.	
GONERIL	An interlude!	90
ALBANY	Thou art armed, Gloucester; let the trumpet sound:	
	If none appear to prove upon thy person	
	Thy heinous, manifest, and many treasons,	
	There is my pledge; [*Throws down a glove*	
	I'll make it on thy heart,	
	Ere I taste bread, thou art in nothing less	95
	Than I have here proclaimed thee.	
REGAN	Sick! O, sick!	
GONERIL	[*Aside*] If not, I'll ne'er trust medicine.	
EDMUND	There's my exchange: [*Throws down a glove*	
	What in the world he is	
	That names me traitor, villain-like he lies.	
	Call by the trumpet: he that dares approach,	100
	On him, on you, who not? I will maintain	
	My truth and honour firmly.	
ALBANY	A herald, ho!	
	Trust to thy single virtue; for thy soldiers,	
	All levied in my name, have in my name	
	Took their discharge.	
REGAN	My sickness grows upon	
	me.	105
ALBANY	She is not well; convey her to my tent.	
	[*Exit* REGAN, *led*	

Enter a HERALD

	Come hither, herald, – Let the trumpet sound, –	
	And read out this.	
OFFICER	Sound, trumpet! [*A trumpet sounds*	
HERALD	[*Reads*] *If any man of quality or degree within*	110
	the lists of the army will maintain upon Edmund,	

The challenge is sounded. On the last note of the trumpet
Edgar appears, his face hidden by his knight's vizor. He
refuses to give his name, but accuses Edmund of treason and
challenges him to fight.

112 **manifold**: many times
Stage directions: *with a trumpet*: with a trumpeter
122 **bare-gnawn**: gnawed to the bone
canker-bit: worm-eaten
124 **cope**: match
129 **it**: drawing the sword
129–130 **privilege...profession**: right of a knight
130 **protest**: solemnly declare
131 **maugre**: in spite of
place: position
132 **victor**: victorious
fire-new fortune: brand new titles
133 **heart**: courage
135 **Conspirant**: conspirator
this high illustrious prince: the Duke of Albany
136 **th'extremest upward**: the topmost part
138 **A most toad-spotted traitor**: stained with treason (as a toad
is covered with spots)

• *How appropriate is Edgar's description of his loss of
name, 'By treason's tooth bare-gnawn, and
canker-bit:' (line 122)?*

supposed Earl of Gloucester, that he is a manifold
traitor, let him appear by the third sound of the
trumpet. He is bold in his defence.

Sound!	[*First trumpet* 115
Again!	[*Second trumpet*
Again!	[*Third trumpet*
	[*Trumpet answers within*

Enter EDGAR, *armed, with a trumpet before him*

ALBANY   Ask him his purposes, why he appears
Upon this call o'th'trumpet.

HERALD   What are you?
Your name? your quality? and why you answer   120
This present summons?

EDGAR   Know, my name is lost;
By treason's tooth bare-gnawn, and canker-bit:
Yet am I noble as the adversary
I come to cope.

ALBANY   Which is that adversary?

EDGAR   What's he that speaks for Edmund Earl of
Gloucester?   125

EDMUND   Himself: what say'st thou to him?

EDGAR   Draw thy sword,
That, if my speech offend a noble heart,
Thy arm may do thee justice; here is mine:
Behold, it is the privilege of mine honours,
My oath, and my profession: I protest,   130
Maugre thy strength, place, youth, and eminence,
Despite thy victor sword and fire-new fortune,
Thy valour and thy heart, thou art a traitor,
False to thy gods, thy brother, and thy father,
Conspirant 'gainst this high illustrious prince,   135
And, from th'extremest upward of thy head
To the descent and dust below thy foot,
A most toad-spotted traitor. Say thou 'No,'
This sword, this arm, and my best spirits are bent

Edmund does not have to accept this challenge from an
unknown opponent, but he fights and is beaten. Goneril says
that he should never have fought. Albany shows her the
letter. She says that she is the ruler and therefore she sets the
laws. She rushes out. Edmund confesses to the crimes he is
charged with, and admits to more.

140 whereto I speak: I speak to your heart
141 In wisdom: because he is not bound to fight someone
   socially inferior
143 say: smack, taste
144 nicely: cautiously
145 I disdain and spurn: I scorn to insist on my rights
146–150 Back do...for ever: I return these accusations of
   treason to your head and heart. They glance off your armour
   but my sword will thrust them straight in your heart where
   they will stay
147 hell-hated: hated as much as hell
148 Which: these treasons
   for: since
   glance: glide
151 Save him!: Albany does not want Edmund's death yet
   practice: treachery
153 opposite: opponent
154 cozened and beguiled: tricked and deceived
155 stople: (stopple means bung, cork) shut
   Hold, sir: to Edgar
156–157 Thou worse...know it: to Goneril
157 know: recognize
158 Say, if I do: what if I do?
159 arraign me: bring me to trial
161 desperate: in a state of despair
   govern: restrain

> • *'Honourable' might describe Edmund's acceptance of
> the challenge, and his confession. Is there any
> explanation for his change of heart at this stage?*

	To prove upon thy heart, whereto I speak, 140
	Thou liest.

EDMUND   In wisdom I should ask thy name;
But since thy outside looks so fair and war-like,
And that thy tongue some say of breeding breathes,
What safe and nicely I might well delay
By rule of knighthood, I disdain and spurn;   145
Back do I toss these treasons to thy head,
With the hell-hated lie o'erwhelm thy heart,
Which, for they yet glance by and scarcely bruise,
This sword of mine shall give them instant way,
Where they shall rest for ever. Trumpets, speak. 150
        [*Alarums. They fight*. EDMUND *falls*

ALBANY   Save him! save him!

GONERIL   This is practice, Gloucester:
By th'law of war thou wast not bound to answer
An unknown opposite; thou art not vanquished,
But cozened and beguiled.

ALBANY   Shut your mouth,
   dame,
Or with this paper shall I stople it. Hold, sir;   155
Thou worse than any name, read thine own evil:
No tearing, lady; I perceive you know it.

GONERIL   Say, if I do, the laws are mine, not thine:
Who can arraign me for't?

ALBANY   Most monstrous! O!
Know'st thou this paper?

GONERIL   Ask me not what I
   know.   160
        [*Exit*

ALBANY   Go after her: she's desperate; govern her.
        [*Exit an* OFFICER

EDMUND   What you have charged me with, that have I done,
And more, much more; the time will bring it out:
'Tis past, and so am I. But what art thou

Edmund forgives the knight, who reveals himself as Edgar.
He tells Albany of his disguise as Mad Tom, and of his
taking care of his father. He regrets that he has only just told
Gloucester his true identity.

165 **this**: brought this
   noble: of good breeding
166 **exchange charity**: forgive each other
168 **more**: more noble
170 **pleasant**: which give us pleasure
171 **plague**: torment
172 **dark...place**: bed outside marriage (dark and vicious also
   bring to mind Gloucester's blinding)
174 **The wheel...circle**: life/history has a way of repeating itself
   and events going in cycles; also Edmund claimed, in Act 2
   scene 1, that Edgar had tried to kill him and this has now
   become fact
175 **gait**: walk, movement
178 **Worthy**: noble
181 **List**: hear
183 **bloody proclamation**: death sentence
184–186 **O! our lives'...at once**: life is so sweet that we would
   rather go through the pain of death every hour than
   actually die
186 **shift**: change
188 **disdained**: scorned
   habit: dress, disguise
189 **rings**: sockets (without eyes, as settings in rings which have
   no jewels)
192 **fault**: mistake
194 **success**: outcome, result

	That hast this fortune on me? If thou'rt noble, 165
	I do forgive thee.
EDGAR	Let's exchange charity.
	I am no less in blood than thou art, Edmund;
	If more, the more th'hast wronged me.
	My name is Edgar, and thy father's son.
	The Gods are just, and of our pleasant vices 170
	Make instruments to plague us;
	The dark and vicious place where thee he got
	Cost him his eyes.
EDMUND	Th'hast spoken right, 'tis true.
	The wheel is come full circle; I am here.
ALBANY	Methought thy very gait did prophesy 175
	A royal nobleness: I must embrace thee:
	Let sorrow split my heart, if ever I
	Did hate thee or thy father.
EDGAR	Worthy prince, I
	know't.
ALBANY	Where have you hid yourself?
	How have you known the miseries of your
	father? 180
EDGAR	By nursing them, my lord. List a brief tale;
	And when 'tis told, O! that my heart would burst!
	The bloody proclamation to escape
	That followed me so near, – O! our lives' sweetness,
	That we the pain of death would hourly die 185
	Rather than die at once! – taught me to shift
	Into a madman's rags, t'assume a semblance
	That very dogs disdained: and in this habit
	Met I my father with his bleeding rings,
	Their precious stones new lost; became his
	guide, 190
	Led him, begged for him, saved him from despair;
	Never – O fault! – revealed myself unto him,
	Until some half-hour past, when I was armed;
	Not sure, though hoping, of this good success,

Edgar explains how he had asked for Gloucester's blessing
before the combat. They were reconciled, but it had been too
much for his father's heart and he had died soon afterwards.
Whilst Edgar was grieving, Kent had arrived and had
collapsed from the trauma of recalling the recent tragic
events. A Gentleman rushes in with a blood-stained knife.

196 **flawed**: cracked
197 **conflict**: between joy and grief
199 **Burst smilingly**: his heart could not take the strain and he
    died with happiness
203 **dissolve**: break down and cry
204 **a period**: an end
205 **such as**: those who
205–206 **another...too much**: to describe another grief in detail
207 **top extremity**: go beyond the limit
208 **big in clamour**: loudly lamenting (Gloucester's death)
    a man: Kent
209 **worst estate**: poorest condition (as Poor Tom)
211 **endured**: suffered
213 **As**: as if
    him: himself
216 **puissant**: powerful
    strings of life: heartstrings
218 **tranced**: unconscious
220 **his enemy king**: Lear had declared himself Kent's enemy,
    Act 1 Scene 1 line 177

> • *Edgar claims that Kent did not want to know him*
>   *when he was Poor Tom. Is this being fair to Kent,*
>   *bearing in mind Act 3 Scene 4?*

| | I asked his blessing, and from first to last | 195 |

(handwritten margin notes:) Shed he / ad cold / Gloucester / Earlier

I asked his blessing, and from first to last   195
Told him my pilgrimage: but his flawed heart,
Alack, too weak the conflict to support!
'Twixt two extremes of passion, joy and grief,
Burst smilingly.

EDMUND   This speech of yours hath moved
      me,
And shall perchance do good; but speak you
      on;   200
You look as you had something more to say.

ALBANY   If there be more, more woeful, hold it in;
For I am almost ready to dissolve,
Hearing of this.

EDGAR   This would have seemed a period
To such as love not sorrow; but another,   205
To amplify too much, would make much more,
And top extremity.
Whilst I was big in clamour came there in a man,
Who, having seen me in my worst estate,
Shunned my abhorred society; but then,
      finding   210
Who 'twas that so endured, with his strong arms
He fastened on my neck, and bellowed out
As he'd burst heaven; threw him on my father;
Told the most piteous tale of Lear and him
That ever ear received; which in recounting   215
His grief grew puissant, and the strings of life
Began to crack: twice then the trumpets sounded,
And there I left him tranced.

ALBANY   But who was this?

EDGAR   Kent, sir, the banished Kent; who in disguise
Followed his enemy king, and did him service   220
Improper for a slave.

Enter a GENTLEMAN, *with a bloody knife*

GENTLEMAN   Help, help! O, help!

The Gentleman announces that Goneril has murdered Regan
by poisoning and then killed herself with the knife. Kent
arrives, looking for Lear. Albany asks Edmund about Lear
and Cordelia.

223 smokes: steams
228 three: Goneril, Regan are dead; Edmund is dying
229 marry: join together
233–234 compliment...urges: courtesy which good manners
  demand should be observed
234 very: mere
235 aye good night: farewell for ever
236 Great thing: important matter
  of us: by me
238 object: spectacle

- *From the entrance of the Gentleman (line 221) to his
  announcement of the identity of the dead woman (line
  226), whom might the audience have supposed to be
  dead? Is it likely that Shakespeare meant to mislead his
  audience in this way?*
- *Is Edmund's ability to engage in black humour, lines
  228–229, at the point of his death, part of his charm
  and attractiveness?*
- *How does Edmund reveal his true self in lines
  239–241?*

EDGAR	What kind of help?
ALBANY	Speak, man.
EDGAR	What means this bloody knife?
GENTLEMAN	'Tis hot, it smokes; It came even from the heart of – O! she's dead.
ALBANY	Who dead? speak, man.
GENTLEMAN	Your lady, sir, your lady: and her sister By her is poisoned; she confesses it.
EDMUND	I was contracted to them both: all three Now marry in an instant.
EDGAR	Here comes Kent.

225

Enter KENT

ALBANY	Produce the bodies, be they alive or dead;

230

[*Exit* GENTLEMAN

This judgment of the heavens, that makes us
   tremble,
Touches us not with pity.
[*To* KENT]   O! is this he?
The time will not allow the compliment
Which very manners urges.

KENT	I am come To bid my King and master aye good night; Is he not here?

235

ALBANY	Great thing of us forgot! Speak, Edmund, where's the King? and where's Cordelia? Seest thou this object, Kent?

[*The bodies of* GONERIL *and* REGAN *are brought in*

KENT	Alack! why thus?
EDMUND	Yet Edmund was beloved: The one the other poisoned for my sake, And after slew herself.

240

ALBANY	Even so. Cover their faces.

Edmund knows that he is going to die. He explains that Lear
and Cordelia are about to be killed. An officer is sent
urgently to prevent their deaths, and Edmund is taken out.
Lear enters with the dead Cordelia in his arms. He cannot
reconcile himself to her death, and wonders if she can
possibly be alive.

245 **brief**: quick
  writ: see line 28
248 **the office**: been given the job
249 **Thy token**: some personal sign
255 **fordid**: destroyed
  The Gods defend her!: irony, because of what follows
  immediately
257 **men of stones**: ie not flesh and blood
258–259 **Had I...crack**: in your place, seeing what you see, I
  would wail and weep enough to make the sky crack
262 **stone**: polished stone or crystal (used as a mirror)
263 **promised end**: the end of the world/the end Lear foresaw
  when he divided the kingdom
264 **image**: representation
  Fall and cease: let the heavens fall and life cease
266 **redeem**: make up for

> • *How is Cordelia's death likely to affect Lear's recovery
> from madness?*

EDMUND	I pant for life; some good I mean to do
	Despite of mine own nature. Quickly send,
	Be brief in it, to th'castle; for my writ 245
	Is on the life of Lear and on Cordelia.
	Nay, send in time.
ALBANY	Run, run! O, run!
EDGAR	To who, my Lord? Who has the office? send
	Thy token of reprieve.
EDMUND	Well thought on: take my sword, 250
	Give it the captain.
EDGAR	Haste thee, for thy life.

[*Exit* OFFICER

EDMUND	He hath commission from thy wife and me
	To hang Cordelia in the prison, and
	To lay the blame upon her own despair,
	That she fordid herself.
ALBANY	The Gods defend her! 255
	Bear him hence awhile. [EDMUND *is borne off*

Re-enter LEAR, *with* CORDELIA *dead in his arms;*
OFFICER

LEAR	Howl, howl, howl! O! you are men of stones:
	Had I your tongues and eyes, I'd use them so
	That heaven's vault should crack. She's gone for
	ever.
	I know when one is dead, and when one lives; 260
	She's dead as earth. Lend me a looking-glass;
	If that her breath will mist or stain the stone,
	Why, then she lives.
KENT	Is this the promised end?
EDGAR	Or image of that horror?
ALBANY	Fall and cease.
LEAR	This feather stirs; she lives! if it be so, 265
	It is a chance which does redeem all sorrows
	That ever I have felt.

Lear has killed the man responsible for Cordelia's death.
Lear recognizes Kent, eventually, but does not listen when
Kent tells him that he is no other than his servant, Caius.
Kent also informs him of the deaths of his other daughters.

274 slave: term of abuse
276 falchion: curved sword
278 crosses: troubles (of old age)
    spoil me: spoil my swordplay
280–281 If Fortune...behold: if fortune were to boast of two
    people whom she both loved and hated, we are each
    looking at one (because we are looking at each other)
282 dull: possibly a reference to his failing sight
283 Caius: the role adopted by Kent to serve Lear
287 that straight: to that immediately
288 first: beginning
    difference and decay: change and decline in fortunes
290 Nor no man else: no one is welcome to such a scene. (This
    completes what he was saying on line 288, but it is also a
    response to Lear's interruption.)
    deadly: death-like
291 fordone: destroyed
292 desperately: in a state of despair

> • *Is it significant that Lear fails to listen to Kent's*
> *revelation?*

KENT	[*Kneeling*] O my good master!	
LEAR	Prithee, away.	
EDGAR	'Tis noble Kent, your friend.	
LEAR	A plague upon you, murderers, traitors all!	
	I might have saved her; now she's gone for	
	ever!	270
	Cordelia, Cordelia! stay a little. Ha!	
	What is't thou say'st? Her voice was ever soft,	
	Gentle and low, an excellent thing in woman.	
	I killed the slave that was a-hanging thee.	
OFFICER	'Tis true, my lords, he did.	
LEAR	Did I not, fellow?	275
	I have seen the day, with my good biting falchion	
	I would have made them skip: I am old now,	
	And these same crosses spoil me. Who are you?	
	Mine eyes are not o'th'best: I'll tell you straight.	
KENT	If Fortune brag of two she loved and hated,	280
	One of them we behold.	
LEAR	This is a dull sight. Are you not Kent?	
KENT	The same;	
	Your servant Kent. Where is your servant Caius?	
LEAR	He's a good fellow, I can tell you that;	
	He'll strike, and quickly too. He's dead and	
	rotten.	285
KENT	No, my good Lord; I am the very man, –	
LEAR	I'll see that straight.	
KENT	That from your first of difference and decay,	
	Have followed your sad steps, –	
LEAR	You are welcome	
	hither.	
KENT	Nor no man else. All's cheerless, dark, and	
	deadly:	290
	Your eldest daughters have fordone themselves,	
	And desperately are dead.	

Lear seems able to understand only Cordelia's death. News is
brought of Edmund's death. Albany intends to restore the
kingdom to Lear, and their titles to Kent and Edgar. Lear
wonders if Cordelia has started breathing again, and then he
collapses and dies. Edgar looks to revive Lear but Kent is
concerned that he should suffer no more.

294 **bootless**: useless, pointless
295 **but a trifle**: insignificant
297 **decay**: wretched situation/wretched Lear
298 **resign**: sign over
301 **boot**: something extra
    addition: titles
    honours: noble deeds
304 **O! see, see!**: looking at Lear, said with pity
305 **poor fool**: term of endearment for Cordelia – or does it refer
    directly to the Fool? What can have happened to him?
    No, no, no life!: let all life cease!
309 **button**: a top button – he is beginning to gasp for air
313 **Vex**: torment
    ghost: spirit
314 **rack**: instrument of torture
315 **longer**: for a longer time/stretched further (play on words)

- *There are two points of view concerning Lear's final
  words (lines 310–311): one school of thought says that
  Lear dies believing Cordelia is alive; the other says he
  dies, having accepted Cordelia's death. Which
  argument do you favour?*
- *What do lines 312 and 313–315 tell us about Kent? Do
  they reinforce earlier opinions of him, or do they
  present him in a new light?*

LEAR   Ay, so I think.

ALBANY   He knows not what he says, and vain is it
            That we present us to him.

EDGAR   Very bootless.

            Enter an OFFICER

OFFICER   Edmund is dead, my Lord.

ALBANY   That's but a trifle
            here.   295
            You lords and noble friends, know our intent;
            What comfort to this great decay may come
            Shall be applied: for us, we will resign,
            During the life of this old Majesty,
            To him our absolute power: [*To* EDGAR *and* KENT
                                           You, to your
              rights,   300
            With boot and such addition as your honours
            Have more than merited. All friends shall taste
            The wages of their virtue, and all foes
            The cup of their deservings. O! see, see!

LEAR   And my poor fool is hanged! No, no, no life!   305
            Why should a dog, a horse, a rat, have life,
            And thou no breath at all? Thou'lt come no more,
            Never, never, never, never, never!
            Pray you, undo this button: thank you, Sir.
            Do you see this? Look on her, look, her lips,   310
            Look there, look there!   [*Dies*

EDGAR   He faints! My Lord, my
            Lord!

KENT   Break, heart; I prithee, break!

EDGAR   Look up, my Lord.

KENT   Vex not his ghost: O! let him pass; he hates him
            That would upon the rack of this tough world
            Stretch him out longer.

EDGAR   He is gone, indeed.   315

Albany asks Edgar and Kent to help him to bring about the
kingdom's recovery, and then to rule with him. Kent
refuses because he says he will soon follow Lear. The three
of them are weary, and sickened by the suffering which they
have had to witness.

317 usurped: wrongfully held on to
320 gored state sustain: help this bloody kingdom to recovery
321 journey: to another world
323 The weight...obey: we must not try to avoid our heavy
responsibilities
324 ought to say: we feel might be appropriate

- *Who do you think is the master to whom Kent refers
in line 322?*

KENT   The wonder is he hath endured so long:
            He but usurped his life.

ALBANY   Bear them from hence. Our present business
            Is general woe. [*To* KENT *and* EDGAR] Friends of
                my soul, you twain
            Rule in this realm, and the gored state sustain.   320

KENT   I have a journey, sir, shortly to go;
            My master calls me, I must not say no.

EDGAR   The weight of this sad time we must obey;
            Speak what we feel, not what we ought to say.
            The oldest hath borne most: we that are young   325
            Shall never see so much, nor live so long.

                            [*Exeunt, with a dead march*

ACTIVITIES

Keeping track

Scene 1

1 Edmund's true position is revealed. Where does he stand? What are his aims?

Scene 2

2 What is the purpose of this brief scene?

Scene 3

3 Lear and Cordelia are prisoners, but how does Lear view the future at the beginning of the scene?

4 '*all three*
   Now marry in an instant' (lines 228–229)
   • What brings about the deaths of Goneril and Regan?
   • How has Edgar arranged his revenge on Edmund?

5 Lear arrives with Cordelia's body almost immediately after Edmund's attempt to do some good. What is the effect of this moment?

6 What actually causes the deaths of
   • Gloucester?
   • Lear?

Drama

1 In threes, rehearse the exchanges between Edmund and Regan at the beginning of Act 5. One of you is the director.
      What is the mood, the atmosphere? Is this a seduction or a calculated negotiation?
      Try it in a variety of styles.

2 Use FORUM THEATRE (see page 273) to examine the inner feelings of both sisters in the moment when Regan says, '*Sister, you'll go with us*?' in Act 5 scene 1 line 34.

3 Consider Edmund at the moment when he says, '*Yet Edmund was beloved*', Act 5 scene 3 line 239. Interrogate someone in role as Edmund – or even two people side by side to represent the 'evil' and 'attractive' aspects of his nature – to try to elicit all his thoughts at this time.

4 Within the structure of a formalized debate consider the arguments

which will be presented to the motion: 'This house
believes that Edmund is an admirable character, much maligned and
misunderstood.'

5 Use FORUM THEATRE to analyse the moment when the Gentleman
   says, '*'Tis hot, it smokes;*', Act 5 scene 3 line 223.

6 The play is over but there are a number of ways in which to record it.
   • What would the gravestones read? There would be epitaphs for
     minor characters, too (the captain killed by Lear, for instance, and
     perhaps some soldier killed in the battle).
        This can be developed to have people standing with arms crossed
     on chests to represent effigies of the dead. These effigies might
     speak the thoughts of the dead.
   • Major characters would merit newspaper announcements
     and obituaries.
   • Survivors would no doubt be interviewed for television and/or radio
     and/or newspapers; newspaper reports would follow.
   • Teams of sculptors could be commissioned to produce rough-casts
     of ideas for a statue to remind people of this story. What might be
     the words inscribed on the plinth?

7 When actors approach a play and consider characterisation, they use
   the script as a starting point for speculation about the life of their
   characters beyond the bounds of what is written. What happened to
   them, for instance, before the events of the play take place? Is some
   childhood experience responsible for a character's current behaviour?
      In groups speculate on one or two characters in *King Lear* in this
   way.
      For example, you might consider the fact that there are no mothers
   in this play. There may be a practical theatrical reason for this in that
   women had to be acted by boys, but take the situation at face value.
   • How might the lack of a mother's influence have affected the
     way that Lear's daughters grew up, and thus their relationships
     with him and with one another?
   • What might Gloucester's relationship with his wife have been
     like, and how might this have affected Edgar's view of him,
     making him ready to believe that his father would turn against
     him?

Close study

1 When Lear anticipates life in prison with Cordelia (Act 5 scene 3 lines
   8–26) what effect is created by the language which he uses?

2 Look at the speeches of Albany in Act 5 scene 3 (for example, his
   contribution to lines 60–96). Considering Goneril's earlier
   criticism of his milky gentleness (Act 1 scene 4 line 341) and

harmful mildness (Act 1 scene 4 line 344), how does he now appear as a character who comes into his own? How does his manner of speaking reflect this?

3 Edmund is another character whose stance and beliefs become clearer in Act 5. Look again at his statement of his own purpose in Act 5 scene 1, beginning at line 55, and then his words when he is challenged and defeated by his brother (Act 5 scene 3 lines 141–150, 162–166, 173–174 and 243–247). What do these lines reveal about him? Why do you think he shows mercy only when he is dying?

4 Lear's entry with Cordelia's body (Act 5 scene 3 line 256), leading up to his own death, is one of the most painful scenes in drama. Kent says he needs to be released from the rack of this tough world.

    How do his words here, when he is clutching at the last straws of hope (for example lines 261–263, 265–267 and 271–272), create an almost unbearable tension for those listening to him so that his death does seem like a release? (See also KEY SCENE, below.)

5 At the end of the play do you feel that the 'good' characters have triumphed over 'evil', or is it simply that the storm has run its course?

6 Who do you think will rule the kingdom from now on? Why are all those concerned apparently so reluctant to take on the responsibility?

Key scene

The deaths of Cordelia and Lear: Act 5 scene 3 lines 257–326

Keying it in

1 This scene presents the tragic denouement of the play in which the hopes raised by the regeneration of Lear at the end of Act 4 are dashed.
    • What is Lear's state of mind at the beginning of scene 3?
    • How does Lear's language differ at this point from the kind of language we have heard from him before?
    • What effect does the mood created at this point have on the tragedy that is to come?

2 After Cordelia and Lear are led out under guard the plot moves rapidly and Edmund receives his death blow in the duel with Edgar.
    • How convincing do you find Edmund's 'death-bed confession'? What do you think motivates him here?
    • Does this confession mark him out as different in his wickedness from Regan and Goneril?

The scene itself

3 lines 257–264

- When Lear enters carrying Cordelia's body does he actually say *'Howl, howl, howl!'*? Do you think he knows whom he is addressing as *'men of stones'*?
- What do the comments of Kent, Edgar and Albany add to the impression created by Cordelia's death?
- What are the emotions felt by these three men at this time?

4 lines 265–278

- What effect does the *'feather'* have, coming moments after Lear has called for a looking glass?
- How do you respond to Lear's rebuffing of Kent?
- What is Lear's state of mind here?
- What is the effect of the reminiscences of himself in times past?

5 lines 278–294

- After a brief moment of memory of more youthful times, Lear again becomes a grief-stricken, broken old man. How is this apparent in his speech?
- What is the effect of Kent's *'All's cheerless, dark, and deadly'*?
- How do you think Kent feels here about the deaths of Regan and Goneril?

6 lines 295–311

- How is the news of Edmund's death received?
- What is the significance of Albany's words? What is the result of his attempt to restore order?
- What picture of Lear is created by his closing words? How does the structure of the language help to create this impression?
- What is the effect of his plea for help with his button?
- How do you interpret Lear's final words:
  'Do you see this? Look on her, look, her lips,
  Look there, look there!' (lines 310–311)?
- Other dramatists might have prolonged Lear's 'dying speech', but Shakespeare is remarkably brief. Why do you think this is?

7 lines 311–326

- How does Kent respond to Lear's death?
- Why do you think he says:
  'I have a journey, sir, shortly to go;
  My master calls me, I must not say no.' (321–322)?
- What is the effect of Edgar's (and the play's) closing lines?

Overview

In this scene the play reaches its dark and tragic conclusion, and the plot has resulted in the deaths of seven of its main protagonists.
- What do you think about the ending of the play?
- Is the play completely pessimistic, or do you see any positive aspects to it?

Writing

1 It is said that, despite his evil doing, there is sometimes a strange attractiveness about Edmund. Do you agree?
Write an assessment of his character, considering:
   - what he has to say about his own status in life and his beliefs (for example, Act 1 scene 2) and how these differ from those of other people such as his father
   - his use of deception in a variety of situations
   - his motives and aims
   - his conduct in the final scene.
2 Throughout the eighteenth century, *King Lear* was performed with an alternative 'happy' ending, written by Nahum Tate in the 1680s. This included a love affair between Cordelia and Edgar.
   What do you think of the view of that time that Shakespeare's ending was just too tragic for audiences to tolerate? Consider particularly the events and structure of Acts 3–5.
3 It has been said that Lear is totally undeserving of the loyalty of a friend like Kent. What sort of character does Kent prove to be?
4 What evidence is there that Lear possesses, or has possessed, qualities which would command the dedication of a loyal friend like Kent?

Explorations

A question of approach

When you study a play, you need to be able to see it from two different perspectives simultaneously. You need to be able to imagine and experience the text line by line, sharing the thoughts and feelings of the characters as they go through the events of the play, but at the same time you need to be able to 'look down on' the play as a whole and see the patterns of character and relationship, of language and imagery, of themes and issues.

A play is essentially an audio-visual experience. No two members of the audience see quite the same 'play' and no two performances are ever exactly the same. Two important lessons should be learned from this. The first is that the printed text is not the play; the play is what you see when you go to the theatre. The text is a set of instructions to be interpreted by the director and the actors, artists and technicians. The second lesson is that there is no one 'right answer' to the play, only a range of possible interpretations. Your view can be just as valid as anyone else's…but only if you can present it clearly and support it by valid arguments derived from the text. For this purpose you need, again, to see it as a whole and as a set of details.

Thinking about the play

By the time you have discussed the text carefully you should be beginning to clarify and organize your response to the play as a whole. Most examination questions concentrate on *content* and *form* and these are useful terms which offer you an approach and a framework within which you can prepare to write successfully.

Your first task is to establish clearly in your mind the broad issues raised by the text and the possible areas for discussion, including major characters. You need to consider and discuss some of the possible views and interpretations of these issues and lay down a sensible framework within which personal response can be convincing and well considered. You also need to get close to the text and identify the key incidents, scenes or even quotations which will form the basis of any essay. When you come to write essays on the whole text, or even a specified passage, the appropriate textual evidence and illustrations should be noted and easily available.

Drama activities

Most of these activities can be done in small groups or by the class as a whole. They work by slowing down the action of the play and helping you focus on a small section of it – so that you can think more deeply about characters, plot and themes.

Hotseating

Hotseating means putting one of the characters 'under the microscope' at a particular point in the play. This is how it works.

1 Begin by choosing a particular character and a particular moment in the play. For example, you might choose Cornwall after he has blinded Gloucester.

2 One person (student or teacher) is selected to be the chosen character.

3 That person sits 'in the hotseat', with the rest of the group arranged round in a semi-circle, or a circle.

4 The rest then ask questions about how the character feels, why s/he has acted in that way, and so on. Try to keep the questions going and not to give the person in the hotseat too much time to think.

Variations

1 The questioners themselves take on roles. (In the example above they could be Gloucester, Regan, and the First Servant.)

2 Characters can be hotseated at a series of key moments in a scene to see how their opinions and attitudes change.

3 The questioners can take different attitudes to the character, for example:
   • aggressive
   • sympathetic
   • disbelieving.

Freeze!

It is very useful to 'stop the action' and concentrate on a single moment in the play. You can do this in a number of ways.

Photographs

Imagine that someone has taken a photograph of a particular moment, or that – as if it were a film or video – the action has been frozen. Once you have chosen the moment, you can work in a number of different ways.

- Act that part of the scene and then 'Freeze!' – you will probably find it easier if you have a 'director' standing outside the scene to shout 'Freeze!'
- Discuss what the photograph should look like and then arrange yourselves into the photograph.
- One at a time place yourselves in the photograph; each person 'entering' it must take notice of what is there already.
- Once you have arranged the photograph, take it in turns to come out of it and comment on it, with suggestions for improvements.

    There are a number of ways in which you can develop your photograph.

- Each person takes it in turn to speak his/her thoughts at that moment in the scene.
- The photograph is given a caption.
- Some members of the group do not take part in the photograph. Instead they provide a sound track of speech or sound effects, or both.

Mirror, Mirror

To use this technique you need to work in pairs. Both play the same character. One person plays the character; the other the character's reflection. The 'character' asks their reflection questions which the reflection answers. You can use this technique to explore a character's reasons for certain actions or to explore their thoughts and feelings about themselves, other characters and events.

Statues/Paintings

Make a statue or a painting like this.

1 Select a moment in the play, or a title from the play (for example, '*O! reason not the need* ').

2 Choose one member of the group to be the sculptor/painter. That person then arranges the rest of the group, one at a time to make the statue or painting.

Statues and paintings are different from photographs in two important ways.

• They are made up by an 'artist' and tell us about the artist's view of the person or event.

• If they talk, they tell us about what they can 'see', for example, how people react when they see the statue or painting for the first time.

Forum theatre

In FORUM THEATRE, one or two people take on roles and the rest of the group are 'directors'. It works like this.

1 Select a moment in the play. (For example, the moment when Edgar reveals his identity after the duel.)

2 Select a member of the group to be Edmund.

3 Organize your working area, so that everyone knows where the other characters are, where characters make entrances and exits, and so on.

4 Begin by asking Edmund to offer his own first thoughts about position, gesture, and movement.

5 The directors then experiment with different ways of presenting that moment. They can:

• ask Edmund to take up a particular position, use a particular gesture, move in a certain way

• ask him to speak in a particular way

• discuss with Edmund how he might move or speak and why – for example to communicate a certain set of thoughts and feelings.

6 The short sequence can be repeated a number of times, until the directors have used up all their ideas about their interpretation.

Character

Judging a character can never simply be a case of putting together all the evidence of the written word and drawing conclusions. It is more complicated than that.

The evidence 1

Characters are revealed by:
- what they say
- how they behave.

Problems

1 Unfortunately (for examination purposes!) characters are rarely consistent. Major characters, particularly, are subject to change because the events on which the action of the play is based are significant enough to affect the main protagonists: the more important the character, the closer to the action, the greater the reaction.

   You must always be aware of how characters are developing.

2 Characters might say or do things for effect: they might be seeking to impress or mislead someone else and not mean what they say at all.

   Decide if the character is being sincere, or if s/he has an ulterior motive.

The evidence 2

Characters are also revealed by:
- what others say about them
- how others behave towards them.

Problem

As in life, whether you accept A's opinion of B depends on how you feel about A. If you believe A is untrustworthy or has a perverted sense of values, then A's criticism of B might prove to be a glowing character reference! Alternatively, an opinion might be based on false information, or, again, might be deliberately misleading. It is essential not to accept one character's opinion of another at face value.

The evidence 3

Characters are also revealed by:
- soliloquies
- asides.

This is the best way to assess a character's personality since s/he is sharing his/her thoughts and feelings with the audience. All pretence is dropped because the soliloquy and the aside are ways of 'internalizing' ideas.

Critical moments

At critical moments in the play you can begin to gain better insight into a character by seeking answers to certain questions. There is no formula which will apply to every situation, but these questions can start you off and might lead you to consider other questions of your own:
- what has the character said/done
- why has the character said/done this
- what will happen as a result of this speech/action
- could/should this reaction (these reactions) have been avoided
- what does this incident tell us about the character
- how does the character change as a result of this incident?

To reassure yourself that this system can work, quickly consider what the following moments from early in the first act of the play tell us about the characters involved, using the CRITICAL MOMENTS questions, above.
- LEAR: '*Which of you shall we say doth love us most?*' (scene 1 line 50)
- CORDELIA: '*What shall Cordelia speak? Love, and be silent.*' (scene 1 line 61)
- KENT: '*See better, Lear;*' (scene 1 line 157)

- GONERIL: '*Pray you, let us hit together;*' (scene 1 lines 302–303)
- EDMUND: '*Now, gods, stand up for bastards!*' (scene 2 line 22)

The CRITICAL MOMENTS approach can be used to highlight key points in the development of a character.

For instance:

1 there is the confidence of Lear's:
'*Know that we have divided*
In three our kingdom...that future strife
May be prevented now.' (Act 1 scene 1 lines 36–44)

2 frustrated by Cordelia and then angered by Goneril, he is determined not to show weakness:
'*Old fond eyes,*
Beweep this cause again, I'll pluck
  ye out,
And cast you, with the waters that you loose,
To temper clay.' (Act 1 scene 4 lines 300–303)

3 he realizes that to resist weeping is to put his sanity at risk:
'*this heart*
Shall break into a hundred thousand flaws
Or ere I'll weep. O Fool! I shall go mad.' (Act 2 scene 4 lines 283–285)

4 not until he is mad does Lear begin to consider others:
'*Poor naked wretches...O! I have ta'en*
Too little care of this.' (Act 3 scene 4 lines 28–33)

5 it is then that he seems eager to re-establish law and order with the mock trial of Goneril and Regan:
'*I'll see their trial first. Bring in their evidence.*' (Act 3 scene 6 line 36)

6 he comes to recognize the unfairness of a society for which he has been responsible:
'*which is the justice, which is the thief?*'
(Act 4 scene 6 line 152)

7 and, at the end, there is the irony that through his madness he has come to a realization of his own personal

weaknesses, which in itself is a sign that he is recovering his sanity:

'*I am a very foolish fond old man,*
Fourscore and upward, not an hour more or less;
And, to deal plainly,
I fear I am not in my perfect mind.'
(Act 4 scene 7 lines 60–63)

Note that CRITICAL MOMENTS are usually occasions when a character undergoes a change of some sort; there will, of course, be other situations in the play which you will wish to refer to, or even quote, which give supporting evidence of characteristics of which you are already aware.

On the other hand CRITICAL MOMENTS might show us in some cases that a character does not in fact change very much in the course of the play: that s/he is the same person at the end that we saw at the beginning. In this case CRITICAL MOMENTS confirm opinions about a character... because s/he will respond consistently in different, and trying, circumstances. For example, see how many CRITICAL MOMENTS you can find to illustrate each of the following characterisitics of Kent:

- loyalty
- directness
- courage
- quick temper.

In the same way that important characteristics can be traced through CRITICAL MOMENTS, so can developing relationships.

The quotations below are concerned with:
a Lear's relationship with Cordelia
b his relationships with Goneril and Regan.

The quotations are given in chronological order. With which relationship is each concerned, and what important stage does it mark in that relationship?

1 '*I loved her most, and thought to set my rest*
On her kind nursery.' (Act 1 scene 1 lines 121–122)

2 '*How sharper than a serpent's tooth it is
  To have a thankless child!*' (Act 1 scene 4 lines 287–288)

3 '*All the stored vengeances of Heaven fall
  On her ingrateful top! Strike her young bones,
  You taking airs, with lameness!*' (Act 2 scene 4 lines
  160–162)

4 '*No, you unnatural hags,
  I will have such revenges...they shall be
  The terrors of the earth.*' (Act 2 scene 4 lines 277–281)

5 '*Is there any cause in nature that make these hard hearts*'
  (Act 3 scene 6 lines 76–77)

6 '*If you have poison for me, I will drink it.*' (Act 4 scene 7 line
  72)

7 '*We two alone will sing like birds i'th'cage:*' (Act 5 scene 3
  line 9)

8 '*Howl, howl, howl! O! you are men of stones:
  Had I your tongues and eyes, I'd use them so
  That heaven's vault should crack. She's gone for ever.*' (Act 5
  scene 3 lines 257–261)

A closer look

Following on from the CRITICAL MOMENTS strategy, a good
way to understand all the elements of the play, including, of
course, the characterization, is to dip into the play at random.
This will test your knowledge of events and increase your
awareness of the implications of any incident.

Choose three or four lines of a speech and answer these
questions:
- who is speaking to whom
- what is the subject of the conversation
- what do we learn of the character/s involved
- what has led up to this incident
- what will follow
- can you comment on the vocabulary and/or the literary
  technique (imagery, metaphor or irony, for instance)?

As examples, with these questions in mind, say what you can about:

1 'Here I disclaim all my paternal care,
   Propinquity and property of blood,
   And as a stranger to my heart and me
   Hold thee from this for ever.' (Act 1 scene 1 lines 112–115)

2 'I pray you, father, being weak, seem so.
   If, till the expiration of your month,
   You will return and sojourn with my sister,
   Dismissing half your train, come then to me.' (Act 2 scene 4
   lines 200–203)

3 'We two alone will sing like birds i'th'cage:
   When thou dost ask me blessing, I'll kneel down,
   And ask of thee forgiveness:' (Act 5 scene 3 lines 9–11)

Imagery and metaphor

In the second scene of the play, Gloucester summarizes the significant events which have already happened and predicts what is about to happen. He speaks in general terms rather than the specific:

> 'These late eclipses in the sun and moon portend no good to us: though the wisdom of Nature can reason it thus and thus, yet Nature finds itself scourged by the sequent effects. Love cools, friendship falls off, brothers divide: in cities, mutinies; in countries, discord; in palaces, treason; and the bond cracked 'twixt son and father. This villain of mine comes under the prediction; there's son against father: the King falls from bias of nature; there's father against child. We have seen the best of our time: machinations, hollowness, treachery, and all ruinous disorders follow us disquietly to our graves.'
> (lines 105–117)

The actions of Lear and Edgar are linked to the whole universe: symbolically, the individual has become a city and the family is a kingdom. The whole of the natural world is involved with the break-up of family life.

Images which are to recur time and again are mentioned here. There is to be constant reference to Nature and natural law, and animal images are particularly prevalent (someone has worked out that there are 133 references to 64 different animals!). The purpose of this is, mainly, to emphasize the sub-human nature of some of the characters, but also to compare the state of man with that of the animals.

We are to see frequent mention of family (son and father), allusions to power (machinations...treachery) and reference to age and sickness (ruinous disorders).

Perhaps the most forceful imagery is of things splitting or breaking or dividing. This might be in connection with the storm, and, therefore, nature; or on an individual level it can refer to the physical pain of the body, and the psychological pain of the cracking of someone's heart and/or mind; and on a national level, the imagery is concerned with the planned division and, later, the threatened break-up of the kingdom.

(It also applies, of course, to the re-allocation of Gloucester's land.)

In this respect, Shakespeare is concerned with physical, geographical boundaries. He also investigates the intangible borders involved in madness and sanity, justice and injustice, and 'natural' and 'unnatural' behaviour. And to mark the contrast between 'civilized' and 'unaccommodated' man, there is the recurring imagery of clothing. In a play which is so concerned with power there are bound to be the 'have-nots'. 'Nothing' is a word which appears frequently. From Cordelia's first refusal to say anything more than '*Nothing*' in response to Lear (Act 1 scene 1) and Lear's response: '*Nothing will come of nothing*' the word is repeated throughout the play. These repeated references to 'nothing' echo '*the thing itself, unaccomodated man*', reduced to nothing in the storm scene. Variations on this image include 0 ('*now thou art an 0 without a figure*', Act 1 scene 4 lines 190–191) and a number of references to egg (crossword enthusiasts will be familiar with the zero/egg link).

One of the recognizable features of Shakespeare's writing is his skill in re-working images and metaphors; in using the same idea in a different and fresh way. With this in mind, look at Albany's angry words to Goneril in Act 4 scene 2 lines 31–50.

Find references to:
- the family
- power
- old age
- nature and humanity
- animals and inhumanity
- boundaries and breaking away.

  '*I fear your disposition:*
  That nature, which contemns it origin,
  Cannot be bordered certain in itself;
  She that herself will sliver and disbranch
  From her material sap, perforce must wither
  And come to deadly use...
  Tigers, not daughters, what have you performed?

A father, and a gracious aged man,
Whose reverence even the head-lugged bear would lick,
Most barbarous, most degenerate! have you madded.
Could my good brother suffer you to do it?
A man, a prince, by him so benefited!
If that the heavens do not their visible spirits
Send quickly down to tame these vilde offences,
It will come,
Humanity must perforce prey on itself,
Like monsters of the deep.'

Issues and themes

As is to be expected in such a complex and many-layered play the issues and themes are interwoven and interrelated. In an attempt to identify the different issues and themes they have been isolated below. It must be remembered, however, that there will be repetition and overlap in tackling this section in this way.

Shakespeare examines these issues:
- good and evil
- ingratitude
- self-seeking
- cruelty
- abuse of power.

He does this by means of the following themes, which we can begin to examine more closely.

Human relationships and conflicts
- Which relationships are essentially relationships of conflict?
- Which relationships are partially relationships of conflict?
- Are there any relationships in which conflict plays no part?

The influence on man of the natural universe
- What is the purpose of the storm which begins in Act 3 scene 4?
- What does 'nature' mean in the play?
- What is 'human nature' as depicted here?
- What is '*unaccommodated man*' (Act 3 scene 4 line 109)?
- Is there a difference between 'natural' and 'civilized' behaviour?
- Which of Gloucester's sons is the more 'natural'?
- Which of Lear's daughters is/are most obviously the child/children of her/their father?
- What remains when the normal ties which bind civilized society and family no longer exist?

The influence of gods and the supernatural

- Lear (Act 1 scene 1 lines 108–111) and Gloucester (Act 4 scene 1 64–66) regard man as being at the mercy of the gods. How – and why – does Edmund see things differently in Act 1 scene 2 lines 1–2?
- Can this be said to be not only a contrast of philosophy, but also a contrast between youth and age?
- Has there been any evidence to support Edgar (Act 5 scene 3 lines 170–171) and Albany (Act 5 scene 3 lines 231–232) when they express faith in supernatural justice?
- How do the gods respond when Gloucester (Act 3 scene 7 lines 63–64) and Albany (Act 5 scene 3 line 255) call on them for help?
- The action takes place in pre-Christian times.
    a Is this significant?
    b What do the characters believe in?
    c What is the difference between 'the stars' and 'the gods'?
    d Are there any 'gods'?
    e If the supernatural is denied, can man look to his own spirit?
    f And/or morality to fill the void?

Justice

- How do different characters' thoughts about justice change, and differ?
- In what sense do characters enact justice as well as discuss it?
- Is the ending of the play 'just'?
- Whatever their failings, is what happens to Lear and Gloucester 'just' ?
- Which character/s do you think suffer/s the greatest injustice?
- Which character/s does justice serve best?

Honesty

- On the evidence of this play, is honesty always the best policy?

  Think about:
  a Edmund's deceptions
  b Cordelia in scene 1
  c Kent's disguise
  d the Fool's observations
  e Edgar's relationship with Gloucester.

The structure of society

- What role/s is/are played by the common man in *King Lear*?
- What is the common man's influence on events?
- Why do you think Shakespeare concentrates on royalty and the aristocracy?

Men and women

- How might it be said to be the tragedy of all Lear's daughters that they appear to live in a world dominated by men?
- In what different ways do they cope with this?
- What is their 'power' and to what extent is it limited?

Kingship and authority

- What is a king?
- On what is his authority based?
- How far may it be legitimately challenged?
- What are the consequences of such a challenge?

Responsibility

- Is Lear abdicating responsibility when he divides his kingdom, or is he showing his real concern to leave a peaceful realm?

- At what point do Edgar and Albany begin to take responsibility?
- Why does nobody seem keen to accept responsibility at the end of the play?

The transfer of power

- Which characters in the play have a personal interest in the transfer of power?
- What is the power which concerns each of them?
- What is their involvement in the transfer of power?

Preparing for an examination

You will be expected to have a detailed and accurate knowledge of your set texts. You must have read your set texts several times and you need to know the sequence of events and the narrative of a text. The plot summaries in this edition should help you with this. It may seem rather unfair but you will get little credit in the final examination for merely 'telling the story', and simply 'going through' the narrative is seen as particularly worthless in an open-book examination. However, you will be in no position to argue a convincing case or develop a deep understanding unless you have this detailed knowledge.

The questions you may be asked

A-level questions are demanding but they should always be accessible and central, a fair test of your knowledge and understanding. They are rarely obscure or marginal. There is actually a relatively small number of questions which can be asked on any text, even though the ways in which they can be worded are almost infinite. They tend to fall into quite straightforward categories or types as outlined below.

Character

You may be asked to discuss your response to a particular character, to consider the function or presentation of a character or perhaps to compare and contrast characters.

Society

You may be asked to consider the kind of society depicted by the text or perhaps the way in which individuals relate to that society.

Themes

You may be asked to discuss the ideas and underlying issues which are explored by a text, and what are the author's concerns and interests.

Attitudes

You may be asked to consider what views or values are revealed by the text, what is valued and what is attacked.

Style or technique

You may be asked to look at the methods a writer uses to achieve particular effects. In essence, you are being asked to examine 'how' a text achieves its effects and you need to consider such matters as diction, imagery, tone and structure.

Personal response

You may be asked to give your own view of the text but this must be more than just unsupported assertion. You need to move beyond 'I think...' to a well-considered evaluation based on close reading and textual evidence. It is worth remembering that there is not an infinity of sensible responses to a text.

'Whole text' questions

These questions require you to consider the text as a whole. You need a coherent overview of the text and the ability to select appropriate detail and evidence.

'Specific' passages

These questions require close reading and analysis but sometimes the specific passage has to be related to another passage or perhaps to the whole text.

Essay questions

1 Lear claims to be '*a man More sinned against against than sinning*' (Act 3 scene 2 line 59–60). Do you agree with his assessment of the situation?

2 The play was called *The Tragedy of King Lear*. What do you see as the tragedy of the play?

3 Gloucester and Lear both learn through suffering, but in what other ways are they similar; and how might their circumstances be said to be different?

4 In what ways do you think Cordelia and Edgar are alike, and in what ways different?

5 a Argue the case that Lear's decision to divide the kingdom and abdicate the throne is a basic error, an act of monumental stupidity. Try to show that there is no way in which his idea could have worked, and that it was doomed from the start.

or

b Argue the case for Lear's decision to split his kingdom between his daughters, with Cordelia's larger share acting geographically as a buffer between her sisters' shares. Show how subsequent events tend to support that original policy for the division, and for his daughters' public affirmation of love, and therefore their consent to Lear's wishes.

6 To what extent are Lear's daughters to blame for his troubles, and how far might he himself be held responsible?

7 Would it be accurate to describe *King Lear* as being primarily concerned with sibling rivalry?

8 How far does *King Lear* represent a clash of generations, and how far a conflict of philosophies?

9 To what extent is cruelty, mental and physical, a feature of the play?

10 One critic has cynically suggested that Goneril and Regan are so alike that Shakespeare could have written about one character only, possibly named Gonerilandregan. How alike do the two sisters seem to you, and in what ways – if any – are they different?

11 Albany is left with the task of restoring order to the land.

From what you have seen of him, are you confident that he has the ability to do this?

12 What is the purpose of the Fool in *King Lear*? Why do you think he is not seen after Act 3 scene 6?

13 Whilst those around him show a willingness to adapt – and sometimes a gift for adapting – to new situations, how is Lear affected by his own inflexibility?

14 '*See better, Lear*' warns Kent in the first scene of the play. The play is full of references to sight, seeing and eyes, in a literal sense or in the sense of perceiving or understanding. Lear and Gloucester learn to 'see better' during the course of the play; but which character/s do you think are capable of seeing clearly throughout?

15 It has been said that from Cordelia's banishment to her death, and from the first signs of Gloucester's gullibility to his death, the events of the play proceed with an inevitable irony. How far do you agree?

16 '*The oldest hath borne most: we that are young*
Shall never see so much, nor live so long.'
(Act 5 scene 3 lines 325–326)
How are old people treated in *King Lear*, and what attitudes to old age are held by the younger characters?

17 How important is it to the effectiveness of the plot that things are not always what they seem; that there is a difference between appearance and reality?

18 *King Lear* is rich in metaphor and imagery. It is the combination and interdependence of metaphors which makes Shakespeare's language so powerful:
'*These late eclipses...'twixt son and father*' (Act 1 scene 2 lines 105–111)

There is reference here to: planetary influences and man's actions in relation to his universe; the cracking or splitting of the natural order of things; and, in particular, the breakdown of family relationships.

Trace the references to one of these ideas throughout the play, and show how the imagery makes a significant contribution to the overall effect of the play's language.

19 '*Robes and furred gowns hide all.*' (Act 4 scene 6 line 163)
   Lear comments on the unfairness of man's system of
   justice. Is nature, or natural law, any fairer, or does man
   suffer from the unfairness of Fate as well?

20 Take any one of the longer scenes from Act 3 or Act 4 and
   show how Shakespeare uses the 'unreal' situation to
   comment on the meaning of life; how he turns an
   observation on a particular circumstance – an event of
   concern to one person perhaps – into a universal 'truth'.

21 Trace one relationship through the play and show in what
   way it is connected with some of the important themes
   which Shakespeare covers.

22 Discuss 'natural' and 'civilized' behaviour as witness in the
   play.

23 '*we make guilty of our disasters the sun, the moon, and
   stars...all that we are evil in, by a divine thrusting on*', says
   Edmund in Act 1 scene 2 lines 123–130.

   Apart from Lear himself (see question 6, above) how far
   are the major characters in *King Lear* responsible for their
   own downfalls, and to what extent might they justly claim
   to be victims of circumstance?

24 It has been said that when characters make a mistake in this
   play they are made to suffer for it out of all proportion to
   their initial transgression.
   a Choose a character of whom you believe this to be true
      and explain your point of view;
      or
   b Choose a character whom you believe deserves all that
      s/he gets, and explain your point of view;
      or
   c Are there dramatic and/or social reasons why some
      characters are made to suffer so extremely?

25 Discuss whether deception is used mainly for good or evil
   in *King Lear*.

26 Do you consider Oswald to be typical of the 'serving class'?
   Support your argument with close reference to the text.

27 What seems to be Lear's opinion of his daughters at the beginning of the play? In what way, and for what reasons, do his feelings towards them change during the course of the play?

28 Do you think that to gain power after Lear's abdication any of the four characters (Goneril, Regan, Albany or Cornwall) reacts in an unpredictable, or even shocking, way? Whose behaviour seems most surprising to you? Compare his/her actions with those of the other three, and explain what it is that you find so unreasonable.

29 What is it about Lear that inspires love and loyalty in Kent, the Fool, Gloucester and, of course, Cordelia?

30 We have been told that, generally speaking, major characters change during the course of this, or any other, play, being affected by developing events and the reaction of others. However, is it possible to make out an argument that Kent shows little, if any, change in this play? Are our early impressions of him merely reinforced as the action progresses? Is it a case of, 'When the going gets tough...'?

Writing an essay

Advice from a Chief Examiner for A-Level Literature
To write a good essay you need to construct a clear argument based on the evidence of the text. Your essay should have a clear sense of direction and purpose and it is better to start with a simple, coherent attitude than to ramble aimlessly or produce a shapeless answer which never gets into focus. Each paragraph should be a step in a developing argument and should engage in analysis of textual detail which is relevant to the question. You must answer the question set – as opposed to the question you wanted to be set – and you must be prepared to discuss a specific aspect of the text or approach it from a slightly new or unexpected angle. You will need to be selective and choose the material which is appropriate to the actual question. An essay which deals only in sweeping generalizations may be judged to lack detail and substance, whilst one which gets too involved in minor details may lack direction and a conceptual framework. The ideal balance is achieved when overview and detailed knowledge combine to allow easy movement from the general to the particular, and back again.

Although different examination boards and syllabuses have their own ways of expressing them, there are basically three criteria against which your work will be judged. They are as follows:
- knowledge and understanding
- answering the question relevantly
- written expression.

There is rarely a single right answer to an A-level essay question, but there is not an infinite range of sensible responses to a text and any interpretation must be clearly based on close reading and supporting evidence.

Here is a fairly typical A-level question:

'*Shakespeare's view of history shows great men at their littlest.*'
How far does this apply to King Lear*?*

The first task is to establish an overview of your broad
response to the question and to get clear in your own mind a
line of argument which engages with the question set. This
question demands an assessment of Lear's response to
adversity: it is not asking for a character sketch, nor a mere re-
telling of events. Time is short in examinations and you will
need to be carefully selective and give your essay a sharp focus
on the question.

The second task is to identify the stages by which Lear is
reduced from greatness to littleness and to emphasize the
influences and implications at each stage. Finally, come to the
conclusion to which your argument has been leading and
make a personal response to the title of the essay.

Here is an answer to the question, written by an A-level
student. It is not the only, nor indeed the perfect answer, but
it is good and it might help you to identify some of the
qualities which contribute to a good essay.

'Shakespeare's view of history shows great men at their littlest.' — KING LEAR

A king was the symbol of secular and divine
authority. However, within this role he was
obliged to reflect the contemporary concept
that the human constitution was similar to
that of the state. Man was a 'little
kingdom' in which the hierarchy of his
faculties resembled the different ranks in
society: reason ruled over will, which
controlled appetite and desire. In the kings
of Lear and Macbeth, Shakespeare drowns
reason with vanity and *'vaulting ambition'*. The
consequences do not only decay the king
himself but assume cosmic significance.

It is Lear's question of identity as king
which leads him to folly. He confuses his

parental and royal functions, expecting courtly flattery from his daughters. France recognizes this confusion:

'love's not love
when it is mingled with regards that stand
Aloof from the entire point.'

Lear 'invests' his love in Cordelia, but receives no return on her capital: *'her price is fallen.'* Cordelia's intransigence is the cause of Lear's catastrophe and salvation and in remaining constant she highlights Lear's decline.

On renouncing the crown, Lear is forced to reassess his role. *'Who is it that can tell me who I am?'* Kent's recognition of authority in Lear's countenance is contrasted with the reality of Goneril and Regan's scheme to strip Lear of his attendants. Lear still sees love measured in physical ways:

'Thy fifty yet doth double five and twenty,
And then art twice her love.'

Although the 'reason' may be seen in Goneril and Regan's argument that Lear's attendants would cause trouble, Shakespeare plays with the labels of 'reason' and 'love' as opposite poles of relationships, in society; a 'reasonable' view does not necessarily comfort the sufferer. Ironically as king, Lear praised Goneril and Regan's reason in love and rejected Cordelia's lack of reason. Here Lear does not reason and he sees it as heartlessness in Goneril and Regan.

'O reason not the need. Our basest beggars
Are in the poorest thing superfluous.
Allow not nature more than nature needs,
Man's life's as cheap as beast's.'

Therefore judgement is based on Lear's feelings not on his daughters' rightness; empathy is sustained with the protagonist.

Juxtaposed with Lear's dependence on emotion as opposed to reason is the Fool. In embodying Reason behind his apparent 'foolishness' he reflects invertedly Lear's original folly behind reason, where reason symbolized the order behind authority The superficial madness of the fool's riddles are paralleled to the puzzles and chaos in Lear's mind: the roles of reason in the king and madness in the fool are ironically reversed.

FOOL: *'Yes, indeed; thou wouldst make a good fool.'*

The chaos in the mind of the king is universalized by the storm.

FOOL: *'This cold night will turn us all to fools and madmen.'*

Lear is both the cause of the natural disorder and also the victim; his suffering may be seen as universal justice. But the disproportion of his suffering to his fault is reflected in:

'I am a man more sinned against than sinning.'

In his madness Lear begins to universalize his own suffering and to penetrate its source more profoundly than he was able to do in his sanity. He explores the ambiguous role of woman provoked by his daughters. Their hypocrisy is a branch of the 'appearance and reality' vein which runs throughout.

'Behold yond simpering dame,
Whose face between her forks presages show;'

Lear's image of women as centaurs shows the division between reason and desire.

'But to the girdle do the gods inherit,

Beneath is all the friend's.'

The upper part of the body is thought of as sanctified and governed by the head or reason, whereas the lower belongs to the devil because it is associated with fleshly lusts.

The subject of lechery which Lear pursues is the symbol of desire in its extreme. Lear sees it ironically as the cause of a bastard yet kind son in Edmund in contrast to his unkind daughters *'got 'tween lawful sheets'*. It symbolizes the distortion in natural order when *'the wren goes to' t and the small gilded fly does lecher in my sight.'*

But Lear's invocations of lust show his celebration of desire overcoming will: *'let copulation thrive'*. It is his counterbalance to Goneril and Regan's heartless reason:

'To 't luxury, pell mell,
for I lack soldiers!'

In pursuing the source of his madness Lear gradually strips off the paraphernalia of life which made him great: honours; power; expectations; illusions. He reduces himself and man to necessity.

On renouncing the crown, Lear's attempt at clinging to the superfluity of his attendants is his only way to maintain any authority. Necessity reduces *'man's life to the cheapness of beast's.'* However, the storm forces Lear to see man at his basest. He is *'bare-headed'* without the crown of authority and the superfluity of clothing.

'Take physic, pomp;
Expose thyself to feel what wretches feel,
That thou mayst shake the superflux to then
And show the heavens more just.'

It is only through madness, where society's imposed structure and civilization is discarded that Lear can see how man really is, and can question the meaning of his existence. *'Is man no more than this?'*

Similarly it is exemplified in Edgar only when he feigns madness.

'Thou art the thing itself:
unaccommodated man is no more but such a
poor, bare, forked animal as thou art.'

Superfluity and civilization is represented by clothing. In wishing to identify himself with the naked beggar in Edgar, Lear attempts to tear off his clothes, which are not essential to man.

'Off, off you lendings! Come, unbutton here.'

In submitting his protagonist to the fall in social hierarchy from king to beggar. Shakespeare explores essential man in relation to his role in society. The point that a king can only identify with man as he really is when he is a mad beggar questions the meaning of society. The fool implies that society is the only thing that can give foolish man meaning.

LEAR: *'Dost thou call me fool, boy?'*

FOOL: *'All thy other titles thou hast given away; that thou*
wast born with.'

Lear recognizes this. In his madness, stripped of society's impositions he sees himself as what he really is: *'I am a very foolish fond old man.'* Shakespeare universalizes him to all humanity.

'When we are born, we cry that we are come
To this great stage of fools'

In reducing Lear to essential man he shows a king who has looked into the abyss of life. His nadir shows him at his littlest in social status, but greatest in his grasp of reality beneath society. After his death Shakespeare leaves the social structure suspended in shock of Lear's revelation. However, they remain ignorant of his enlightenment. Edgar, who significantly exemplifies essential man in feigning madness, is the only character who is seen to acknowledge any degree of Lear's experience.

> 'The oldest hath born most; we that are young
> Shall never see so much, nor live so long.'

There are several points to note about this essay.

1 The opening paragraphs clearly show an appreciation of what is being asked. After a general statement about the authority of kings, the attention is concentrated on Lear. (It is a good idea to include – even in passing – a relevant reference to another of Shakespeare's plays.)

2 The point is then developed that it is Lear himself who must take the responsibility for his loss of greatness. It is argued that it is a weakness in Lear's character which reduces him to 'littleness'.

3 Lear's descent into madness is contrasted with the Fool's wisdom; and, it is argued, his self-realization is only possible when he is at his 'littlest'.

4 In conclusion the point is made that 'littlest' in this respect is a social definition, not a humanitarian one.

5 In assessing this essay an examiner would note the depth of knowledge and understanding, the complexity and detail in the argument and the appropriateness of the language.

6 You will notice how quotation is also used skilfully and purposefully in short, apt extracts which are invariably integrated into the developing argument.

Ken Elliott

Glossary

Alarum: A call to arms, often a trumpet call.

Alliteration: A figure of speech in which a number of words close to each other in a piece of writing begin with the same sound:

'Here I disclaim all my paternal care,
Propinquity and property of blood'

Alliteration helps to draw attention to these words.

Anachronism: In a historical drama the writer may accidentally or deliberately allow characters to refer to things from a later period, which they would not have known about. This is called 'anachronism':

'with a sigh like Tom o'Bedlam'

Bedlam/Bethlehem (the Hospital of St. Mary of Bethlehem) was an asylum from the mid-sixteenth century only.

Antithesis: A figure of speech in which the writer brings two opposite or contrasting ideas up against each other:

'Have more than thou showest,
Speak less than thou knowest,
Lend less than thou owest,
Ride more than thou goest,
Learn more than thou trowest,
Set less than thou throwest'

Apostrophe: When a character suddenly speaks directly to someone or something, which may or may not be present:

'Thou, Nature, art my goddess'

Dramatic irony: A situation in a play when the audience (and possibly some of the characters) know something that one or more of the characters do not. In a pantomime, for example, young children will often shout to tell the heroine that a dreadful monster is creeping up behind her, unseen. An example from *King Lear* is when Edmund has turned Gloucester against Edgar and then reports to his brother that Gloucester is for some reason displeased with him:

> EDGAR: *'Some villain hath done me wrong.*
> EDMUND: *That's my fear.'*

Exeunt: A Latin word meaning 'They go away', used for the departure of characters from a scene.

Exit: A Latin word meaning 's/he goes away', used for the departure of a character from a scene.

Hendiadys: A figure of speech expressed by two nouns joined by 'and' ('*milky gentleness and course*') rather than by an adjective and a noun (mild and gentle course of action).

Hyperbole: Deliberate exaggeration, for dramatic effect: '*every hour He flashes into one gross crime or other.*'

Irony: When someone says one thing and means another, often to make fun of, tease, or satirize someone else:
'*Since that respect and fortunes are his love,*
I shall not be his wife.'

It is also *irony* when someone is unable to see/understand something which should be obvious. Such a case is Gloucester's hasty condemnation of Edgar on the word of Edmund, and yet he sympathizes with the injustice of Kent's treatment by Lear:
'*Find out this villain, Edmund; it shall lose thee nothing; do it carefully. And the noble and true-hearted Kent banished! his offence, honesty! 'Tis strange.*'
See also *Dramatic irony*

Metaphor: A figure of speech in which a person, or thing, or idea is described as if it were something else:
'*Think'st thou that duty shall have dread to speak*
When power to flattery bows?'
Kent is saying that Lear (power) has been misled by his daughters (flattery) and Kent himself (duty) is not afraid to tell him so.

Onomatopoeia: Using words that are chosen because they mimic the sound of what is being described:
'*Rumble thy bellyful! Spit, fire! spout, rain!*'
Lear's words echo the sound of the storm.

Oxymoron: A figure of speech in which the writer combines two ideas which are opposites. This frequently has a startling or unusual effect:

'*Fairest Cordelia, that art most rich, being poor;*
Most choice, forsaken; and most loved, despised!'

Personification: Referring to a thing or an idea as if it were a person:

'*Ingratitude, thou marble-hearted fiend*'

Play on words: see *Pun*

Pun: A figure of speech in which the writer uses a word that has more than one meaning. Both meanings of the word are used to make a joke. Gloucester is explaining to Kent that Edmund is his bastard son:

KENT: '*I cannot conceive you.*

GLOUCESTER: *Sir, this young fellow's mother could.*'

Sometimes a pun may be used to make a more serious point.

Cordelia takes leave of her sisters, not in tears, but knowing them for what they are:

'*The jewels of our father, with washed eyes Cordelia leaves you.*'

Simile: A comparison between two things which the writer makes clear by using words such as 'like' or 'as':

'*Such smiling rogues as these,*
Like rats oft bite the holy cords a-twain
Which are too intrince t'unloose'

Soliloquy: When a character is alone on stage, or separated from the other characters in some way and speaks apparently to himself or herself.